Infiltrating Society

The **ISEAS – Yusof Ishak Institute** (formerly Institute of Southeast Asian Studies) is an autonomous organization established in 1968. It is a regional centre dedicated to the study of socio-political, security, and economic trends and developments in Southeast Asia and its wider geostrategic and economic environment. The Institute's research programmes are grouped under Regional Economic Studies (RES), Regional Strategic and Political Studies (RSPS), and Regional Social and Cultural Studies (RSCS). The Institute is also home to the ASEAN Studies Centre (ASC), the Singapore APEC Study Centre and the Temasek History Research Centre (THRC).

ISEAS Publishing, an established academic press, has issued more than 2,000 books and journals. It is the largest scholarly publisher of research about Southeast Asia from within the region. ISEAS Publishing works with many other academic and trade publishers and distributors to disseminate important research and analyses from and about Southeast Asia to the rest of the world.

Infiltrating Society

The Thai Military's Internal Security Affairs

PUANGTHONG PAWAKAPAN

 YUSOF ISHAK INSTITUTE

First published in Singapore in 2021 by
ISEAS Publishing
30 Heng Mui Keng Terrace
Singapore 119614
E-mail: publish@iseas.edu.sg
Website: http://bookshop.iseas.edu.sg

All rights reserved. No part of this publication may be reproduced, stored in a retrieval system, or transmitted in any form or by any means, electronic, mechanical, photocopying, recording or otherwise, without the prior permission of the ISEAS – Yusof Ishak Institute.

© 2021 ISEAS – Yusof Ishak Institute, Singapore

The responsibility for facts and opinions in this publication rests exclusively with the author and her interpretations do not necessarily reflect the views or the policy of the publishers or their supporters.

ISEAS Library Cataloguing-in-Publication Data

Name(s): Puangthong Pawakapan, author.
Title: Infiltrating society : the Thai military's internal security affairs / Puangthong Pawakapan.
Description: Singapore : ISEAS – Yusof Ishak Institute, 2021. | Includes bibliographical references and index.
Identifiers: ISBN 9789814881715 (soft cover) | 9789814881722 (PDF) | 9789814881739 (epub)
Subjects: LCSH: Thailand—Armed forces—Political activity. | Internal security—Thailand. | Administrative agencies—Thailand. | Civil-military relations—Thailand. | Thailand—Politics and government—1988-
Classification: LCC DS573 P57

Illustration on front cover reproduced by permission of Chinatip Egkantrong.

Typeset by Superskill Graphics Pte Ltd
Printed in Singapore by Markono Print Media Pte Ltd

Contents

Thai Language Convention	vi
List of Tables and Figures	vii
Abbreviations	viii
Foreword by Michael J. Montesano	ix
Preface	xviii
Acknowledgements	xxi
1. Introduction	1
2. Rationale, Legitimacy, and Development	19
3. The Making of the Development Military	62
4. Establishing State-Dominated Mass Organization	91
5. Remobilization of the Royalist Mass Since 2006	119
6. Conclusion	145
Bibliography	151
Index	175
About the Author	182

Thai Language Convention

For most Thai words, this book adheres to the phonetic transcription of the "General System of Phonetic Transcription of Thai Characters into Roman" devised by the Royal Institute, Bangkok, in 1954. In the case of a name which is widely known or which can be checked, the owner's transcription is used. The English names of certain Thai royals, such as Chulalongkorn, Bhumibol, and Vajiralongkorn, have been adopted rather than the lengthy official titles. Thai people are referred to by their first names while Westerners are referred to by their surnames. In the text and bibliography, Thai names are entered according to first names.

List of Tables and Figures

Tables
2.1	Budget of Ministry of Defence for Fiscal Year 2009	31
2.2	Budget of Ministry of Defence for Fiscal Year 2018	33
2.3	Budgets of ISOC, 2009–18	56
3.1	Budgets for *Isan Khiao* Project, 1988–91	71
5.1	Partial Number of ISOC's Mass in March 2012	128

Figures
2.1	Command Structure of ISOC Introduced by the Government of Prem Tinsulanonda in 1987	34
2.2	Command Structure of ISOC According to the Internal Security Act of 2008	47
2.3	Command Structure of ISOC According to Thaksin Shinawatra's Prime Ministerial Order No. 158/2545, dated 29 May 2002	48
2.4	Command Structure of ISOC at Community Levels According to Thaksin Shinawatra's Prime Ministerial Order No. 158/2545, dated 29 May 2002	50

Abbreviations

Mass Organizations

CDV	Civil Defence Volunteers (*Asa samak pongkanphai fai phonlaruen*)
RNS	Reservists for National Security
TNDV	Thai National Defence Volunteers (*Thai a-sa pongkanchat* or *Tho.so.po.cho.*)
VDC	Volunteer Defence Corps (*A-sa raksa dindaen* or *O.So.*)
VDSD	Volunteers for Development and Self-Defence (*A-sa phatthana lae pongkan ton-eng* or *O.pho.po.*)
VDSV	Village for Development and Self-Defence Volunteers programme (*Muban a-sa phatthana lae pongkan ton-eng*)
VSU	Village Security Unit (Chutraksa khwamplodphai muban or Cho.ro.bo.)
VPH	Volunteers for Public Health
VHV	*Village Health Volunteers (Asasamak satharanasuk pracham muban* or *O.so.mo*)

Others

ARD	Accelerated Rural Development
BPP	Border Patrol Police
CIA	Central Intelligence Agency
CDD	Community Development Department
CPM	Civilian-police-military joint command
CPT	Communist Party of Thailand
CSC	Central Security Command
DDPM	Department of Disaster Prevention and Mitigation
DOPA	Department of Provincial Administration
DOLA	Department of Local Administration
LAD	Local Administration Department
MOI	Ministry of Interior
MOPH	Ministry of Public Health
NCPO	National Council for Peace and Order
NESDB	National Economic and Social Development Board
NPKC	National Peace Keeping Council
NRC	National Reform Council
NSCT	National Student Centre of Thailand
PWD	Public Welfare Department
RFD	Royal Forest Department

Foreword

Michael J. Montesano

Infiltrating Society opens up new and valuable perspectives on three concerns central to serious understanding of modern Thailand. The first of these concerns is the means by which the military in fact involves itself in the country's politics and governance. The second concern is the specific challenge posed to Thai democracy by the military's employment of those poorly understood means. The last concern is Bangkok's relationship with the Thai provinces—and by extension the country's and society's historically fraught quest for and contest over what, with apologies to modernization theorists of yore, it is appropriate to call national integration.

* * *

The closing years of the reign of King Bhumibol Adulyadej and the opening years of that of his successor King Vajiralongkorn have aroused renewed interest in relations between Thailand's military and its monarchy. Attention has focused above all on the inactivity to which King Bhumibol's infirmity condemned him during the last years of his life and its consequences for the partnership of palace and Army, on the loyalty to the royal institution of the high command of that latter force, on the apparent strength or weakness of various senior officers' ties to King Vajiralongkorn, and on the new king's decision to assume direct control of certain units of the country's military.

Puangthong Pawakapan denies the importance of none of these foci. But she argues in *Infiltrating Society* that an effort to understand the bonds between military and monarchy demands that we look well beyond coup plots hatched among senior officers in Bangkok and those same officers' extravagant poses of loyalty to a notionally timeless and essential Thai monarchy. For the bonds between soldier and sovereign in recent history have in fact owed much to the era of counterinsurgent operations—focused on the perceived security threat of the Communist Party of Thailand (CPT) and undertaken above all in rural and even remote reaches of the Thai provinces—from the 1960s into the 1980s. At levels both institutional and personal, rural counterinsurgency brought monarchy and military into close and sustained collaboration.

While violence and coercion most marked Thai counterinsurgency, it was not in the main their use that gave rise to this collaboration. Violence and coercion shared prominence with another approach to besting the CPT in the countryside: the military's programme of *kitchakan phonlaruean*, or what are in *Infiltrating Society* termed "civil affairs projects". At the centre of that programme stood military involvement in "development for security" and in the creation of an array of mass organizations. The armed forces of the Bangkok state sought through development projects meant to win "hearts and minds", and through the mobilization of—above all—rural Thais into mass organizations, to prosecute a "political offensive" against the CPT. The state's goal of cultivating royalism notwithstanding, this latter strategy of mobilizing the populace followed the example of communist revolutionary practice. Its adoption reflected an awareness that the Bangkok state faced a political challenge rather than a primarily military threat. This awareness resulted in the politics-first strategy of *kanmueang nam kanthahan*, pursued in the main under the auspices of the Communist Suppression Operations Command (CSOC)—later and still today called the Internal Security Operations Command (ISOC).

Infiltrating Society suggests that, in its original Cold War context, much about this approach was essentially fantasy. The Thai military's attempt to wage a political offensive from the mid-1960s and through the 1970s proved largely ineffective. Coercion, including the often heavy-handed use of force, remained the defining trait of counterinsurgency practice. Efforts at popular mobilization through the creation of mass organizations proved a poor fit with the realities of rural society, despite the frequent willingness of local notables to participate in or support those organizations. Those efforts proved one more chapter in the long history of the Bangkok state's and Thai metropolitan elites' sociological misapprehension or mismapping of the provincial hinterlands that they sought to dominate.

*   *   *

The decidedly indifferent results of the Thai military's civil affairs projects notwithstanding, those projects outlasted the demise of the CPT in the 1980s. The involvement of the Bangkok state's military in internal security became so routine that it rarely drew comment, let alone analysis or criticism. But the survival of an approach to internal security dating from the counterinsurgency era gave that military a repertoire of stratagems that it could remobilize at any time. Puangthong offers the first comprehensive account of just such a remobilization, initially undertaken as a deliberate response to the energetic electoral politics that marked the first decade of the present century in Thailand.

On one level, and not least as it concerns mass organizations, that remobilization has reflected a lack of imagination or of new thinking. It has revealed a decision to double down on the not terribly successful approach of the past to meet the challenges of a very different present. On another level, however, it reveals just how central to the Thai military's understanding of both its political role and its relationship to society internal security and civil affairs projects have remained all along. *Infiltrating Society* offers invaluable perspective on the implications of that understanding for Thai democracy. It argues that counterinsurgency as ostensibly pursued by political means and through civil affairs projects served as a "springboard" for the military's lasting involvement in the socio-economic and political realms. The book thus makes clear that the challenge to democracy and democratic government posed by the military is far more fundamental than a storied propensity to mount coups and install dictatorial rule, naked or otherwise, in the aftermath of those coups.

Central to this point is Puangthongs's analysis of two prime ministerial orders promulgated by the government of General Prem Tinsulanonda, himself a veteran of counterinsurgent activities in Northeast Thailand, in 1980 and 1982. The near-universal understanding of these orders as "magic spells" cast to bring about the ultimate defeat of the CPT by political rather than military means has always been puzzling. It is hard to square with the historical record. In *Infiltrating Society*, Puangthong has no time for this understanding, or in fact for this puzzle. The import of these orders, the book points out, has lain far less in their long-exaggerated relevance to the defeat of the CPT than in their crystallizing the military's politics-first, notionally civil-affairs-oriented, approach to counterinsurgency into what proved a robust political vision.

Central to that vision, as it had been implicit in counterinsurgency for much of the fifteen years preceding the promulgation of the two orders, was the integration of the people of a still predominantly rural Thailand— the subjects of the ninth Chakri monarch—into the nation as members of mobilized but pliable masses. That socio-political vision motivated the launch and oversight of mass organizations on the part of the CSOC, then of the ISOC, and also of numerous other organs of the Bangkok state.

The prominence of those organizations went hand in hand with that of "community development" during the counterinsurgency era. Indeed, the mobilization of rural people into mass organizations and the submission of their settlements to community development work were grounded in a single ideological project. Programmes in community development brought at least superficial material benefits to the settlements in which rural Thais lived.

Perhaps more significantly, they also had the goal of reinforcing pseudo-organicist conceptions of the village community. While those conceptions were destined to have a long, strange afterlife in the thinking of putative progressives in Thailand, their significance to the counterinsurgency project was straightforward. Members of the rural masses lived in communities, and those villagers need not concern themselves with public affairs at scales greater than that of the community. Or so the vision had it.

At the core of the vision, as embodied no less in the mobilization of mass organizations than in community development, stood a determination to forge an unmediated relationship between state and society. An energetic sovereign and his consort, willing during the era of counterinsurgency and for some years thereafter to undertake an active programme of visits across provincial Thailand to promote "development" and to link rural people to the kingdom's exemplary centre, also served this purpose admirably for several decades. Numerous familiar, iconic photographs underline the direct contact with rural people that these visits afforded King Bhumibol. For all their brevity, the photogenic immediacy of such encounters was crucial.

That immediacy was of a piece with the attempts on the part of the Bangkok state's military to shape and then to manipulate, as if in the management of a vast front organization, a large segment of Thai society. Complemented by royalist ideology—and almost certainly by the progressive resacralization of the Thai monarchy—and touted as democratic, the vision outlined in Prem's famous orders of the early 1980s prescribed what amounted to an illiberal project of depoliticization, *um integralismo à tailandesa*. Like many corporatist visions, this one afforded ample opportunities for major business concerns. In the Thai case, the interest of such concerns was in penetrating and exploiting the countryside. Puangthong notes the example of the infamous military-backed "Green Isan" project. Initiated in the same decade that saw the promulgation of Prem's orders, the project sought to foster large-scale commercial forestry on land cultivated by tens of thousands of Northeastern small-holders.

Infiltrating Society makes repeated reference to the apparent obliviousness of the leadership of elected governments and of much of the public to the implications of the expansive internal security role of the Thai military. This obliviousness has led democratic forces in Thailand to forfeit oversight of the military's deep engagement with—or infiltration of—Thai society. Perhaps more significantly, and for the same reason, those forces have also effectively tolerated the military's active promotion of a form of state-society relations incompatible with liberal democracy.

The crux of that incompatibility is the role in mediating between state and society that political contestation, elections and parties play in a liberal democratic order. The illiberal and depoliticizing vision that the Thai military of today has inherited from the counterinsurgency era cannot abide either that role or the closely related substantive function of political parties as vehicles for the articulation of competing interests. Recent indicators of this intolerance are abundant, and clear.

The constitutionally binding twenty-year National Strategy published in October 2018 by the National Council for Peace and Order junta assigns—or rather reassigns—a leading role to "communities" as points of interface between state and society. It thus both demarcates a radically constricted sphere of legitimate political participation and ideologically obviates the need, above all among the residents of provincial Thailand, for recourse to political parties as vehicles for the expression of their will. At the same time, and in another distinct echo of the 1980s, the document outlining the strategy would foster metropolitan business interests' economic domination of the provinces, following a model that two influential Thai political scientists label "hierarchical capitalism".

Similarly, the three-year National Security Policy and Plan released in November 2019 stresses the importance of building "immunity" to political contestation, and thus to the appeal of political parties and politicians, among individuals and communities and in society as a whole. This same determination to immunize and depoliticize accounted for the dissolution of the maverick new Future Forward Party in February 2020 and the use of the legal system to harass its leadership. That party's decidedly liberal orientation, its programmatic challenge to the place of the armed forces in the Thai order and to the power of oligopolistic business interests, and its remarkable appeal to young and impatient voters presented an elemental challenge to the political vision of the Thai military.

As these developments unfold, *Infiltrating Society* emphasizes, Thailand continues to witness the reinvigoration of extant state-sponsored mass organizations and the mobilization of new ones. The project to render society pliable carries on. But persistent efforts of Thailand's "military state within the state" in the realm of internal security have left it above all in the role of spoiler. Events of recent decades make evident that its illiberal and depoliticizing vision is an even poorer fit with contemporary Thai society than with the less complex and sophisticated Thai society of the counterinsurgency era. There is no place in that vision for what scholars have variously called a "middle-income peasantry", "cosmopolitan villagers" and "urbanized villagers", let alone for the young people for whom the ideals of the Future Forward Party had such strong appeal. At the same time, Puangthong observes pointedly, pending the cessation of the military's internal security activities in all their ambitiousness, electoral democracy in Thailand remains condemned to fragility and instability.

* * *

In demonstrating both the chronic ineffectiveness of the Thai military's approach to internal security affairs as a socio-political vision and its effect in undermining the prospects of an alternative, liberal democratic order, *Infiltrating Society* speaks to the central issue in Thai history in the past century and a third. This issue is the quest for national integration in all its dimensions—political, economic, social, cultural, ideological and even linguistic. Contests over who in state or society sets the terms for that integration, whether those terms are exclusionary or aim at inclusiveness, what means of and social bases for that integration are viable and realistic, and how to structure a balanced and just relationship between the great primate city of Bangkok and its broad and varied provincial hinterlands have long defined that quest. They continue to define it today.

A number of the most noteworthy developments in the history of modern Thailand have reflected efforts to set those terms. The 1890s saw Prince Damrong Rajanubhab give momentum to the work of centralizing provincial administration, often at the expense of local lords, under the *thesaphiban* system. Following the end of the absolute monarchy, the 1930s brought the introduction of a parliament featuring members whose explicit function—a remarkable innovation that historians seem to take for granted—was to represent individual provinces and the residents of those provinces. In a related development, that same era saw the promotion of constitutionalism as an integrative ideology across the length and breadth of the country. Beginning a quarter-century later, during the 1957–63 dictatorship of Field Marshal Sarit Thanarat, the promotion of the Thai monarchy would have the same integrative or unifying aim.

Still other efforts to set the terms of Thai national integration have included the Bangkok state's creation of organs to promote "community development" in the late 1950s and early 1960s, noted above, and the still contested steps towards meaningful administrative decentralization introduced in Thailand's 1997 Constitution. The pair of widely heralded if misunderstood orders promulgated by Prime Minister Prem in the early 1980s were also very much part of the tradition of attempts to effect and to control national integration in Thailand, as is the equally poorly understood but much less discussed 2018–37 National Strategy crafted by the dictatorial National Council for Peace and Order regime.

The vision laid out in the Prem-era orders had an unmistakable influence on that strategy. As Puangthong stresses, that lasting influence reflects the importance of Cold War counterinsurgency as the crucible for the Thai military's internal security activities and the vision that informs them. While the power of that legacy certainly points to stagnation in military thought during the last thirty years, it would be wrong to dismiss it as a matter of mere ideological anachronism. Rather, the Bangkok state's continued recourse to a repertoire of stratagems conceived to counter the CPT reflects an understanding, conscious or not, that the insurgency mounted by that party and the effort to defeat that insurgency together represented one more episode in the long quest for national integration and contest over its terms. That contest predated by many decades the threat posed by the CPT, and the demise of the party in no way signalled its end. Nor did it necessarily indicate the obsolesce of stratagems conceived in the face of that specific threat, as the discussion in *Infiltrating Society* of the Thai military's ever-broader understanding of security illustrates.

Puangthong highlights the preparatory function of the prime ministerial orders of the 1980s that gave explicit expression to the stratagems developed in the Bangkok state's contest with the CPT. Those orders lay the foundation for the Thai military's continued active role in national integration. Among younger historians of Southeast Asia, scholarship scrutinizing the impact of the Cold War on, its long-term legacies for, the region has become fashionable. On one level, today's Thai military and its internal security activities, the Thai monarchy of the reign of King Bhumibol, and the relationship between the two institutions that has so distorted Thai political life for decades would appear to represent just such a legacy. But to restrict oneself to that level of understanding is myopic, and to view those two integrative institutions and the durability of the stratagems for national integration associated with their relationship in a time horizon of just sixty or even eighty years is an historiographic misstep. Those institutions' prominence in the post-1945 era notwithstanding, the story of Thailand's quest for integration and contest over the appropriate and just means to effect it long predated the Cold War. They have outlasted the counterinsurgency era. That attempts on the part of the Bangkok state, no matter how futile, to apply tools forged in that era continue is no surprise. Likewise, in the history of that quest and that contest, the recent prominence of Thailand's soldiers and its sovereigns comprises but a brief chapter—to be followed by other, perhaps very different, chapters, in which other, perhaps very different, actors may figure as the protagonists.

* * *

In its treatment of the internal security activities and civil affairs projects of the Thai military, *Infiltrating Society* invites comparison between the example of Thailand and those of other countries, both in Southeast Asia and outside the region. The volume can certainly inform understanding of the long, prominent and continuing "civic action" tradition of the Armed Forces of the Philippines and of the political implications of that tradition, just as that tradition can inform understanding of the Thai experience. The same is true of the socio-political vision associated with the concepts of the "family state" and the "floating mass" in New Order Indonesia. Further, the Thai military's adoption of a strategy of counterinsurgent mobilization occurred in the same period that saw the governments of the United States and the Republic of Vietnam move to enhance "pacification" efforts in rural southern Vietnam under the broad framework of "Civil Operations and Revolutionary Development Support", or CORDS—with its development cadres and determination to match the communists' revolution with the Saigon government's own. To turn to comparisons beyond Southeast Asia, the concerns of *Infiltrating Society* overlap with those of scholarship on the "professionalism"—whether "old" or "new"—of Latin American militaries in the twentieth century and on the political attitudes and political involvement associated with it.

Puangthong Pawakapan's most pressing concern is, however, the state of her own country, the unending involvement of whose military in politics is of more than historical interest. *Infiltrating Society* draws on Puangthong's historical perspective, her masterful use of sources and, above all, on her deep—and increasingly widely shared—conviction that much in Thailand need not be as it is. Her book makes clear the ineffectiveness of the Thai military's involvement in internal security affairs as an approach to both political manipulation and national integration, despite the persistence of that involvement. The roots of this chronic failure to build a viable relationship between Bangkok and the society of its provincial hinterlands by militarized means lie in that approach's long-evident and ever-increasing irrelevance to Thai social realities. This failure has meant that almost all that the military's civil affairs projects and internal security activities have to show for themselves is the stunting of Thailand's electoral democracy.

Read with this outcome in mind, Puangthong's closely considered study amounts to a trenchant argument for giving Thai liberal democracy a chance. It underlines Thailand's need to double down this time on elections, political parties and contestation among those parties—to bet on representative structures whose design ensures the participation in the national life of provincial voters and of urban voters whose origins lie in the provinces. This bet holds out integrative possibilities with the flexibility to meet the demands of ongoing and unpredictable social change.

The title of *Infiltrating Society* is apt: Thai national integration must work as a social project, and not just a spatial one. In one of just a few, perhaps unwitting, gestures towards poignancy in her book, Puangthong leaves little doubt about who may stand to benefit from Thailand's taking a genuine chance on liberal democracy. The Bangkok state's mass organizations—with their uniforms and the sense of power and authority that those uniforms convey, and with the possibility of forging connections with influential patrons that participation in those organizations may bring—have long had particular appeal for marginalized Thais of modest means and modest levels of education, Puangthong writes. Membership in those organizations has thus held out at least an imagined refuge from precarity in Thailand's infamously unequal society. Taking a moment to think about the nature of that attraction will break the heart of any reader who knows Thailand. It will also bring home the urgency of replacing the failed, six-decade-old, military-led approach to national integration with one that better matches Thai realities and better meets Thai needs.

Preface

I grew up in an area adjacent to Bangkok's Ratchadamnoen Avenue, the centre stage of many significant events in modern Thai politics. I had the opportunity to witness several popular demonstrations, beginning with the 14 October 1973 uprising, and too many military coups d'état. Even before the generals made a public announcement, I knew we had another coup when the phone line at home was cut off and the area was swarming with soldiers and military trucks. Despite being familiar with this vicious cycle of civilian government and military rule, I refuse to accept that military rule is the norm for Thailand. It is frustrating to see the growing popularity of the military among a large section of people, the consolidation of military power, the increasing militarization of society in various aspects, the lack of accountability for those involved in violent crackdowns, and the impunity that the military and the rightist elite enjoy. Still, like the majority of Thai people, I have long overlooked the political apparatus of the military. Like most others, I paid attention to the military mainly when the country was under its rule.

The sweeping and heavy-handed attempts of the National Council for Peace and Order (NCPO), the junta of the 22 May 2014 coup, to impose its version of security and order in civil space triggered my curiosity. The first unusual activities of the NCPO I noticed took place soon after the coup. For example, there were forced evictions of small farmers from the forest reserve areas, an obsession with management of traffic and street food in Bangkok, remobilization of many mass organizations, the resurfacing of the Internal Security Operations Command (ISOC) in news headlines, and the establishment of ISOC-led popular surveillance mechanisms in Bangkok and the provinces. The longer the NCPO stayed in power, the more expansive and intensive the military's political control over civilian lives became, justified on grounds of the nation's internal security. I could not find a satisfactory answer to why all this happened. The matter was too important to ignore. I decided to dig for more information. This became my first research project on the Thai military, a topic I had never thought I would address, mainly because I do not enjoy the politics of cliques and classes, a dominant feature of Thai military studies, and partly because the military's machoism dulls my interest. This may be my weak point. Fortunately, my research mainly deals with the military's civil affairs.

At the beginning of my research, I began to notice that the attempt to impose firm control over the people and electoral politics began soon after the 2006 military coup, which brought down the hugely popular elected government of Thaksin Shinawatra. Development for security programmes, the ISOC-dominated mass organizations, state surveillance in various forms, ideological indoctrination and the counter-democracy psychological warfare proliferated from then onwards. These were once the major components of Thailand's counterinsurgency operations. The military has given them a new euphemistic label as *kitchakan phonlaruen khong thahan* or the military's civil affairs.

To understand what the military is doing with its political apparatus at present, I had to look back to the counterinsurgency period, when the foundations were laid for the Thai military's internal security operations, including the definition of national security, and the key concepts and methods to fight the internal threats, which are still relevant today. On the one hand, these old concepts and methods are obsolete, indicating the military's failure to catch up with the modern world. On the other hand, their continued use shows that the military and its conservative allies never abandoned the remnants of the counterinsurgency operations despite the demise of communism decades ago. They proudly believe that these old methods will bring them victory over internal threats, just as they did over the Communist Party of Thailand. I argue that such a belief is a political myth. However, in Thailand a myth may give life to a gigantic political apparatus which grants greater power to the military and the establishment.

ISOC is known as the key agency in charge of Thailand's internal security affairs since the counterinsurgency period. In fact, all branches of the armed forces have been actively involved in various internal security programmes. The military has never waged a large-scale warfare with an external enemy since its modernization in the early twentieth century. Internal security has become the *raison d'être* of the Thai armed forces, defining its main mission, operations, perception of its role towards national institutions, the people and its political power. This book is, therefore, not just about ISOC. The agency's coordinating authority enables the military to dominate and direct other government bodies, even when the country is under a civilian government.

Whether or not Thailand is under military rule, the bureaucracy of internal security is present on a routine basis. The attempt to keep society under control requires persistence and patience. The military coup is a convenient way for the military and its allies to amplify its power in the short term, but commanding the loyalty of the people and mobilizing them in mass organizations is more effective in the long run. On the one hand, this strategy allows the military and conservative elites to dictate the country's long-term political direction. On the other hand, this strategy creates division among the people and thus makes democratization in the future more difficult. Thailand will not escape the vicious cycle of coups and weak civilian governments as long as the infrastructure of power is controlled and manipulated by the military and its conservative allies. As an academic and a citizen, I wish this book could help reshape the understanding of military-state-society relations in and beyond Thailand. I feel an obligation to inform people about what the military and its allies are doing. Thailand may soon return to civilian rule but a genuine reform of the security sector will never happen until the role of the military's political apparatus is understood and addressed.

Since embarking on this book in 2017, I have written a few articles in Thai and English, given talks in public and closed-door forums, and been interviewed by the press. I believe that a good proportion of politically active citizens are now aware of the political projects of the military and ISOC. However, there are constraints on what I can say to the press and in open forums in Thailand. Writing in English allows me to put these constraints aside and write with greater freedom.

I do not deny that I have a firm political position and I make no effort to hide it. I believe in a free and fair political system with good governance, transparency, and accountability, all of which military governments have failed to provide for the Thai people in the past, and will continue to fail in the future. Under military-led authoritarian rule, people have paid too high a price for too long a time. I hope readers will appreciate the research, the substantial evidence and the serious arguments in this book.

Puangthong Pawakapan
Bangkok in the time of Covid-19
March 2020

Acknowledgements

I am indebted to many people and institutes for giving me trust, support, encouragement, and friendship during the course of this research project. First of all is Michael Montesano, who helped me in many invaluable ways from the beginning to the end of this book. It began with his invitation for me to take up a research fellowship at the ISEAS – Yusof Ishak Institute right after the coup d'état in 2014, allowing me a quiet time to carefully watch the actions of the National Council for Peace and Order regime and its allies. This was when the research questions emerged. Later when I was ready to begin the writing, Michael again helped me get the second fellowship to work on the introductory part at ISEAS. Comments and suggestions from Michael and two anonymous referees helped improve this book significantly. I am also very grateful to the former ISEAS Director Tan Chin Tiong and Deputy Director Terence Chong for their generous support and kindness. Many thanks to the wonderful assistance of the members of the ISEAS Publishing, Ng Kok Kiong, the Managing Editor, Rahilah Yusuf, and Catherine Ang. I truly appreciate ISEAS and former Director Tan for their valuable support and promotion of Thai studies since 2014.

This book would not have been possible without another two research fellowships of the Center for Southeast Asian Studies at Kyoto University, between February and July 2018, and the Harvard-Yenching Institute at Harvard University, between August 2018 and May 2019. The staff of all three institutes were kind and helpful to me, and made my away from home times very pleasant. I would like to express my sincere appreciation to my colleagues at Department of International Relations of Chulalongkorn University, Supamit Pitipat in particular, for allowing me to take a long leave to complete this project.

I received valuable comments and suggestion when I presented various issues and parts of the work at the 2017 International Conference on Thai Studies, the 2018 Council of Thai Studies at University of Wisconsin-Madison, Kyoto University, the Harvard-Yenching seminar and the Thai Studies program at Harvard University, the Genocide Studies program at Yale University, Political Science at Chulalongkorn University, the National Graduate Institute for Policy Studies in Tokyo, the 2019 Thailand Update Conference at Columbia University, and the 2019 EUROSEAS conference. I thank all for the comments and the organizers for those presentations.

My gratitude is extended to several interviewees, whom I cannot name, due to their safety; to Sarayut Tangprasert and Neeranuch Niempradit for introducing me to several former communist cadres in the Phuphan area, to Daorueang Naewthong, the librarian at the Thammasat Univeristy Archives, for helping me locate important materials; to Paul Charbonneau for editing the first draft of my manuscript.

My mentors, friends, and colleagues helped me in many meaningful ways. I am deeply indebted to Chris Baker, who kindly responded to my urgent call for help. His attentive editing, comments, and suggestions helped improve the manuscript a great deal. Chris's generosity and kindness was appreciated beyond words can express. Thanks to Nidhi Eoseewong, Chaiwat Satha-anand, Kasian Tejapira, Tyrell Haberkorn, Tamada Yoshifumi, Masaaki Okamoto, Junko Koizumi, Yoko Hayami, Ben Kiernan, Michael Hertzfeld, Duncan McCargo, Jay Rosengard, Surachart Bamrungsuk, Prajak Kongkirati, Julalak Phookerd, Athukkit Sawaengsuk, Anekchai Ruengrattanakorn, Kritdikorn Wongsawangpanich, Pitch Phongsawat, and Viengrat Netipho for their encouragement, helps, suggestions, and friendship. Special thanks to Thongchai Winichakul for being a good cheerleader, mentor, and friend for over thirty years.

I owe so much to Niti Pawakapan for his unwavering support and encouragement for me to pursue my wish. Thanks to Pian Pawakapan for being my pride and joy.

I am very fortunate to be among these wonderful people. Having said all of this, I am, certainly, solely responsible for all the ideas, good or bad, in this book.

Introduction

This book is my first research project on the Thai military. My interest began soon after the coup d'état mounted by the National Council for Peace and Order (NCPO) on 22 May 2014 but my interest was not in the NCPO junta itself, but in the junta's non-military activities. One incident in particular piqued my curiosity: the forced eviction of thousands of families from the forest reserves. Less than a month after the coup d'état, on 14 June 2014, the junta leader General Prayut Chan-o-cha issued an order about encroachment and destruction of forest resources. Several thousand people were forcibly rooted out of forest reserve land immediately. Their crops were destroyed. Several hundred people faced charges. Then, in August, the junta introduced a master plan to resolve the problems of forest destruction, citing encroachment of forest land by small farmers as one of the major causes. The Internal Security Command Operations (ISOC), together with the Ministry of Natural Resources and Environment, was entrusted with the task of determining and implementing a strategy in coordination with other state agencies. The master plan claimed that the principal objective of this effort was to increase the forest coverage in Thailand from 31.57 per cent of the country's total area to 40 per cent within ten years, which meant around 26 million *rai* of land (approximately 10.24 million acres or 4.16 million hectares) had to be expropriated (Internal Security Operations Command and Ministry of Natural Resources and Environment 2014, p. 2; *Prachatai*, 15 June 2014; 17 December 2014).

To begin with, it is intriguing that the management of natural resources would become one of the priorities of the military junta. Perhaps even more intriguing is the fact that the forced eviction took place so soon after the coup and that the junta was able to introduce the master plan within a few months, indicating that the military has been deeply involved in the management of forest reserves long before. The question is when and how did this begin and what was the source of the junta's legitimacy for claiming this role (Puangthong 2015b). I asked experts on the Thai military, staff of non-governmental organizations working with the affected people, and a member of the Phuea Thai party who was an army general in charge of the national security and military affairs. None could give me a satisfactory answer.

The book *Khor Jor Kor: Forest Politics in Thailand* by Oliver Pye (2005) was useful as it provided me with background on a similar incident that had occurred in 1991–92 under the military junta, the National Peace Keeping Council (NPKC). Pye's research shows that the military involvement in this area went back to the counterinsurgency period when the idea of development for security was formulated. The main questions that stood out to me while conducting this preliminary research were: why has the military's involvement in natural resource management continued until the present day, and what sort of political or legal legitimacy has the military acquired to justify its role in the area?

Apart from the question of land management, I also wondered what other non-military areas was the Thai military involved with. I found that the military has been very active in a wide range of non-military affairs since the coup d'état in September 2006, which toppled the elected government of Thaksin Shinawatra (February 2001–September 2006). Indeed, it turned out that the origins of their involvement in non-military activities extended back over decades. To my astonishment, ISOC often appeared in these activities after the 2006 coup.

The main duty of ISOC (its original name was the Communist Suppression Operations Command or CSOC) is to carry out intelligence, ideological, psychological and political programmes in the name of internal security. It is known to have employed both violence and propaganda techniques during the counterinsurgency period against student, peasant and worker movements. Importantly, ISOC is not officially a branch of the military, but rather falls under the authority of the Prime Minister Office. Hence, it looks like a civilian agency. However, this is only nominal as the army has managed and controlled ISOC from its inception in 1965 until the present day, with army officers holding key positions across the organization. It is not an exaggeration to claim that ISOC is the political wing of the military.

ISOC's activities became increasingly visible again when the country was engulfed in the polemics of colour-coded politics. Some of its activities at this time were reminiscent of its role in the Cold War era, including establishment of mass surveillance of political dissidents, remobilization and expansion of the ISOC-controlled mass organizations, and threats to and coercion of political opponents. Other of its activities appeared new, such as forcing people from forest reserve areas and narcotic suppression. Below are some examples of these activities.

In March 2009, during the government of Abhisit Vejjajiva (December 2008–August 2011), Jatuphon Phromphan, leader of the United Front for Democracy against Dictatorship (UDD), known as the Red Shirts movement which supports the former prime minister Thaksin and his parties, accused the government of funding and using ISOC to block its activities. In response to Jatuphon, Colonel Thanathip Sawangsaeng, ISOC's spokesperson, countered that the budget of 1,000 million baht (approximately US$28.57 million) was aimed at promoting the sufficiency economy philosophy of the late King Bhumibol Adulyadej (5 December 1927–13 October 2016) in the Red Shirts-dominated areas. He, nevertheless, admitted that ISOC was monitoring the activities of the Red Shirts in the northern region (Channel 3 News, 25 March 2009). Then, in April 2011, ISOC authorities shut down thirteen local radio stations belonging to Red Shirts groups, accusing them of insulting the monarchy (*Thairath*, 28 April 2011).

After the coup of 2014, ISOC assumed authority over cyber surveillance. In 2015, the spokesperson for ISOC disclosed to the media that the agency had discovered 143 websites, with 5,268 separate URLs, carrying content deemed insulting to the monarchy. It ordered the Ministry of Information and Communication Technology (ICT) to shut down 3,426 of these URLs (*Manager Online*, 7 September 2015). This action bypassed the authority of both the police and the judiciary. ISOC and the ICT did not need to explain to the public or to the administrators of the websites how the content insulted the monarchy or threatened national security, thanks to section 44 of the Interim Constitution of 2014, which provided the Head of the NCPO, General Prayut, with absolute power.[1] Section 44 stipulates that in any case deemed necessary by the head of the NCPO, he shall issue orders, restrain or perform any acts, with the approval of the NCPO, regardless of whether the enforcement of such acts falls to the legislature, executive or judiciary; all orders, acts as well as performance in compliance with such orders shall be deemed lawful and constitutional. On 22 May 2014, General Prayut issued NCPO Order No. 26/2557, authorizing the ICT to shut down or remove websites, social media, video and audio clips that were deemed to violate laws, instigate disorder and unrest, or contravene the NCPO's policies and actions (*Royal Gazette*, 29 May 2014).

Immediately after the coup d'état that toppled the elected government led by the Phuea Thai party on 22 May 2014, many Red Shirt leaders in the northern and northeastern provinces were detained, summoned or threatened by soldiers (*Prachatai*, 1 July 2014; BBC, 9 June 2014). These local Red Shirt leaders had to request permission from the military chief in their province if they wanted to travel to other provinces. As a result, some of them took refuge in neighbouring countries, while many others decided to leave their localities and lie low in other provinces. Some were still afraid to return home almost three years after the coup.[2] Whenever the military junta was worried that the Red Shirts might gather together to show opposition to the junta and support for the Shinawatra family, many Red Shirts in the provinces received phone calls from police or military officers ahead of time, warning them not to join the gathering.[3]

During the counterinsurgency period, the Thai army and ISOC mobilized several mass organizations in the rural areas. The demise of communism from the mid-1980s, which subsequently led to the repeal of the Anti-Communist Act in 2000, resulted in a decrease of paramilitary activities. The emergence of the colour-coded political conflict in the mid-2000s evidently reinvigorated the paramilitary and civic groups under ISOC command. A 2012 progress report of the Thai National Defence Volunteers (TNDV or *Thai asa pongkan chat*), one of ISOC's paramilitary organizations, indicates that the activities of TNDV had been in decline since 1992 but were revived in 2006, the year the Thaksin government was toppled by a military coup. The report quotes the order of General Prayut, then army commander and deputy director of ISOC, that the agency must hastily re-establish a strong TNDV network nationwide and link it with other mass organizations (ISOC 2012, pp. 6–7, 9–10).

In advance of the referendum on the NCPO's draft constitution scheduled for 7 August 2016, ISOC's spokesperson claimed that over 500,000 people were ready to support the referendum campaign (*Post Today*, 7 May 2016). At the same time, opponents of the draft constitution were prohibited from campaigning by threats of criminal charges.

In November 2016, social media was ignited by a controversy sparked by a famous royalist speaker, Oraphim Raksaphon, nicknamed Best. Her sensational speaking skill, particularly on the topic of the benevolence of King Bhumibol, often drove audiences to tears. One of her famous lines, widely quoted across social media, was "even if one is reincarnated ten times, one would not be able to find a great monarch like King Bhumibol". The controversy began when people criticized one of her talks, posted on YouTube. In that talk, she had suggested that the people in the northeast, known as the base of the Red Shirts movement, appeared not to love the king enough, even though he had done many great things for them. People accused her of being divisive and of insulting people in that region. Oraphim has been a regular speaker for ISOC, and the talk in question was organized by ISOC as part of a project called "Promoting the works of King Bhumibol and the royal members". Over 3,000 students from thirty-five schools and four vocational schools in Maha Sarakham province in the northeast were assembled for the talk. Despite the controversy, ISOC senior officer insisted that Oraphim was a useful resource person for the programme (*Manager Online*, 16 November 2016; *The Nation*, 28 November 2016).

In recent years ISOC and army websites along with YouTube have carried posts on ISOC's engagement with high school students, along with numerous military training programmes about imbuing the love of the king and the nation, the wisdom of the king's sufficiency economy philosophy, and watching out for threats against the nation.[4]

The case of Oraphim gave the public insight into the activities of ISOC's modern mass organization and psychological warfare. The military government of General Prayut appeared to especially favour the services of ISOC. Prayut himself was once the deputy director of ISOC and is currently its director. The ongoing activities of ISOC have, however, gone unnoticed and unquestioned by political parties and civil society.[5]

The role of ISOC/military has quickly expanded from managing political order to managing social order, such as the traffic problem in Bangkok and beyond. The motorcycle taxi and vans business in Bangkok is a source of lucrative under-the-table money for the authorities. These services help people to commute faster but also cause congestion in many areas, especially where streets are turned into temporary parking lots for motorcycles and minibuses. The military appeared to take this issue seriously. Immediately after the 2014 coup, the NCPO ordered the minibuses on many congested roads to move to the suburbs immediately, causing problems for both the commuters and the minibus drivers. ISOC admitted that it had taken over the management of the motorcycle taxis and minibus services in Bangkok and surrounding provinces since 2014 (*Thairath*, 19 June 2019). In July 2014, the army officer, who was in charge of the matter, told me that he had been annoyed by this problem for a long time because he had to drive past a congested area twice every day.[6] The Thai military is clearly obsessed with establishing social order with military-style measures. Dictatorial power allowed the military to act on this obsession.

The above examples suggest that the junta and ISOC reactivated their Cold War apparatus in order to exert control over civil society. As I will show in the following chapters, the Thai military's role in the socio-political and economic arena has been much more intensive and extensive than the examples above. In response to the persistent political conflict since 2006, the military and conservative elites have carefully reconstructed their infrastructure of power. One of their crucial political weapons is the internal security apparatus under the command of ISOC and the armed forces.

Studies of the Thai Military

Thailand's intransigent political crisis and polarization, marked by two military coups and persistent mass demonstrations since 2006, is often seen as the orchestrated work of an anti-democratic alliance of the old powers against the rise of electoral politics. The alliance is conceptualized as "network monarchy" by Duncan McCargo (2005), a "parallel state" by Paul Chambers (2015), "deep state" by Eugénie Mérieau (2016), and "royal democracy" by Thongchai Winichakul (2019). Despite their differences in some aspects, these authors agree that the monarchy is the bedrock of the alliance while the military is its least popular component, especially since the violent crackdown on the popular uprising in May 1992 by the military government led by General Suchinda Kraprayoon (7 April–24 May 1992). Following the May 1992 crackdown, the military was perceived to have retreated to its barracks (Surachart 1998, p. 17). These studies seem to consider only coups and military governments as political intervention by the military. They overlook the military's Cold War-era political apparatus.

A study of the Thai military's internal security apparatus is needed for understanding the entrenched power of the Thai conservative elites. These networks operate actively and openly even when the country is under elected civilian governments. Particularly after the 2014 coup, the military appeared so confident in its power that it made no attempt to conceal the widespread activities of the internal security apparatus, backed by budgetary support and legal power. While the concept of a "deep state" suggests that conspiracy is the dominant mode of operation used to undermine elected governments, the Thai establishment has always worked openly to undermine its political rivals. Bureaucracy is the major apparatus used to perpetuate its power. Given the transparency of this aspect of ISOC's operations, the concept of a "deep" state does not apply.

Since the coup in 1947, which effectively brought Thailand under a full military regime with Field Marshal Phibunsongkhram (1948–57) as prime minister, the Thai military has never restricted itself to an exclusively military role. The military believes itself to be the core institution responsible for protecting the Thai nation from internal and external threats, maintaining peace and order, and actively engaging in national development. Its victory over the Communist Party of Thailand (CPT) further increased its confidence. A "coup-prone" politics has become a mark of the country's recent history. Since the end of the absolute monarchy in 1932, the country has been governed by military rulers for fifty-seven years in total, much longer than the thirty years under democracy (1932–33, 1947–73, 1976–88, 1991–92, 2006–8, 2014–19).

Some historians have argued that the Thai army from its very beginning was formed for internal security, not external defence (Baker and Pasuk 2005, p. 61). However, studies of the Thai military's internal security operations have been few and all of them focus on the counterinsurgency period only. Works of Chai-anan, Kusuma, and Suchit (1990), Suchit (1987), Suchit and Kanala (1987) and McCargo (2002) have contributed to a good understanding of the origin of the Thai military's internal security operations, which defined the military's extensive role in the nation's social, economic and political life. Despite their warnings about the military's attempt to sustain its political power and influence through its internal security apparatus after the end of the counterinsurgency period, there have been few studies focusing on the matter since the coup in 2006. Most studies of the Thai armed forces tend to focus on internal factionalism, conflict between elected civilian governments and military leaders, networks of cliques and classes, and personal ties between military leaders and the palace (Chambers and Napisa 2016; Surachart 1998, 2016; Yoshifumi 2008).

This is rather astonishing as studies of the military role in internal security affairs in other military-dominated authoritarian states, such as Indonesia, Pakistan, and various countries in Latin America, have been abundant for decades (Crouch 1988; Mietzner 2008; Lowenthal and Fitch 1986; Farooq 2012). Studies of the Thai military have left a big research gap. Possibly, the plummeting political legitimacy of the military after the bloody crackdown of the popular uprising in May 1992 led to a general belief that there would be no further coups, and a decline of research into Thai military affairs until the coup in 2006. As many believed that the Thai military had retreated from politics after 1992, this led to a misunderstanding that its continuing socio-economic and political programmes, disguised under a euphemistic term "*kitchakan phonlaruen khong thahan*" or the civil affairs of the military, were apolitical in nature.

The name ISOC, the nerve centre of the state's internal security affairs, disappeared from public view after the demise of the CPT. People may have thought that ISOC's function had ended long time ago. Despite the fact that ISOC has always been mentioned in studies of the Thai military, rightist movements, and problem in the three southern Muslim-dominated provinces (Bowie 1997; Ball and Mathieson 2007), there has been no serious dedicated study of ISOC. Although the threats to internal security in the post-counterinsurgency period have moved away from the battlefield to civil space, such as environmental issues, disaster management, illicit drugs and human trafficking, ISOC and the army comfortably sustained their leading role. The involvement of ISOC and the army in these non-militaristic areas began without any serious objection from elected governments, which seemed to lack a solid understanding of the implications of the military's internal security operations.

Moreover, while ISOC has been known publicly as the key agency in charge of internal security, all branches of the Thai armed forces have been active in internal security affairs. They have had their own operations and budgets. In fact, internal security projects account for a significant part of their activities. This study shows that the power of the Thai military lies not only in its use of force but also in its political arm. Its seemingly apolitical projects can be turned into dangerous weapons when the situation demands. This political weapon was initially created in order to counter the communist insurgency. After the collapse of the CPT in the mid-1980s, the establishment has consciously expanded these internal security operations and has worked to legitimize the military extensive role in the socio-economic and political sphere.

Since the creation of the modern Thai armed forces by King Chulalongkorn in the early twentieth century, the Thai military has never fought a full-scale war on Thai territory. When the Japanese imperial troops invaded and occupied Thailand in 1941, military leaders quickly gave in to their demands without resistance (Thaemsuk Numnon 2005). Internal security affairs, rather than external threats, have long been the raison d'être of the Thai military, the justification of its power, and the leading mission of the Thai military from the counterinsurgency period to the present day.

The military and its conservative allies have distrusted and despised civilian politicians and have not accorded them the authority that is standard in functioning democracies around the world. Although it has become increasingly difficult to suppress parliamentary democracy since the popular uprising in 1973, civilian control of the armed forces in Thailand has always been weak and ineffective. When the country was controlled by elected civilian governments between 1992 and 2006, politicians and civil society made little attempt to carry out any substantial reform of the security forces.

The main strategy to enhance civilian control over the armed forces was to appoint trusted generals in top positions of the army, simply to prevent another coup (Chambers 2015). Though some civic groups and scholars call for the military to "return to their barracks" in an effort to enhance democratic governance and civilian control over the military, none of them advocate dismantling the military's internal security apparatus or closing down its extensive involvement in socio-economic and political matters. The lack of any attention to the military's extensive role in the socio-political arena is reflected in most recommendations for security sector reform, which tend to follow the standard guidelines for professional militaries in democratic societies, such as reducing the size and budget, increasing capacity and technological know-how, adapting to the dynamics of globalization and new security threats, and strengthening civilian control over the armed forces (Surachart 1999; Chambers 2015, p. 9). As Raymond (2018, pp. 131–32) argues, the fear of coups deters civilian politicians and governments from any attempt to exert civilian control over the armed forces. They lack understanding of defence issues, military strategy and strategic planning. They try to placate the military leaders by giving in to their demands, particularly over the annual military budget and arms purchases. Moreover, after the defeat of the CPT, politicians, academics, and civil society possibly thought that the military's internal security operations no longer functioned. This area has thus been left solely in the hands of the military.

In *Thai Military Power: A Culture of Strategic Accommodation* (2018), Gregory Raymond argues that deterring and defending Thailand from external threats has been at the core of the Thai military's strategic and organizational culture since the establishment of the modern Thai armed forces by King Chulalongkorn in the late twentieth century. In his comprehensive analysis, the root causes of the Thai military's weakness and inefficiency in this defensive role lie in royal nationalist history, the hierarchical interdependence between the military and the monarchy, and civilian-military power relations. In contrast, this book will show that the Thai military has been heavily invested in internal security affairs, particularly in the post-counterinsurgency period, when Thailand's concern over external threats significantly declined.

Issues and Scope

The main topic of this book is Thailand's internal security affairs, which have been under the domination of the Thai army and ISOC, its political arm, since the counterinsurgency period. This study will show that, not only the ISOC, but all branches of the Thai armed forces, including the supreme command, the air force, the navy, and especially the army, have been active in internal security affairs in the post-counterinsurgency period until present day. Their activities are similar to those of ISOC. However, ISOC alone has coordinating power over other state agencies concerning matters of internal security. ISOC's special role is to coordinate and control other civilian agencies in order to discreetly and effectively infiltrate the society. ISOC thus figures prominently in this study.

The conservative elites have given great importance to maintaining the military role in the country's socio-political life even after the CPT was defeated. In order to maintain the relevance of internal security organizations after the demise of the CPT, the definition and scope of threats to national security were modified and expanded. The major questions of this book are:

- How did the Thai state's counterinsurgency approach open a gateway for the military's intrusion into the socio-economic and political sphere?
- How and why did such a role continue after the fall of the communist insurgency?
- How were threats to national security defined in the post-counterinsurgency period and how did the change of definition help perpetuate the military extensive role and power?
- What were the objectives and rationale used to legitimize the military's socio-political role?
- How was the internal security apparatus employed by the ruling elites to protect their power and interests, especially after the coup in 2006?
- How were state-dominated mass organizations turned into an apparatus of mass surveillance and ideological reproduction?

In the counterinsurgency period between the 1960s and 1980s, the military's framework, ideology and methods were formed for the internal security battle in the decades to come. The legacy of this period is still prevalent in the age of electoral politics. This book thus covers three major phases of the development of the military's internal security operations. The first phase was the counterinsurgency period, which was marked by the emergence of the concept of political offensive as part of counterinsurgency operations, the incorporation of socio-economic and political and psychological measures in the counterinsurgency strategy, the establishment of the Communist Suppression Operations Command (CSOC), later ISOC, in 1965, and the forging of the modern monarchy-military tie.

The second phase covers the semi-democratic period under General Kriangsak Chamanan (October 1977–March 1980) and General Prem

Tinsulanonda (March 1980–August 1988). This period witnessed a crucial transition: demise of the CPT, reform of counterinsurgency operations, and preparations for sustaining the military's internal security apparatuses in the post-counterinsurgency period. The Prime Minister Order Nos. 66/2523 and 65/2525 under the Prem government have been vaunted as the origins of a political offensive leading to triumph over the CPT. This study will offer a new interpretation of these orders and their implication for the military's power in the post-counterinsurgency period. The ramification of these orders extended far beyond the struggle against communism. From their inception they were intended to lay the groundwork for the military's political activity in the post-counterinsurgency period.

The third phase began with the coup in 2006 and continues until the present day. This phase was marked by the looming royal succession, the unprecedented popularity of Thaksin Shinawatra, polarization of Thai politics and society, the rise of the Yellow Shirts and Red Shirts movements, two military coups and the NCPO's authoritarian military rule. Alongside these political developments, ISOC was empowered to an astounding degree and the internal security apparatus, especially the military-dominated mass organizations and royalist ideological indoctrination programmes, were vigorously revived.

Frameworks

Internal security has been broadly defined as "the act of keeping peace within the borders of a sovereign state or other self-governing territories, generally by upholding the national law and defending against internal security threats". Crucial factors affecting security include social, political and economic conditions. The modern definition of internal security as "human security" extends the scope to include environmental degradation, poverty, migration, illicit drugs, human trafficking, and so on. Maintaining internal security requires the state to manage all kinds of threat to the well-being of its people (Katoch 2016, p. 18).

In the Cold War era, many post-colonial and developing countries faced challenges to their nation-building process, ranging from poverty, political and ethno-religious secession, and radical insurgent movements. The major task of the armed forces, which often captured political power, was to eliminate threats to internal security. Because internal security depended on domestic socio-economic and political well-being, the military expanded its role in politics. As Alfred Stepan (1986) has suggested, during the counterinsurgency period, the armed forces not only developed their standards of professionalism, armed strength, strategies and missions, but also became increasingly politicized. In other words, internal security affairs preoccupied the armed forces and acted as a justification for the expansion of their roles within, and authority over, other areas of governance. Such was the case of many military-dominated authoritarian regimes, such as those in Brazil, Peru, Argentina, and, alas, Thailand. The Thai military's leading role in internal security affairs during the counterinsurgency operations served as a springboard for its massive expansion into activities concerned with the country's socio-economic and political development. Any obstacle to the military's role in these areas was easily overcome when the military controlled the government.

The definition of threats to internal security can shift in accordance with changing situations. The broader the definition of internal security—such as the defence of the national pillars of nation, religion, and particularly monarchy—the greater the sphere of military power. Repeated calls by civil society, both nationally and internationally, for the Thai military to stop intervening in politics fell on deaf ears among the military and its conservative allies. The military's leading role in the counterinsurgency operations and the defeat of the CPT certified its high status within internal security affairs.

This study benefits from several studies on the Thai monarchy and military. Under the seventy-year reign of the late King Bhumibol Adulyadej, the monarchy shaped the unique character of modern Thai politics. The special relationship between the monarchy and the military underpinned the expansive role of the army. The military should, therefore, be viewed as part of the conservative elites, consisting of the military, top bureaucrats, judiciary and business elites, or what McCargo (2006) has termed "network monarchy". This conservative alliance has intervened in the political process through the palace and its proxies. King Bhumibol's royal hegemony was a licence for the network to exercise considerable influence over important issues. The various elements of the network were adaptable to changing situations. Some might be prominent at particular political moments, but keep a low profile when their roles were increasingly questioned. This study will show that collaboration among these conservative elites has been essential for the expansive role of the military in internal security affairs.

Several scholars have confirmed how the interdependent relationship between the monarchy and the military, with support from the US government during the anti-communist period, is essential for understanding the rise of the monarchy's political hegemony after the end of absolute monarchy in 1932. The military government of Field Marshal

Sarit Thanarat and the US government enthusiastically promoted the role of King Bhumibol and the palace members as a symbol of Thainess and the Thai state in fighting against the alien communist threat. The synergistic relationship, in which the military became subservient to the monarchy, became the major source of legitimacy for the military's political power. In return, the military has been committed to promoting a royal-nationalist ideology, depicting the monarchy as the embodiment of the nation (Thak 1979; Kobkua 2003; Hyun 2014; Chambers and Napisa 2016; Thongchai 2019). Chambers and Napisa (2016) suggested that the close association between the palace and generations of military leaders has turned the Thai armed forces into a "monarchized military", which in turn helped build and sustain the monarchy-centred political power. This book shows that the military-monarchy nexus has developed far beyond the personal or informal relationship between the palace and military leaders. It has involved the establishment of an infrastructure of political power for the military. The monarchy has been active in supporting and promoting the military's socio-political and economic role since the counterinsurgency period. In return, the military has pledged loyalty to the monarchical institution.

"Royal democracy" is a socio-political order which the network monarchy has been trying to entrench. The official name is "the Democratic Regime with the Monarch as the Head of the State". According to Thongchai (2019) royal democracy operates within an ostensibly normal parliamentary democratic polity, yet the power of elected bodies are restricted within parameters prescribed by the palace. Civilian governments do not have substantive power because true power is with the monarchy and its network. Despite the image of "being neutral and above politics", King Bhumibol often appeared as a source of legitimacy, particularly for military regimes, and a determining factor in major political issues. The palace often intervened via the network of the military, bureaucracy, judiciary and the Privy Council. The royal hegemony of the monarch is pivotal to the success or failure of the network's operations. For the Thai conservative elites, this Thai-style democracy, which honours and allows purportedly moral or good people to rule and intervene when it is necessary, is more suitable to Thailand than Western-style liberal democracy.

Internal security mechanisms have proven essential for ensuring the military plays a leading role in entrenching and protecting this socio-political order in the aftermath of the counterinsurgency period. The military employs hard power, such as coercion, oppression, and execution as well as soft power, including royal-nationalist indoctrination, propaganda, development and other incentive programmes, and the deployment of mass organizations.

Soft power strategies aim to create a sense of social unity by binding people together with the royal-nationalist ideology. According to Thongchai (2014), the narrative used to justify royal nationalism is based on two main strands. One claims that Thailand is facing constant external aggression, as exemplified by the fall of Ayutthaya to the Burmese on two occasions, and the loss of territories to the French and British. The second strand exalts the capabilities of the past monarchs, who had built the Thai nation to the present day and are responsible for the relative prosperity that has been achieved along the way. Such royal nationalist history has prevailed in the military's indoctrination programme until today.

Planting royal nationalism into the hearts and minds of the Thai people is seen as vital for building *khwam samakkhi khong chat*, or national unity. As Raymond (2018, pp. 32–36) argues, national unity is of paramount importance in the Thai military's strategic culture. It has been emphasized by the Thai kings and the military from the reign of King Chulalongkorn until today. They contend that disunity will lead the nation to another tragedy like the fate of Ayutthaya. Only the royal hegemony of the monarch is able to unify Thailand and lead the country out of deep-rooted conflict. National unity has been a matter of grave concern among the military since the political polarization after the 2006 coup. As this book will show, the remobilization of a royalist mass by the military and the revival of royalist indoctrination programmes through mass organizations shows how the military are trying to protect the social order through internal security mechanisms.

However, soft power is not the only measure the Thai state has used for building national unity. It has not hesitated to use coercion and violent force to suppress dangerous political opponents, particularly those accused of being un-Thai or anti-monarchy. This unity is a unity without diversity and hence is unrepresentative of the complexity of Thai society today.

Structure of the Book

The presentation is not based on chronological order, but structured around three major aspects of the military's internal security operations: first, their development, rationale and legitimacy; second, socio-economic development programmes; and third, mass organizations and mobilization programmes.

Chapter 2 is divided into two sections. The first provides a historical background of Thailand's counterinsurgency operations and the vital role of the monarchy, the military and the United States. It then explains the origin of *kanmueang nam kanthahan* or the political offensive, and the development of the concept of security, and civilian-police-military operations during counterinsurgency operations in the 1960s, and shows how these concepts were modified for the expansive role of the military in the post-counterinsurgency socio-political sphere. It shows that all branches of the Thai armed forces have been engaged in internal security. The second section examines the sources of political and legal legitimacy for the military's wider socio-political role from the counterinsurgency period until the present day.

Chapter 3 discusses the emergence of the development military in parallel with the development monarch, and the expansion of the military's development programmes into new areas. This chapter argues that the concept of development for security and the perception of threats were modified to facilitate the military' role in the post-counterinsurgency period. The military's early development programmes in the rural areas were transformed and extended into urban areas. On the one hand, the role of the monarchy was crucial in the expansion and transformation of the military's development role. On the other hand, the military was enthusiastic in promoting the image of King Bhumibol as a development monarch.

Chapter 4 begins with a discussion of the state-sponsored mass organizations during the counterinsurgency period, including their objectives and practices, and an assessment of the success and limitations of the military's political offensive operations. This will lead to a new interpretation of the Prime Ministerial Orders Nos. 66/2523 and 65/2525. These two executive orders have been praised as the most successful policies behind the Thai state's victory over the CPT. The treatment here explains why the governments during the subsequent semi-democracy period continued the same mass control operations. Importantly, the bad reputation of the ISOC-dominated rightist groups following the student massacre on 6 October 1976 had little impact on their operations.

Chapter 5 focuses on the remobilization of mass organization since the coup in 2006. State-sponsored mass organizations were in decline immediately following the counterinsurgency period. However, once the Thai establishment could claim to be facing new political enemies, they easily revived the remnants of the Cold War organizations as well as creating new ones. As the politics became more polarized, the mass organizations became larger and more varied. This chapter looks at the objectives of the mass control programmes, the membership, and methods used by ISOC and the military government to establish a broad base of loyalist citizens and mass surveillance by deploying Cold War methods.

Research Materials

When I was first drawn to this subject, I was not sure if I could do research on this topic. I thought it would be difficult to obtain empirical data related to security affairs because it would be highly classified. I do not have connections with personnel in the armed forces either. Despite these obstacles, curiosity got hold of me. The more I searched for data on the military's non-military affairs and ISOC, the more interesting information I found, including websites, Facebook accounts, photographs, and video clips on YouTube channels belonging to various branches of the army, ISOC, paramilitary forces, and mass organizations. Some of the sources are official documents from meetings between ISOC officers and members of mass organizations. In this Internet age, the military and civilian government agencies utilize cyberspace to promote their activities, connect with their members, and conduct psychological operations. Numerous pictures and video clips about their activities which appear on the web were possibly intended to impress their superiors about the success of their operations.

The websites and Facebook accounts of ISOC headquarter, ISOC regions, and army regions provide rich information on the military's civic activities and their network of collaborators. ISOC's provincial branches have regularly uploaded their training activities onto YouTube.[7] Whenever ISOC had a new programme, it would create a new Facebook account to promote and persuade people to join the programme. One interesting programme is the *007 sai khao khwammankhong* or *007 Intelligence*, which is a channel for people to report intelligence information to ISOC. The unit also has an account on the social media *Line*.[8] Many ISOC-dominated mass organizations created Facebook accounts to display their group activities and to invite people to join them.[9] Numerous video clips, particularly about ISOC's ideological training programmes, have been uploaded to YouTube. One only needs to type the names of those mass organizations to get the results.[10] Websites and Facebook pages of the Supreme Command, army, air force, and navy are useful as well.[11] Thammasat University Archives carry numerous documents related to the Thai state's counterinsurgency operations. They have been underutilized.

Although it was difficult to find ISOC officers willing to be interviewed, it was possible to interview government officials who worked with ISOC and people who were recruited for training and ideological programmes. This was possible partly because many activities took place outside the military barracks, in the public civic sphere, such as schools, village meeting places, and the forest reserve areas. Their confidentiality was lax. It is also possible that the military regime under the NCPO was overly confident in its power. ISOC often organized press conferences to inform the public, if not to show off, what it was doing. If one tuned into a rural radio channel, one would often hear the voices of military officers talking about various problems in the area and how the military was trying to solve them. This happened during my trip to the northeastern provinces during floods in late 2017. A minibus driver turned on the radio and instead of hearing the voice of a provincial governor talking about the floods, as one would expect, I heard a top military officer of the Second Army Region talking about the military's role in mitigating natural disaster. All these sources are useful for understanding internal security operations since 2006.

Notes

1. Article 44 of the Interim Constitution of 2014 states that in any case deemed necessary by the Head of the NCPO, with the approval of the NCPO, shall authorize, issue an order, restrain or perform any act regardless of whether such act enters into legislative, executive or judicial force. In this regard, all orders, as well as actions and performances in compliance with such orders shall be deemed lawful and constitutional.
2. Interview Mr Wat (pseudonym), 30 March 2017, Bangkok. He is the leader of the United Front for Democracy against Dictatorship (UDD).
3. Interview with Somchit (pseudonym), 21 August 2017, Ubon Ratchathani. She identified herself as a Red Shirt who holds a leading position in the government-sponsored programme of promoting women's role in community development.
4. "Op-rom phunam yaowachon kongthap thai" [Training Young Leaders by the Thai Armed Forces], 8 March 2014, https://www.youtube.com/watch?v=rga76bHeZU4 (accessed 14 December 2017); *Chiangmai News*, "Yaowachon Thai ru rak samakkhi" [Thai Youths United], 27 January 2020, https://www.chiangmainews.co.th/page/archives/1244426 (accessed 20 February 2020); Interview with a vocational student, 2 November 2018, Kanchanaburi.
5. I gave a public seminar on the anti-democracy role of ISOC and the military's civil affairs project at the Faculty of Political Science, Chulalongkorn University on 14 November 2017. The seminar was reported by the press: *Prachatai*, 17 November 2017; *Way Magazine*, 15 November 2017; and *Khom Chad Luek*, 15 November 2017. Later, it was followed by two in-depth interviews I gave to *Prachatai* (27 February 2018) and The 101 World (14 December 2017).
6. The army officer's name is Major Colonel Pasakon Kulrawiwan. On 3 July 2014, he escorted me to the NCPO headquarters at the 1st Infantry Regiment Camp on Phahonyothin Road for the junta's "attitude adjustment" of people considered to be anti-military. He bragged that he was in charge of reorganizing the minibuses in Bangkok. He was also involved in many arrests of anti-military activists.

7. For example, www.isoc.go.th (previously www.isocthai.go.th until 4 July 2017), www.facebook.com/isocnews1/ of ISOC Headquarter; http://www2.army2.mi.th/th/category/isoc2 and //th-t.facebook.com/pg/กอรมนภาค-2-176558233055660/posts/?ref=page_internal of the Army Region 2; https://www.isoc.go.th/?tag=%E0%B8%A0%E0%B8%B2%E0%B8%84-3 of ISOC Region 3; https://www.isoc.go.th/?tag=%E0%B8%A0%E0%B8%B2%E0%B8%84-4-%E0%B8%AA%E0%B8%99 of ISOC Region 4; https://www.isoc.go.th/?tag=%E0%B8%A0%E0%B8%B2%E0%B8%84-4-%E0%B8%AA%E0%B8%99 of the Army Region 4; https://www.facebook.com/massisocsmtpr/?__tn__=%2Cd%2CP-R&eid=ARBQQ5_A_i4GggrZ1ClIEF9oz5X-GV_PhTL5pvBb2mSqDUYiqoqjDwPRYxi05tMVPUOhNVTa89HCwlHp of ISOC News.
8. See https://www.facebook.com/isoc007/?__tn__=%2Cd%2CP-R&eid=ARD2wHDTzvnsXUdPSvFWVsZnKQDmgaShgq64Ico9R_8inb-EAsSTHjFWT34Gxg-F-kHbtDwpnK8O7oS9
9. Such as https://www.facebook.com/thai.asa.pongkanchat/ of the Thai National Defence Volunteers; https://www.facebook.com/groups/1581194052132176/ of the Military Reservists for National Security of Phuket province; Such as *Chomrom bikbaithai chairakphaendin ko.o.ro.mo.no.* (Club of Thai Big Bikers Love the Nation, ISOC), see its Facebook, https://www.facebook.com/Bigbike.center/; https://www.facebook.com/profile.php?id=100006388475830 of Club of Village Scouts, Bangkok.
10. Such as https://www.youtube.com/watch?v=wGXU9iIhl5s of the Thai National Defence Volunteers (TNDV); https://www.youtube.com/watch?v=mlXc7ZjFl7Y of the TNDV, The Military Reservists of National Security and the Military Veterans.
11. Directorate of Civil Affairs of the Air Force's Facebook page https://www.facebook.com/กรมกิจการพลเรือน-ทหารอากาศ-1468497056773884/?ref=page_internal; Directorate of Civil Affairs of the Army's Facebook page https://www.facebook.com/pg/doca.thaiarmy/posts/; Directorate of Civil Affairs of the Navy's Facebook page https://www.facebook.com/navalcivil/; Directorate of Joint Civil Affairs' website https://j5.rtarf.mi.th/web/index.php

Rationale, Legitimacy and Development

Since the end of the absolute monarchy in 1932, Thailand has spent more time under a military regimes than under civilian rule. The military and its conservative allies have tended to define what are the threats to national security. Despite a change in socio-political circumstances in the post-counterinsurgency period, new threats have been defined which provide the rationale and legitimacy for the military, especially the army, to expand its socio-political role. In contrast, civilian governments have paid little attention to this matter. This chapter examines the development of the power of the military—the army in particular—over internal security affairs.

The chapter contains two sections. The first provides the basic understanding of the Thai state's counterinsurgency operations against the Communist Party of Thailand (CPT) since the 1950s. It begins with a brief description of the origin of the struggle against the CPT and how this struggle defined the Thai state's perception, strategy and operations on internal security affairs. The cooperation among the military, the monarchy and the United States is discussed. Then, I trace the emergence of the two key concepts of Thailand's counterinsurgency operations: the concept of political offensive (*kanmueang nam kanthahan*) and the concept of development for security (*yutthaphatthana*). These two concepts were the basis for the expansion of the military role in the socio-economic and political development spheres during the counterinsurgency period, and were sustained with modifications in the post-counterinsurgency period. I demonstrate that ISOC was not the only agency involved in internal security operations as commonly understood. All branches of the Thai armed forces, including the army, navy, air force and the Supreme Command, have been extensively involved in the country's socio-political affairs at least since the early 1980s when the communist threat was in decline. Internal security has been the leading mission of the Thai armed forces.

In the post-counterinsurgency period the threats to national security no longer involved combat and hence should have been the responsibility of civilian agencies, yet the military continued to claim that managing these threats was its main mission. The second section shows how the military secured legal and political legitimacy to continue its wider socio-political role from the counterinsurgency period until the present day. It also examines how the political conflict since the 2006 coup resulted in the empowerment of the military-dominated internal security apparatus, including discussion of the content and the hidden objective of the Internal Security Act of 2008, the vital political legacy of the coup in 2006.

PART ONE: INCEPTION OF COUNTERINSURGENCY OPERATIONS

The Alliance of the Military, the Monarchy and the United States

While the support and influence of the United States were crucial for the Thai military's adoption of modern counterinsurgency operations, the role of the monarchy was no less essential. The counterinsurgency operations were the key sphere where the close alliance of the military, the monarchy and the United States was formed.

The communist movement was present in Thailand from the 1920s but Thai governments did not take it seriously in the early years. Some members of the Chinese Communist Party migrated to Thailand and began to promote communism among Chinese migrants. The CPT was established during World War II with a main objective of mounting resistance against the Japanese. After the war ended, the CPT began secretly promoting revolutionary ideas among peasant and workers. No armed unit was formed yet. Most CPT members were Chinese migrants (Suthachai 2008, pp. 76–77).

The military coup d'état in 1947, led by General Phin Choonhavan, Colonel Kat Katsongkhram, and Police General Phao Siyanon, returned Field Marshall Phibun Songkhram to the premiership in 1948, beginning a long sequence of military regimes. Meanwhile, the dramatic expansion of communist regimes and movements in Asia after the end of World War II, and particularly the outbreak of the Korean War, deeply worried the United States, which began to provide socio-economic and security assistance to allied countries. Thailand became a partner in the US containment strategy in Southeast Asia until the end of the Vietnam War.

For Phibun, the US containment policy provided crucial economic and political support for his regime (1948–57). As Phibun was no longer a commander of the armed forces, his security depended on gaining support from the coup group and counterbalancing two rising and rival younger officers, General Sarit Thanarat and Police General Phao Siyanon. These three were the country's all-powerful triumvirate at the time. Phibun understood that acquiring huge military aid from the United States would gain him support among the military, while economic and development assistance was essential for building up his popularity in the context of post-war economic hardship. He seized the opportunity presented by the outbreak of the Korean War to secure US support. On 3 July 1950, Phibun announced that Thailand would dispatch 4,000 troops along with rice supplies to South Korea to assist the United States. Thailand was the first country to do so and thus greatly impressed Washington (Thak 2007, pp. 68–69; Fineman 1997, pp. 104–14; Natthaphon 2020).

Phibun knew that he must demonstrate a staunch anti-communist stance to the United States. He thus agreed to the US request for Thailand to recognize the uncharismatic Bao Dai as leader of South Vietnam in February 1950. In 1952, the Anti-Communist Activities Act was promulgated. Phibun's government began anti-communist campaigns and closed down newspapers accused of spreading communist propaganda. As a result, US economic and military aid increased. Phibun's anti-communist position is seen as a ploy to win US support for his personal benefit, rather than a reflection of his concern over a domestic communist threat (Fineman 1997, pp. 101–4).

After Sarit seized power from Phibun in a coup in 1957, the new regime treated communism more seriously. In his declaration at the 1958 coup, Sarit cited the rise of communism as one of the threats Thailand was facing. However, the Thai ruling elites still perceived the movement as external in nature and believed that revolutionary ideology remained alien to Thai people, and the Chinese-dominated movement was simply a minority problem (Chai-anan, Kusuma and Suchit 1990, pp. 49–50).

Thailand's relationship with the United States became increasingly solid, particularly when the United States began its full-scale engagement in South Vietnam right after the end of French colonial rule in Indochina in 1954. Washington launched gigantic containment policies in Southeast Asia, including nation-building projects in South Vietnam and Thailand, support for anti-communist regimes in Laos and Cambodia, and converting Thailand into an air base to support its Vietnam War operations.

By the early 1960s, communist movements inside Thailand and neighbouring countries increased their offensive activities. In December

1960, the communists in South Vietnam announced the establishment of the National Liberation Front, known as the Viet Cong, with the objective of driving American troops out of Vietnam and unifying the country. After Vice-President Lyndon Johnson returned from a trip to Southeast Asia in mid-1961, he made a report to President John F. Kennedy that if the United States wished to prevent Thailand and South Vietnam from being the next dominoes to fall, the United States must provide major support to the two countries (Williams et al. 1985, pp. 191–94). In Laos, the forces of the rightist faction were defeated by the communist Pathet Lao. In Thailand, communists from Laos and North Vietnam were reportedly recruiting people in the northeast and ethnic groups in the hills for training. The CPT also began propaganda work among peasants in the northeast. In light of this situation, Sarit established the Central Security Command (CSC) under the Supreme Command in 1962 (Chai-anan, Kusuma and Suchit 1990, p. 51).

The Thai armed forces, particularly the army, would not have been developed and modernized without comprehensive military assistance from the United States, covering almost all aspects, such as its professional outlook, fire power, personnel training, psychological warfare and intelligence gathering (Chai-anan, Kusuma and Suchit 1990, pp. 20–21; Randolph 1986; Natthaphon 2013). US aid served the vested interests of Thai military leaders and strengthened the country's military regime (Kusuma 1985, pp. 250–51). Thailand's socio-politico-economic development and foreign affairs were so comprehensively shaped by US policies that Benedict Anderson called this period in Thailand the American era (Anderson and Mendiones 1985).

The late King Bhumibol Adulyadej (5 December 1927–13 October 2016) was the most important leader involved in the counterinsurgency operations from the beginning. King Bhumibol and his family members began royal development projects as part of the political offensive against the communist movement in the remote rural and hill areas as early as 1954. Throughout his seventy-year reign, over 3,000 royal development projects were created. As Natthaphon Chaiching (2020, pp. 149–67) shows, the monarchy occupied a central position in the US's psychological operations and propaganda to counter communism in Thailand. His projects and his frequent visits to the poor in the remote countryside were vital components of the monarchy's image. The royal institution became a symbol of Thainess unifying the people to fight against communism.

The palace developed a close relationship with Phao and the Border Patrol Police (BPP) from the Phibun period onwards. The monarchy and the BPP carried out civil activities, including providing primary education, forming schools, arranging medical assistance, and advising people of job opportunities. They also recruited and trained local paramilitary forces. The BPP was the first armed unit active in the political offensive strategy. It was created in 1951 with the assistance of the CIA and placed under the command of the police. After the fall of Phao as a result of Sarit's coup in 1957, the role of the police and BPP in the counterinsurgency operations was reduced because Sarit distrusted Phao's armed forces. The army took over the leading role in counterinsurgency operations. King Bhumibol cultivated a good relationship with the military (Hyun 2014, pp. 127–31).

Sarit is known as a trusted knight of King Bhumibol, unlike Phibun, who tried to limit the role of the monarchy in the public domain. The king had tacitly supported Sarit's seizure of power from Phibun and Sarit showed a strong commitment to promote the king's political role, domestically and internationally. The king accepted the honorary positions of Commandant of the Army Academy, and Commander of the 1st Infantry Regime, the 11th Infantry Regiment, the 1st Calvary Regiment, the 1st Artillery Regiment, and the 1st Engineers Regiment. Queen Sirikit became the honorary commanding colonel of the army's 21st Regiment. All these units were part of the royal guard. A royal ceremony conferring *chaichaloemphon* flags on regiments was created to make allegiance to the monarchy a sacred duty of military officers (Thak 2007, p. 210).

The king's endorsement in the form of speeches and overseas trips also assisted in building up support for Thai military cooperation with the United States in the Vietnam War (Puangthong 2013, pp. 50–51). In return, the relationship with the monarchy was a vital source of legitimacy for Sarit's military rule. The relationship significantly transformed the role of the constitutional monarchy in that the king's interest in politics and his appeal to the populace increased tremendously (Thak 2007). By the time of the military regime of Field Marshal Thanom Kittikhachon and Field Marshal Praphas Charusathian (1963–73), the king's high moral authority had become the source of his political power. His tacit support was indispensable for future governments.

Counterinsurgency operations were the primary area where the personal and institutional relationships between the monarchy and the military were formed. During their co-operation throughout the period from the 1950s to the 1980s, a strong and hierarchical relationship developed. The royal institution spearheaded the Thai state's effort to fight the anti-communist war, while the military played an active role in numerous royal development projects, thanks to its well-organized manpower and equipment throughout the country. The monarchy was both the active operator of the political offensive strategy and the most valuable legitimator of the military's civil activities. The interdependency of the monarchy and the military, where the latter acted as the subordinate to the former, strengthened the political power of both (Thak 2007; Kobkua 2003, p. 168; Chambers and Napisa 2016, p. 426). I will illustrate this close cooperation in detail when I discuss the military's development work in Chapter 3.

The Political Offensive Approach

The "political offensive" or *kanmueang nam kanthahan*, which literally means politics leading the military, was a central concept in the Thai state's counterinsurgency operations. The approach is commonly associated with Prime Ministerial Order No. 66/2523, entitled the "Policy to Win over Communism", issued by Prime Minister General Prem Tinsulanonda on 23 April 1980, supplemented two years later by Prime Ministerial Order No. 65/2525, entitled "Plan for Political Offensive to Win over Communism". In this subsection, I argue that the political offensive approach had emerged since the mid-1960s, symbolized by the creation of the Communist Suppression Operations Command (CSOC) on 14 December 1965, renamed as the Internal Security Operations Command (ISOC) in 1974. In practice, the political offensive was translated into socio-economic development projects, mass organization, ideological indoctrination and psychological programmes.

The Central Security Command (CSC), established in 1962, was the first organization in charge of communist suppression and was tasked with coordinating various state agencies involved in anti-communist operations. But CSC failed to subdue communist activities and armed attacks. The belief that it would defeat the CPT within six months evaporated when the rural areas under communist influence and infiltration expanded. CSC was unable to coordinate various state agencies to work with them because these agencies did not yet take the communist threat seriously enough. Even the majority of the military did not see the significance of the political offensive. Armed suppression continued to dominate the counterinsurgency operations. Then, on 7 August 1965, the CPT officially announced the beginning of armed struggle against the Thai state and launched armed attacks against state security forces in Na Kae District in Nakhon Phanom Province (Chai-anan, Kusuma and Suchit 1990, pp. 58–59).

The political offensive approach was established within the context of the Thai state's frustration at the expansion of the communist insurgents.

When the Thai communist movement began to emerge in the mid-1950s, the Thai military was confident that it could eradicate the insurgents from Thailand within six months. But by the mid-1960s, the insurgents' strength had increased. They were able to capture more areas in the provinces and caused more casualties to state authorities. Finally, they announced the official establishment of the Communist Party of Thailand in 1965. Against the background of the growing communist movements in the neighbouring countries, the CPT compelled the ruling elites to admit that the use of armed suppression alone was inadequate to end the armed struggle, and that communism could not be viewed simply as an external invasion because the root cause of the armed conflict lay with domestic socio-economic and political injustice (Chai-anan, Kusuma and Suchit 1990; Saiyud 1986).

In the early years of CSOC, its architects still believed that the CPT was by nature an external threat and tried to convince the public that people remained loyal to the government, as shown in Saiyud's speech in 1968 (Saiyud 1986, p. 35). The military gradually learned from the CPT's guerrilla warfare that its strength was based on the support it gained from villagers in the insurgent areas. Because of their inferior fire power, the insurgents tried to expand their popular base, support, and loyalty by deploying ideological, political, socio-economic, psychological and military methods in their struggle. Mass organization was a vital element of the communist guerrilla operations. By contrast, the heavy use of force by the Thai state failed to win over the people. It drove more and more people to join the insurgents.

In response to the deteriorating situation, the military government of Thanom and Praphas began to take the counterinsurgency more seriously. Praphas established the CSOC, just a few months after the CPT officially announced the beginning of armed struggle. In his capacity as army commander, Praphas was its first ex-officio director. The political-cum-military offensive became CSOC's mantra. CSOC was assigned to plan, coordinate and command the police, civilian and military units involved in counterinsurgency operations (Saiyud 1986, pp. 28–30).

General Saiyud Kerdphol helped to establish CSOC/ISOC, where he held the positions of the chief of staff and then director before retiring as the supreme commander of the armed forces. In his various speeches in the late 1960s, Saiyud talked of the importance of integrating rural economic development and popular participation in the counterinsurgency programmes in order to build villagers' trust and confidence in the Thai state. He emphasized this idea more firmly in his speeches in the early 1970s when the Thai armed forces were facing increasing challenges from the CPT (Saiyud 1986, pp. 30, 42, 116). In a confidential letter in 1971, Praphas as CSOC director asked Prime Minister Thanom to persuade other related state agencies to give their full cooperation to the government's anti-communist policy as a priority. He emphasized that all state agencies must align with the political offensive approach and make use of force or legal measures as a supplement when necessary. Praphas repeatedly stressed the importance of persuading the people to be on the side of the government (Thammasat University Archive [hereafter TUA], So.bo.9.7.2/65).

Saiyud often emphasized civilian-police-military joint operations (CPM). The term "civilian" here meant civil servants and the people, especially the locals living in the areas under the counterinsurgency operations. CPM was based on the doctrine that the communist guerrilla warfare was a people's war, and that the insurgents were trying to win the people's support by various means, such as indoctrination, anti-government propaganda, and pro-poor economic policies. The Thai state must therefore try to compete with the insurgents, winning the hearts and minds of the people as opposed to ruling through brute force alone. The state would win over the insurgents only when it could mobilize popular cooperation and support for a variety of programmes. The assumption was that active participation of the people would ensure the success of these programmes and would eventually lead to widespread public loyalty (Tanham 1974, pp. 72–84; Saiyud 1986, pp. 30–31).

This idea gave birth to state-controlled mass organizations, through which several programmes were administered, including village development projects, vocational and skill training programmes, royal-nationalist indoctrination, propaganda, paramilitary forces, intelligence gathering and surveillance (ISOC 1972, pp. 2–14; TUA, So.bo.9.7.2/70, pp. 2-15–2-40). Mass organizations, therefore, were the crux of the political offensive approach. The first mass organizations set up by ISOC in 1966 were the Village Security Teams (VSTs). In 1967, VSTs were organized in about 140 villages (Saiyud 1986, pp. 30–31). The CPM approach of joint operations by state agencies and mass organizations has remained at the core of ISOC's operations.

The United States certainly had influence over the establishment of state-controlled mass organizations. The administration of President Dwight D. Eisenhower saw the significance of organizing and mobilizing indigenous paramilitary forces in order to strengthen village-level security. In an internal US intelligence report from 1954 on psychological strategies deployed in Thailand, the CIA detailed counterinsurgency projects aimed at assisting anti-communist psychological operations. It proposed to transform paramilitary forces into village self-defence units, loyal to the Thai state (Hyun 2014, p. 122). I will discuss in detail the topic of state-sponsored mass organizations in Chapter 4.

In sum, the concept of political offensive emphasized that armed operations must be carried out in tandem with socio-political and economic measures. The experience of armed struggle against the CPT shaped the military's doctrine and operation of the counterinsurgency. Its strategists realized that they could no longer rely on the brute force tactics of the past and must now compete for the hearts and minds of the people, especially those in the communist infiltrated rural areas. In short, it was seen as necessary for the military to have an active role in the nation's development and security (Chai-anan, Kusuma and Suchit 1990; Saiyud 1986).

Development for Security Concept

With the inauguration of the Sarit regime, Thailand entered the era of the developmental state. But the meaning of development according to Sarit focused on nation-building, initially different from the path that the United States wished Thailand to follow, namely development as a strategy for fighting the communist threat. The concept of development for security, *yutthaphatthana* or *kan phatthana phuea khwam mankhong*, became an essential component of the counterinsurgency's political offensive approach and was absorbed into the military's mandate. National security and socio-economic-politico development became two sides of a single coin.

As Washington was increasingly concerned about its overall strategic plan in Indochina, it was willing to approve Thailand's requests for financial and military aid. The US aid no doubt came with advice on the planning and implementation of aid programmes to suit the strategic requirements of the US. Under Sarit, it was easier for American security experts to convince the Thai government of the domestic and regional communist aggression. Sarit's rural development programmes were easily absorbed into the US counterinsurgency idea. Originally, the Sarit government's rural development programmes were aimed at all regions. But from 1961, they focused on the northeastern region, the proximity of which conveniently served the US operations in the Vietnam War. The region was also the stronghold of the CPT. Infrastructure development projects, rather than agriculture and irrigation projects, were prominent in the American-dominated plans. Numerous community development projects and administrative centralization served the objective of preventing the spread of communism (Thak 2007, pp. 168–69).

The Sarit regime originally pursued development, *kan phatthana*, as part of nation-building. The focus was on improving the living standards in the rural areas nationwide through the extension of water and electricity facilities, constructing and repairing village roads, improving sanitation and health, developing agriculture, constructing small reservoirs, and expanding education. As Thak (2007, pp. 9, 167) elaborates, when Sarit staged his second coup in 1958 he claimed he had two objectives, *patiwat* and *phatthana*, revolution and development. The terms did not imply radical change to the socio-economic and political order but were a framework for nation-building. In Sarit's usage, the term *patiwat* meant the stabilization of the traditional hierarchical political and economic order, while *phatthana* was interpreted as the means to achieve *patiwat*. The well-being of the nation and the people would be taken care of by macroeconomic planning under an authoritarian government. Because of US influence, however, the meaning of development shifted to mean a strategic response to the rising communist threat.

Another important point which allowed the United States to advance its development for security strategy rather smoothly was the fact that US aid was channelled through the Thai armed forces, making the Thai military government and armed forces dependent upon its benefactor. President John F. Kennedy preferred increased use of civilian measures to counter communism. Economic, political and social developments would supplement military measures, not replace them. Significantly, the civil activities were disguised under the rhetoric of "development for security" and "modernization" to provide ideological justification for covert counterinsurgency programmes in US-allied countries (Hyun 2014, p. 142). In addition, the United States Operations Mission played an important role in directing the works of the Community Development Department, established in 1960. The Mission also heavily financed the army's three Mobile Development Units, established in 1962. These units allowed the army to spearhead national development work in critical areas (Thak 2007, p. 171).

As the military undertook major civil action programmes in remote areas, rural developmental work was linked to national security. Since protecting national security was the major task of the military, development was then automatically integrated into the army-led counterinsurgency programme (Chai-anan, Kusuma and Suchit 1990, p. 93). Security and development, thus, became the Thai military's dual strategy from the mid-1960s until the present day. Unfortunately, ISOC and the army became infamous for their oppressive approach. I will make an assessment of the military's political offensive and the true implications of Prem's Order 66/2523 in Chapter 4.

The Modern Political Offensive

Although the Thai military nowadays seldom uses the term "political offensive", the reality remains. The military continues to undertake various development and socio-political projects, but has devised a new euphemistic term to make such activities sound less threatening and intrusive. *Kitchakan phonlaruean* literally means civilian affairs or civil activities. The army, navy, air force and Supreme Command have all established a Department of Civil Affairs which oversees activities concerning internal security.

In 1982, at the demise of CPT, the Prem government established a new department under the army, called *Kong kitchakan phonlaruean* or the Directorate of Civil Affairs. Later, the Supreme Command, navy and air force established their own civil affairs departments. The three main missions are:

1. to unite manpower and resources of the military, civilian state agencies and the populace to support military-led operations on civil affairs, psychology, public relations and information operations, with the objective of maintaining internal security and order;
2. to use the military's resources to support the works of civilian administrative bodies in order to maintain peace and order in both normal and critical times; and
3. to promote and protect the three pillars of the Thai nation (Rakrat 2016).

The activities of the Directorate of Civil Affairs of other armed forces appear redundant alongside those of ISOC.[1] According to Surasak's study (1993, p. 89), ISOC's Department worked with civilians, meaning state-sponsored mass organizations and the public in general, while those of the branches of the armed forces involve only their own personnel. This principle was applied in the 1990s, but the Directorates of Civil Affairs of the army, navy, air force and Supreme Command no longer limit their activities to their personnel, as shown on their websites in May 2019. They have recruited students and people of different professions for their various programmes. The major activities include promoting royalism, especially the *Chit-a-sa* or the Volunteer Spirit, a programme initiated by King Vajiralongkorn. Other activities are cyber surveillance training, promoting royal-nationalism, public disaster preparation training and anti-illicit drugs programmes.[2] The army even established a Cyber Center, which is discussed in Chapter 5.[3]

In addition, the Armed Forces Development Command unit or *Nuai banchakan thahan phatthana* is involved in development of infrastructure and agriculture, particularly through numerous royal development projects. In essence, the scope of the armed forces' civil affairs activity has expanded beyond its original objective. All the branches are engaged in internal security affairs. All are parts of the political apparatus of the military. Among the four branches, the army is certainly the most active.

The expenditure budget of the Defence Ministry indicates the major task of the Thai military. Table 2.1 shows the allocation of the defence budget for fiscal year 2009 to various policies and projects of all branches of the armed forces. Only two of ten policy areas (items 7 and 8) are truly related to external threats. Seven of them are clearly concerned with internal security. They are: problems in the three southernmost Muslim-dominated provinces; building reconciliation among the people and restoring democracy; combating narcotic problem and influential people; improving public health; structural improvement of tourism and service sector; keeping internal security and order (defending the monarchy); and preventing and restoring public and natural disaster. Table 2.1 also indicates that all branches of the armed forces were given budgets for these internal security issues. The army has undertaken the highest number of plans.

This situation remains unchanged today. The defence budget for fiscal year 2018 shows that under the military government of Prayut, development projects under the armed forces have expanded further into areas which have nothing to do with internal security and are beyond the military's expertise, such as: enhancement of domestic economic strength and sustainability; development of special economic zones; development of the Eastern Economic Corridor; and development of transportation and logistics systems (see Table 2.2).

ISOC as the Army's Political Arm

The Anti-Communist Activities Act of 1952, revised in 1969, provided the legal legitimacy for anti-communist operations and the existence of ISOC until April 2000, when the government of Chuan Leekpai (1997–2001) repealed the Act. Although ISOC has officially been under the command

TABLE 2.1
Budget of Ministry of Defence for Fiscal Year 2009

Policy Programme	Agency in Charge	Value (million baht)
1. Building reconciliation among the people and restoring democracy	Total	62.3545
	Office of Permanent Secretary	26.7545
	Supreme Command	5.0000
	Army	30.0000
	Air Force	0.6000
2. Solving problems in the three southernmost provinces	Total	7,824,4026
	Supreme Command	50.8436
	Army	6,273.0000
	Navy	1,025.5590
	Air Force	475.0000
3. Combating narcotic problem and influential people	Total	277.4316
	Office of Permanent Secretary	2.2700
	Army	46.4440
	Navy	32.7555
	Air Force	16.5355
4. Improving public health	Total	94.3728
	Office of Permanent Secretary	0.3287
	Supreme Command	0.9000
	Army	12.5000
	Navy	3.7330
	Air Force	67.0111
5. Structural improvement of tourism and service sector	Total	29.7340
	Supreme Command	9.0000
	Navy	0.7340
	Air Force	20.0000
6. Keeping internal security and order (Defending the monarchy)	Total	1,222.3684
	Office of Permanent Secretary	11.5573
	Royal Bodyguards Dept.	660.6896
	Supreme Command	249.5125
	Army	280.0000
	Navy	5.6090
	Air Force	15.0000
7. Enhancing the nation's defence system	Total	158,247.54051*

continued on next page

TABLE 2.1 — *cont'd*

Policy Programme	Agency in Charge	Value (million baht)
7.1 The country is free from both external an internal threats.		155,300.9725
7.2 Enhancing military relations with neighbouring and friendly countries.		1,274.4790
7.3 Improving living conditions of people living in the military operated areas.		1,498.000
8. Preventing and solving terrorism. Defending national interest both inland and maritime areas.	Total Army Navy	1,831.3270 230.0000 1,601.3270
9. Preventing and restoring public and natural disaster	Total Office of Permanent Secretary Supreme Command Army Air Force	530.7200 2.3000 10.0000 479.7700 15.0000
9.1 A warning system	Navy	23.6500
10. Public administrative management	Total Office of Permanent Secretary Supreme Command Army Navy Air Force	47.1424 2.7824 10.0000 30.3600 2.0000 2.0000

Source: Budget Bureau, Thailand. *Expenditure Budget of Fiscal Year 2009*, vol. 1, pp. 419–24, http://www.bb.go.th/bbweb/?page_id=604 (accessed 21 February 2018).

of the Office of the Prime Minister, it does not bear any resemblance to a civilian agency. From its founding until today, ISOC has always been controlled by the army.

Until 1987, the army commander was ex-officio director of ISOC. The first director was Praphas, who simultaneously held the positions of army commander, deputy prime minister and minister of interior. The deputy director was the deputy commander of the army; four assistant director posts belonged to two assistant army commanders, the permanent secretary

TABLE 2.2
Budget of Ministry of Defence for Fiscal Year 2018

Policy Programme	Value (million baht)
Enhancing security of the nation's institutions	163.6809
Building national reconciliation and unity	54.3511
Solving problems in the three southernmost province	1,260.2339
Problems of alien workers and human trafficking	50.1760
Narcotic drugs suppression and rehabilitation of drug addicts	327.9422
Enhancing international relations in security area	77.2000
Enhancement of national defence system	74,947.5242
State personnel (security sector)*	104,335.0216
Security foundation	36,774.0759
Expansion of tourism and service revenue	95.0533
Enhancement of domestic economic strength and sustainability	170.3722
Development of special economic zones	33.6268
Development of Eastern Economic Corridor	443.0100
Development of transportation and logistics systems	9.5600
Research and innovation	78.9226
Total	220,523,650,700

Note: * Salary and wages.
Source: Budget Bureau, Thailand. *Expenditure Budget of Fiscal Year 2018*, vol. 2, pp. 310–11, http://www.bb.go.th/topic-detail.php?id=6494&mid=545&catID=863 (accessed 21 February 2018).

of the Ministry of Interior (MOI) and the national police chief; and the position of ISOC chief of staff went to the army chief of staff. Under Praphas's leadership, the revised Anti-Communist Activities Act of 1969 created posts of provincial ISOC directors, held ex-officio by the provincial governors under the supervision of regional directors, posts held ex-officio by the commanders of the army regions (TUA, So.bo.9.7.2/46). This means civilian agencies are under the power of the military in all matters concerning internal security. The provincial ISOC deputy directors are also army officers. ISOC has its own office at every provincial headquarters so that it can conveniently work with the MOI, a relationship that continues to the present day.

In 1987, the prime minister became the ex officio director of ISOC, and the commander of the army became the deputy director. This change took place under the government of Prem. Prem did not want to establish civilian control over internal security affairs but was under challenge from the army chief, General Arthit Kamlang-ek, once his trusted ally and now his rival. Arthit used the political apparatus of ISOC's mass organizations to build up his own popularity and to advance his political ambitions. Prem responded by moving ISOC under the Office of the Prime Minister and became its director, demoting the army commander to deputy director (see Figure 2.1) (Chai-anan, Kusuma and Suchit 1990, pp. 100–2; Suchit 1987, pp. 52, 57–62).

Placing ISOC under the prime minister appeared to fulfil Saiyud's wish. Since 1976, Saiyud had wanted the prime minister to take direct charge

FIGURE 2.1
Command Structure of ISOC Introduced by the Government of Prem Tinsulanonda in 1987

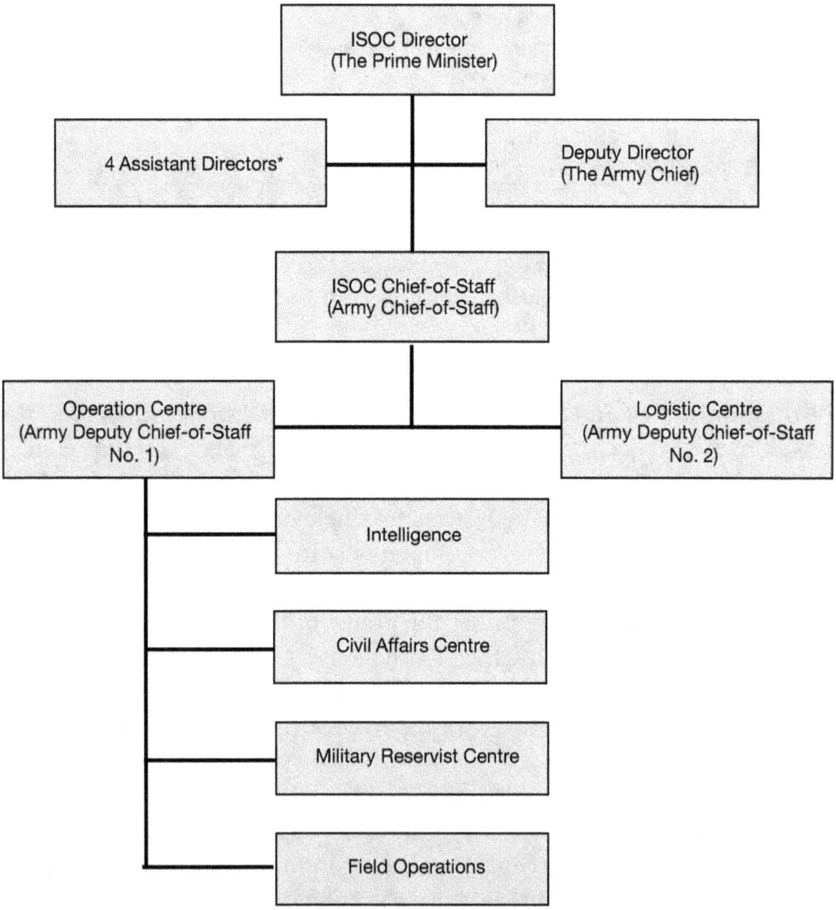

```
                    ISOC Director
                  (The Prime Minister)
                          |
        ┌─────────────────┴─────────────────┐
  4 Assistant Directors*              Deputy Director
                                      (The Army Chief)
                          |
                  ISOC Chief-of-Staff
                  (Army Chief-of-Staff)
                          |
        ┌─────────────────┴─────────────────┐
   Operation Centre                    Logistic Centre
   (Army Deputy Chief-of-Staff        (Army Deputy Chief-of-Staff
    No. 1)                             No. 2)
        |
        ├── Intelligence
        |
        ├── Civil Affairs Centre
        |
        ├── Military Reservist Centre
        |
        └── Field Operations
```

Notes: The Assistant Directors were two Assistant Army Chiefs, Permanent Secretary of the Ministry of Interior and the Police Chief.

of ISOC so that ISOC would have real authority over other state agencies (TUA, So.bo.9.7.2/147). The change did not modify the army's domination of ISOC because Prem was not a civilian leader.

In December 2018 Prayut announced that his government planned to make ISOC more civilian so that it would not be seen as the army's political apparatus. The agency would recruit more civil servants and police personnel (*Post Today*, 25 December 2018). But given the military's grip on power since the 2014 coup, such change would have no real substance. As of May 2019, all command positions of ISOC from the national director to heads of all departments and units are held by army officers.[4]

ISOC AND OTHER STATE AGENCIES

There are several state agencies that participate in the counterinsurgency operations. As mentioned earlier in this chapter, the army took command of operations after the coup in 1957. Despite the establishment of ISOC in 1965, the role of other state agencies, including the BPP, remained necessary and crucial.

Though ISOC is the primary authority over internal security for strategic planning, supervising and coordinating with all state agencies and the military's civil affairs projects, the major operations on the ground are carried out by regional agencies which have easy access to the targeted local populations. These agencies are under the authority of the Ministries of Defence, Interior, Education and Public Health. There are other agencies under various branches of the military that operate their own civic work projects. These include the Royal Thai Armed Forces (formerly the Supreme Command Headquarter), the army, air force and navy. Many of these initiatives are part of the royal development projects (see Chapter 3).

The key agencies involved in the government's development programme are the Community Development Department (CDD), Accelerated Rural Development (ARD),[5] Local Administration Department (LAD), and Public Welfare Department (PWD), which all report to the MOI. These are the civilian agencies most active in military-led counterinsurgency operations. Their territorial units throughout the country, along with subdistrict heads (*kamnan*) and village heads (*phuyaiban*), have assisted the military on countless projects. In this sense, they can be considered the administrative and civil wing of the military (Connors 2007, p. 111). As these civilian agencies appeared less threatening than the military, it was easier for them to work with local communities. The locally based village heads and subdistrict heads in particular proved to be excellent bridges between the Bangkok-based Thai state and the periphery. Their pivotal role in the success of executing development programmes across the country has continued to the present day. Since the 2006 coup, ISOC has worked more with the Ministry of Education, organizing many military and royalist indoctrination programmes for school students (see details in Chapter 5).

ISOC's enormous power is shown in its ability to mobilize the personnel of other state agencies to assist in its operations. ISOC does not have many staff. As of May 2018, ISOC had only 200 permanent personnel and 1,452 borrowed personnel, mostly military officers (*Manager Online*, 16 June 2018). Many more state officials worked under its command. For example, in 2014, Prime Minister Prayut, in his capacity as the ISOC director, authorized ISOC Region 4 Forward, which has been in charge of the unrest in the three southernmost Muslim-dominated provinces of Pattani, Yala, and Narathiwat, to mobilize 70,738 personnel from various state agencies. Of that figure, 61,221 were combat forces (32,958 soldiers, 18,583 policemen and 9,680 paramilitary), and 2,489 were civilians from the ISOC provincial offices and thirty-seven Centres for Sub-district-level Operations under the MOI in the three provinces. The remainder were experts at various tasks, such as intelligence operation, ideological struggle, explosives and ordnance, development assistance, and land patrolling (*Royal Gazette*, 30 December 2014, p. 40).

PART TWO: PROVIDING LEGITIMACY

Royal Hegemony

> The duty of soldiers is not limited to the use of force in war. They must also work in civilian affairs. They must employ their knowledge, thinking, psychology and wisdom, or their intellectual weapons, to develop local communities so that people can have a better livelihood, safety, and a good morale to do good deeds and progress for themselves as well as for the public. (King Bhumibol's speech given to the graduates of the Chulachomklao Royal Military Academy, the Royal Thai Navy Academy, the Royal Thai Air Force Academy, at the King Mongkut Medical College on 29 April 1993; *Lak Mueang* 2016, p. 1).

Under the leadership of the late King Bhumibol Adulyadej, the monarchy was the most important institution involved in the development of security strategy. Throughout his seventy-year reign, over 3,000 royal development projects were created. Most of them were located in the rural and hill areas.

They were an essential component of the US-supported psychological operations to combat communism in Thailand. Counter-insurgency operations were the primary area where the personal and institutional relationship between the monarchy and the military was formed. Cooperation between the monarchy and the military on counterinsurgency operations throughout the 1950s and 1980s formed the core of their hierarchical relationship. As the royal institution spearheaded the Thai state's effort to fight the anti-communist war in remote rural and upland areas, the military played an active role in numerous royal development projects. The monarchy was both the active operator of the political offensive strategy and the most valuable legitimizer of the military's role in civilian affairs. The interdependency of the monarchy and the military, where the latter acted as the subordinate to the former, strengthened the political power of both (Thak 2007; Kobkua 2003, p. 168; Chambers and Napisa 2016, p. 426).

State-sponsored mass organizations were another area where the special cooperation between the monarchy and the army took place. Members of mass organizations pledged loyalty to the monarchy and received royal patronage and support in return. Creating a force of compliant royalist citizens is the primary objective of the royalist elite and one which they have been largely successful at accomplishing. While politicians claim their political legitimacy from ballots, the military and its conservative allies claim to have immense support from the citizenry.

Royal patronage was essentially a licence to draw funds and cooperation from both government agencies and private firms. The king's moral authority possesses magnetic power that is capable of drawing popular support for state projects, and shielding the projects from public criticism (Bowie 1997 pp. 81–87; Chanida 2007, pp. 131–32). King Bhumibol's speeches often emphasized the necessity of the armed forces' involvement in national development programme, thus justifying the military's expansive role in civil work (Usani 1999, p. 32). It is not difficult to find messages similar to the king's speech quoted above. The king not only urged the armed forces to be actively involved in the nation's socio-political and economic development, particularly in the post-counterinsurgency period, but also provided them with legitimacy. I will provide more examples of royal legitimation of the military's expansive development works in Chapter 3.

His frequent visits to the countryside, and the initiation and promotion of thousands of rural development projects, were vital components of the image of *kasat nak phatthana*, the development monarch. The active participation of King Bhumibol and his family members was indispensable for the success of US-supported anti-communist operations in Thailand.

The United States launched the royal institution as a symbol of Thainess to combat the alien invasion of communism from the time of the government of Phibun (Natthaphon 2020). Even the Western press in the 1960s was able to see through the strategic objective of the US support of the Thai monarchy. In a *Time* magazine report from May 1966, an official from the United States Information Service (USIS) in Bangkok, who was actively involved in anti-communist psychological operations and propaganda, acknowledged that "USIS funds could not be better employed than spreading the likeness of His Majesty" (Puangthong 2019, p. 312).

The monarchy gradually appropriated the US-Thai government-sponsored development programmes and merged them into the royal development projects. Despite this direct political involvement, the projects were able to maintain a public image of being apolitical. These projects strengthened the king's popularity and supreme moral authority, which was then translated into his ability to intervene in politics. Although he had ascended the throne amid a tussle for power among prominent military generals, by the 1980s King Bhumibol had successfully built up the power of the monarchy. While the image of the military's credibility was strained by its leaders' corrupt practices, King Bhumibol emerged as the figure of the highest moral authority in Thai society. The royal projects were often cited as evidence of the king's devotion and sacrifice for the people. Such seemingly apolitical development projects became emblematic of King Bhumibol's public image as a righteous king, and formed the basis of his royal hegemony as well as the hyper-royalist ideology that burgeoned in the public imaginary. King Bhumibol was the biggest winner of the counterinsurgency operations in Thailand (Thongchai 2016, pp. 15–16; Hyun 2014).

By the mid-2000s, a discourse of royal nationalism was deployed to counter the increasing strength of electoral politics and popular politicians like Thaksin Shinawatra. Promotion of the royal development projects, King Bhumibol's ideas on the sufficiency economy, and love for the monarchy were the heart of indoctrination programmes by the armed forces and ISOC. This issue will be elaborated further in Chapters 3 to 5.

Legal Legitimacy

In addition to the Anti-Communist Activities Act enacted by Phibun's government, the civilian and military governments after the popular uprising of October 1973 provided constitutional and legal guarantees for the armed forces' role in socio-political and economic development projects.

The toppling of the military regime of Thanom-Praphas by a student-led popular uprising on 14 October 1973 brought a sudden political change, releasing previously suppressed social forces onto the streets. Students, peasants and workers expressed ideals of democracy, human rights and freedom to an unprecedented degree, to the point of being a real threat to the established social order. The student movement, led by the National Student Centre of Thailand, was increasingly radicalized towards Maoist-Marxist ideology. At the same time, the military, especially ISOC, was criticized harshly for its authoritarian and oppressive actions in remote areas. The students and press called for the dissolution of ISOC on grounds that its oppressive behaviour was socially divisive and pushed people to join the communist movement (Chai-anan, Kusuma and Suchit 1990, p. 103; Saiyud 1986, p. 195).

Concurrently, the number of CPT armed attacks on government sites in rural areas increased. Cambodia, Vietnam, and Laos fell under communist regimes in 1975. The establishment increasingly viewed the student movement as an enemy of the state and of its own interests. The ruling elites sought methods to counteract the new social movements. Several right-wing mass movements grew much stronger with support from the palace and the military. Left-wing activists increasingly faced attacks by right-wing thugs and some were assassinated (Morell and Chai-anan 1981). The US military withdrawal from Thailand and South Vietnam exacerbated anxiety among the establishment. In this context, attempts began to strengthen the legitimacy of the military's socio-economic and political role.

The primary step was to provide constitutional legitimacy for the military's expansion into internal security and development (Suchit 1996, p. 57). According to the Constitution of 1932, the role of the armed forces was limited to protection of national independence and interest. But in 1974, the National Legislative Assembly passed a constitution, in which section 70 stipulated five duties for the armed forces:

1. engaging in war;
2. protection of the monarchy;
3. suppression of rebellions and riots;
4. protection of state security; and
5. national development.

The first duty, engagement in war, is a standard responsibility for armed forces worldwide. But the second to fifth missions paved the way for the military's role in other socio-political-economic affairs.

Protection of the monarchy has become the primary objective of the Thai military nowadays and has taken on an almost sacred status. The law on *lèse majesté* was widely applied after the coup in 2006 to silence and threaten critics of the monarchy and the ruling elites (Streckfuss 2014). Defending the royal institution from the threat of communism has been the rationale for several military coups, including those by the National Reform Committee in 1976 (Order of the National Reform Committee, 6 October 1976), the Council for National Security in 2006 and the National Council for Peace and Order in 2014 (*Manager Online*, 20 September 2006 and 2 June 2014).

Rebellions and riots are caused by domestic strife rather than external threats. The job of suppression should fall to the police rather than the armed forces, which have no training in crowd control. The excessive use of force by the military in crackdowns on protesters in October 1973, May 1992, and April–May 2010 proved fatal to many civilians. As for protection of state security, the Thai state tends to make a broad interpretation of the term, such as in the case of the *lèse majesté* law. Insulting, critiquing, or threatening the king, the queen, the heir or the regent are considered threats to national security. The fact that the number of people charged under this law skyrocketed after the coup of 2006 indicates how national security has been exploited for political objectives. ISOC's current conception of national security has expanded to cover the affairs of minorities and illegal migrants, drug trafficking, cybercrimes, terrorism, deforestation, conflict over natural resources, "influential people" and mafia gangs, and even natural disasters (ISOC n.d a and b). Under the 2014 coup regime, critical comments about General Prayut were considered a crime of sedition (Human Rights Watch, 18 April 2017).

Lastly, the military role in "national development" encompasses a wide range of socio-economic and political affairs. The 1974 Constitution became a precedent for similar clauses in Thailand's later constitutions. The more power the military holds, the more broadly and arbitrarily these terms are interpreted.

Based on the 1974 Constitution, the army issued a supplementary Order No. 298/2519 in June 1976, specifying that the objectives of ISOC's programmes were to provide support to the government's community development and to supplement other government agencies' development work; to ensure that civilians maintain a friendly attitude towards soldiers and support armed forces' operations; to monitor intelligence and to promote national security; and to support the army's plan for communist suppression (Suchit 1996, pp. 7, 57; Suchit 1987, pp. 49–50).

In 1975 the Kukrit government made national security the primary objective of national planning. The theme of the fourth National Economic and Social Development Plan, covering 1977–81, was "development for security" to contain the communist threat (Chanida 2007, p. 125). Publications by the armed forces often quote the clause in the 1974 Constitution along with a statement by Kukrit, pledging to support the military's role in national development to ensure that people have a positive attitude towards the military (Usani 1999, pp. 35–38). With the force of law and public rhetoric behind the military, this period saw a substantial expansion of military-dominated mass organizations (see Chapter 4).

Despite the popular uprising of October 1973, which led to the end of over two decades of military rule, and despite the reaction against the military's failed crackdown on the revolt, which severely harmed the military's political legitimacy, the military's socio-economic and political work, as well as its constitutional legitimacy, ironically continued under civilian governments. This continuation of military influence under the cloak of civilian government was possible because of the Thai ruling elites' widespread fear of domestic and regional communist expansion at that time, and the fact that all three civilian prime ministers after October 1973—Sanya Dharmasakti, Seni Pramoj and Kukrit Pramoj—were conservative royalists. Needless to say, the use of military force still dominated the counterinsurgency operations throughout the 1970s.

The Danger of Ultra-Rightist Politics

The newborn democracy ended with a massacre of protesters at Thammasat University on 6 October 1976. The police, right-wing thugs and members of paramilitary groups, including the BPP, the Village Scouts, the Red Guars, and many others, were the primary perpetrators of this barbaric attack, responsible for killing, torture, lynching, burning and desecration of corpses in front of hundreds of Thai and foreign journalists (Puangthong and Thongchai 2018). Following the massacre, a military junta, known as the National Reform Committee (NRC) and led by Admiral Sangad Chaloryu, staged a coup d'état and appointed an ultra-royalist judge, Thanin Kraivichien, as prime minster. The widespread oppression that both preceded and followed the coup, drove thousands of students, peasants and activists to join the CPT in the hills.

As Thanin's oppressive ultra-rightist regime effectively strengthened the CPT militarily and politically, the ruling elites had to adjust their anti-communist strategy. During this time, the number of armed clashes between communist insurgents and state forces increased dramatically. The Thanin government's foreign policy led Thailand onto a dangerous path, risking the country's territorial security and the lives of villagers on the borders. Its extreme hostility towards the communist regimes in Vietnam, Laos and Cambodia resulted in border clashes with Cambodia's Khmer Rouge forces on an almost daily basis (Puangthong 2004). The junta, which installed Thanin's government in October 1976, saw the danger of his extreme domestic and foreign policies. Seeing an opportunity to consolidate power more firmly in the hands of the National Reform Committee, the junta leader, Admiral Sangad, staged another coup to remove Thanin on 20 October 1977. King Bhumibol offered Thanin a position on the Privy Council. General Kriangsak Chamanan, then Supreme Commander of the Armed Forces and one of the coup leaders, became prime minister.

The 1977 coup also made space for a dovish faction in the armed forces to rise. By 1978, a group of military officers calling themselves the Democratic Soldiers, *Thahan prachathipatai*, emerged as a leading intellectual force in the army. One of its members was General Chavalit Yongchaiyudh. This group had been influenced by Prasert Sapsunthorn, a communist defector working for the military since 1958. They had been trying to promote political-based measures in the counterinsurgency operations since the late 1960s (Chai-anan, Kusuma and Suchit 1990, pp. 67–68, 147). The crisis that the Thai state faced after the 1976 Thammasat massacre paved the way for this group to rise and subsequently to reform the counterinsurgency strategy. They were influential behind the Prime Ministerial Orders Nos. 66/2523 and 65/2525, which shaped the political offensive to defeat the CPT.

The Semi-Democratic Regime's Political Offensive

A semi-democratic regime began with the government of Kriangsak Chamanan (November 1977–March 1980) and was continued by that of General Prem Tinsulanonda (March 1980–August 1988). These governments were labelled as semi-democratic because the military remained a dominant power over both the executive and legislature despite the restoration of an electoral system in April 1979. The Constitution of 1978 gave an appointed Senate the same power as that enjoyed by the elected House of Representatives, and allowed non-MPs and active-duty bureaucrats and military officers to hold political positions, including the premiership. The semi-democratic system aimed to perpetuate the power of the military and conservative elites which refused to be subordinated to electoral power (Chai-anan, Kusuma and Suchit 1990, p. 182).

Kriangsak launched a political offensive by offering conciliation to the leftist students and activists. In September 1978, he granted an amnesty to the eighteen student leaders who had been imprisoned and charged with serious offenses after the Thammasat massacre. He also aimed for a diplomatic rapprochement with Vietnam, Laos and Cambodia (Puangthong 2004).

One month after he took over the premiership, Prem issued Prime Ministerial Order No. 66/2523, followed by Order No. 65/2525 two years later. These directives heralded an end to the hardline anti-communist military offensive in favour of a more political approach. Students, activists, and peasants who decided to depart from the CPT were allowed to return and resume normal lives without facing prosecution. Introducing at a time of weakening international support for the CPT, this policy presented a considerable challenge to the dwindling communist movement. These two orders also marked a new approach to the military's quest for means to justify their intervention in politics.

New Power in the Semi-Democracy Period

The two orders required all state agencies at all levels to comply with their implementation. ISOC was responsible for policy implementation, issuing directives, and coordinating the work of ministries, bureaus, departments and organizations. Its director was empowered to reward or punish civilian officials, police, military officers and others whom he appointed from various governmental organizations. Although the two Orders seemed to confirm the power that ISOC already exercised, Prem elevated them to a level of national policy that state agencies at all levels had to comply with. The two Orders overrode any directives, rules or regulation that were in contravention with them. The two Orders thus significantly increased ISOC's power.

In addition, Prem's Prime Ministerial Order No. 83/2526, dated 1983, further enhanced ISOC's immense power by placing civilian, military and police agencies under its command, along with mass organizations previously under other ministries, such as the Volunteer Defence Corps (*kong asa raksa dindaen*), formerly under the MOI (Ball and Mathieson 2007, p. 101). Again, in March 1986, Prime Ministerial Order No. 47/2529, signed by Prem, reiterated the priority of the Order Nos. 66/2523 and 65/2525. It directed all government agencies to fully participate in promoting the democratic regime with the monarch as the head of the state, and to focus on combating the united front activities which had emerged after the demise of the CPT and might subvert national security (Suchit 1987, pp. 68, 75, 100–4).

ISOC top commanders had been pushing for this increased power for some years. Although the agency had been tasked with leading and coordinating the counterinsurgency operations from the beginning, by the 1970s its officers were frustrated over the absence of a unified counterinsurgency strategy, which they blamed on weak coordination between the military, police, and civil servants. In 1971, Praphas as CSOC director wrote asking Thanom as prime minister to impress on other armed force units and civilian state agencies to give utmost importance to the counterinsurgency operations (TUA, So.bo.9.7.2/65). General Saiyud, then deputy director of CSOC, submitted a proposal to the minister of defence on 5 August 1976 to establish a unified command structure for civilian-police-military joint operations, under the command of the military (TUA, So.bo.9.7.2/148). With his two orders Prem created a unified system for internal security activities under ISOC, and ordered all state agencies to comply with their directives as a matter of national priority, thus granting ISOC unprecedented authority.

Other Legitimacy in the Post-Counterinsurgency Period

The semi-democracy regime of Prem ended in 1988, but the military managed to retain state support and legitimacy for its socio-political and economic activity. As mentioned earlier, the Constitution of 1974 had bestowed on the armed forces the constitutional right to engage in national development, and similar clauses were included in the constitutions of 1978 (section 56), 1991 (section 61), 1997 (section 72), 2007 (section 77) and 2017 (section 52). Despite the army's violent crackdowns on popular uprisings in 1973 and 1992, the attempts by political parties, elected governments and civil society to reform the armed forces were ineffective. Even under the Constitution of 1997, which was drafted with the participation of civil society and academics, the role of the armed forces in civil affairs remained unscathed. Those who drafted the Constitution of 1997 seemed uninterested or unknowledgeable about the military's civil activities. The military continued to claim constitutional legitimacy and support from elected civilian leaders for its role in civil affairs (Usani 1999, pp. 35–38).

The military role in the nation's socio-political affairs was also granted legitimacy through development planning. As mentioned earlier, national security was incorporated into the national development framework in the post-counterinsurgency period. "Development for security" became a policy in the Fifth Plan (1982–86), and the Sixth Plan (1987–91) reiterated that socio-economic development must support security and military policies (NESDB, 1987–91). Military leaders and Sumet Tantiwetchakun, a technocrat at the National Economic and Social Development Board (NESDB) and a key figure in the royal development projects, played important roles in incorporating security objectives into national development plans (Chanida 2007, pp. 128–29). Such legitimacy is often cited in military publications (e.g., Panya 1988, pp. 89–97; Sumet 1988, pp. 113–17).

In the period after the bloody suppression of protesters in May 1992, elected governments broadened the Thai military's role in the non-military sphere. In his inaugural address to parliament, Prime Minister Chuan Leekpai (November 1997–February 2001) emphasized that his government would support the military's participation in economic development, public health provisions, disaster relief operations, protection of natural resources and solving environmental problems (*Biznews*, 21 November 1997). On 1 April 2000, Chuan's cabinet repealed the Anti-Communist Activities Act, but did not dismantle ISOC, instead handing it responsibility for coordinating operations against narcotics (Ball and Mathieson 2007, p. 101).

Perhaps the Chuan government thought that redirecting the armed forces' mission towards socio-economic initiatives would lessen the military's interference in politics. After the popular outcry against the military's violent crackdown in May 1992, the army "retreated to the barracks" with its political role severely reduced, yet it remained a threat to elected governments by virtue of its armed force alone. As Yoshifumi demonstrated, the military's demands could not simply be ignored. In the post-1992 era, civilian governments paid attention to the annual military reshuffle with the objective of decreasing the possibility of a coup (Yoshifumi 2008, pp. 72–109). But the civilian governments underestimated the political implications of the military's civil projects. After the May 1992 violence had damaged its popularity and reduced its political role, the military welcomed the opportunity to expand its civil role. While the public called for the military to return to the barracks and reform itself in line with democratization and globalization, the civil projects, which were assigned to the military by elected governments and thus had the appearance of transparency and accountability, provided the military with an excellent opportunity to claim that its troops contributed to society.

These new socio-economic projects emerged at the time when global security studies took up the concept of "non-traditional security threats", meaning terrorism, drug trafficking, human trafficking, migration, disease and environmental problems. In Thailand, interest in the concept among security experts appears to have begun around the end of 1990s (e.g., Surachart 2000, 2002). The military was happy to adopt these new security threats into its mission. General Prayut wrote a research paper on "Adjustment of the Thai Armed Forces to Handle New Security Threats", as part of his training at the elite National Defence College in 2007–8 (Prayut 2008). The current ISOC organizational structure is designed to handle such a wide scope of internal security areas (see Figure 2.2). Academics seem to have sensed no danger as there is no scholarly critique of the military's expansion into these areas. Recently, the army commander General Apirat Kongsompong said in public that a good professional military must be involved in defending the monarchy, as well as suppressing illicit drugs, arms smuggling, and illegal immigration (*Khaosod*, 13 May 2019).

Thaksin's Limited Reform

A limited attempt to place the armed forces under civilian control took place after Thaksin Shinawatra became prime minister (February 2001–September 2006). He appointed his cousin and other associates to top positions within the armed forces, a move which was roundly condemned by his opponents as self-serving reform (Chambers and Napisa 2016, p. 431). Continuing his structural reconfiguration of the military, Thaksin issued Prime Ministerial Order No. 158/2545, dated 29 May 2002, which amended the mission, role, and responsibility of ISOC. Its ex-officio director remained the prime minister and the army chief of staff was its secretary. Thaksin appointed the supreme commander of the armed forces, and the permanent secretaries of the MOI and another civilian agency as its deputy directors while five assistant directors were the commanders of the army, the navy, the air force, the police and director general of the Department of Provincial Administration. Although he put a couple of civil servants on the ISOC executive, the restructuring did not significantly reduce military domination (Prime Ministerial Order No. 158/2545) (see Figure 2.3).

Thaksin's policy of restructuring the bureaucracy led to a cut in the military budget from 7.5 per cent of the national budget in fiscal year 2002 to 6.3 per cent in fiscal year 2006. The military budget, however, had declined steadily since 1991, when it was allocated 16 per cent of the national budget (Suehiro 2014, pp. 329–30). He also oversaw a reform of all ministries, including security agencies, with an aim to increase their

FIGURE 2.2
Command Structure of ISOC According to the Internal Security Act of 2008

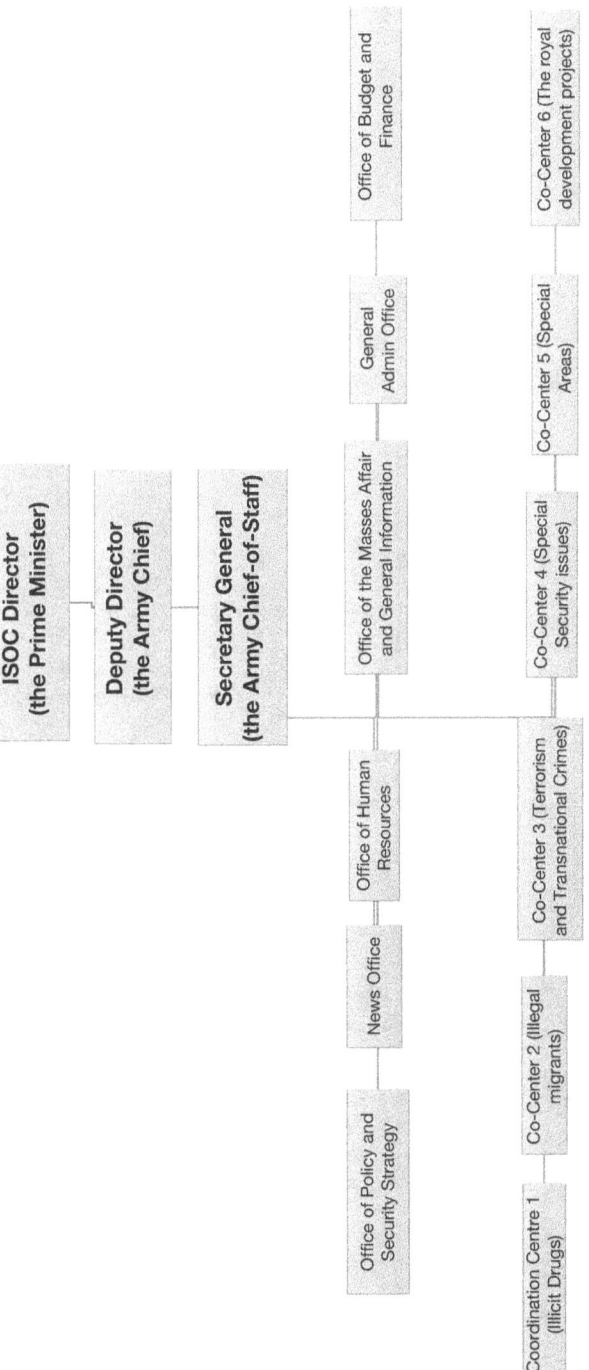

FIGURE 2.3
Command Structure of ISOC According to Thaksin Shinawatra's Prime Ministerial Order No. 158/2545, dated 29 May 2002

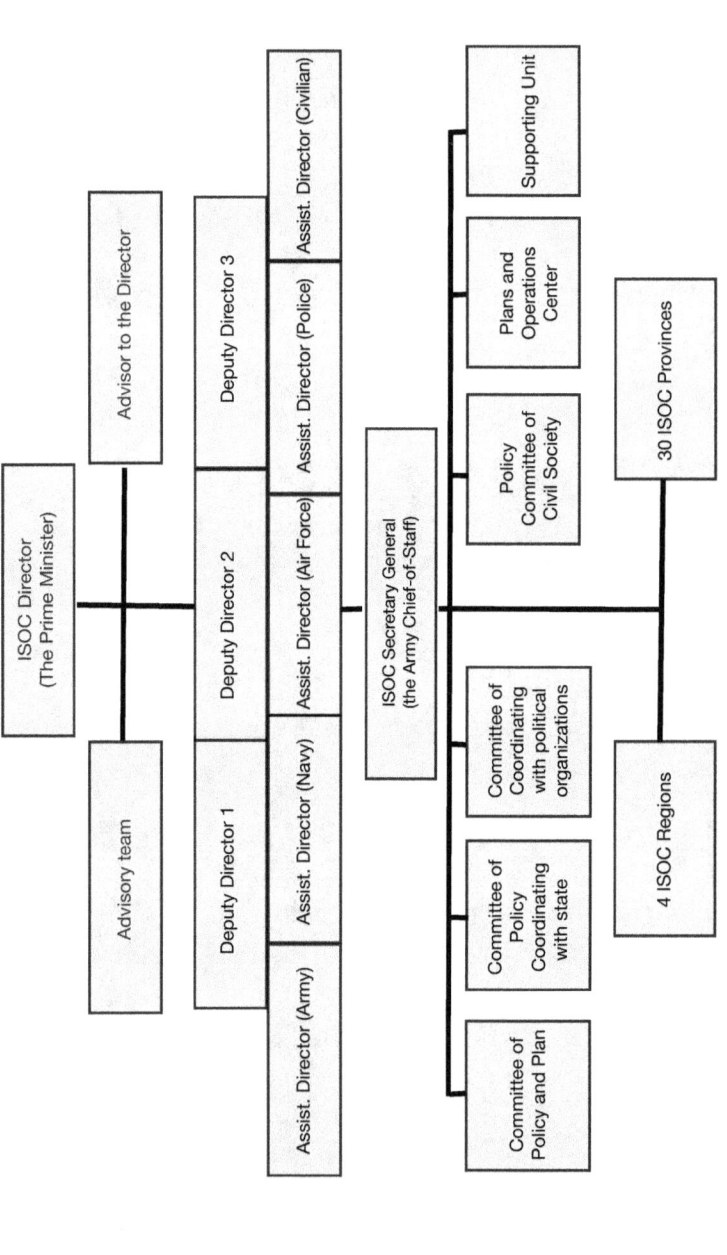

Source: Internal Security Command Operations, *Khrongkan chumchon mankhong* [Stable Community Programme], 2002, Appendix.

efficient response to the fast-globalized environment. In addition, Thaksin's government enacted a new security decree, titled the "Executive Decree on Public Administration in an Emergency Situation", which made the prime minister the head of any agency set up to oversee an emergency (Chambers 2015, p. 21). He wanted to modernize the Thai bureaucracy and security sector and tighten civilian control. Despite the limited extent of his reform, his attempt backfired. As Suehiro (2014, p. 299) points out, Thaksin's reforms "were too radical and too speedy for all the people including the royalists, the military, government officers, as well as conservatives".

There was a contradiction in Thaksin's policy regarding ISOC's role. With the rising concern over the widespread use and trafficking of methamphetamine (*ya ba* in Thai), Prime Ministerial Order No. 158/2545 gave ISOC a central role in planning, implementing and coordinating with various state agencies in different ministries to combat the drug problem as well as other emerging new security threats along the borders. As a result, ISOC's structure expanded to several administrative levels: ISOC Province, ISOC District (*amphoe*), ISOC Minor-district (*king-amphoe*), ISOC Sub-district (*tambon*), ISOC Municipality (*thetsaban*), ISOC Town Community (*chumchon mueang*) and ISOC Village (*muban*) (see Figure 2.4). Further, the order gave ISOC authority to mobilize popular participation in combating new national security threats. All the agencies had to integrate local business people, civil servants, journalists, teachers, students and so on in their campaigns.

When the insurgency in the three southernmost provinces re-emerged in 2004, Thaksin did not hesitate to authorize military operations under the supervision of the Forward Section of ISOC Region 4 (Srisompob 2013, p. 558). As a result, ISOC became the most powerful agency in charge of the southern conflict. Again, a civilian government was unaware that it was creating an opportunity for the military to penetrate deep into the civil area.

After a failed plot to assassinate Thaksin with a car bomb was disclosed in August 2006, he was reportedly planning to revamp ISOC again. He believed that ISOC's deputy director, General Phanlop Pinmanee and three other ISOC military officers were behind the assassination plot (*The Nation*, 25 August 2006). However, before Thaksin had the opportunity to enact this reform, his government was toppled by a coup on 19 September 2006.

The civilian government led by Abhisit Vejjajiva of the Democrat Party also enjoyed utilizing the Internal Security Act of 2008 (ISA 2008), which is currently the foundation of ISOC's power. Using the ISA 2008 automatically means employing ISOC for operations. The United Front

FIGURE 2.4
Command Structure of ISOC at Community Levels According to Thaksin Shinawatra's Prime Ministerial Order No. 158/2545, dated 29 May 2002

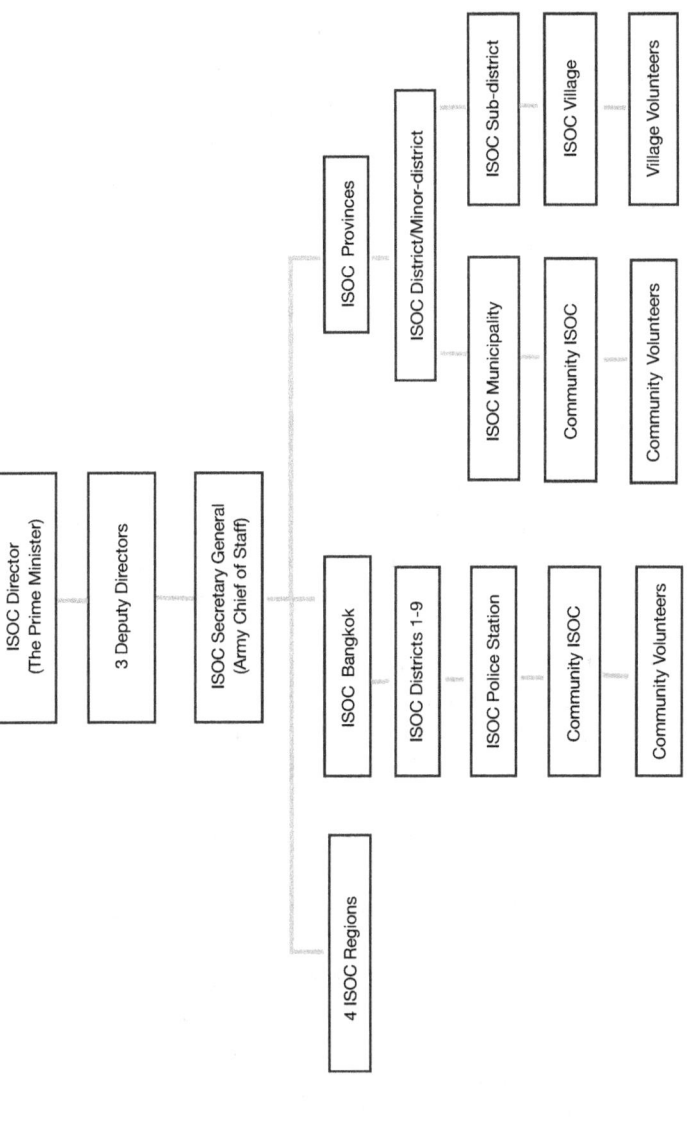

Source: Internal Security Command Operations, *Khrongkan chumchon mankhong* [Stable Community Programme], 2002, Appendix 2/1.

for Democracy against Dictatorship (UDD) or the Red Shirts movement became increasingly confrontational to the Democrat government. The UDD twice organized lengthy rallies occupying streets in the heart of Bangkok, and calling for Abhisit to dissolve the parliament and hold early elections in the expectation that the majority of voters would prefer the Thaksinite party. The first rally took place between 26 March and 14 April 2009 and the second between 14 March and 19 May 2010. Both ended in violent crackdowns and defeats for the Red Shirts.

In response to this situation, Abhisit, in his capacity as the ex-officio director of ISOC, used Article 15 of the ISA 2008 to establish a temporary unit named *Sun amnuaikan raksa khwam sa-ngop riaproi* or the Centre for Peace and Order. One of its important duties was to keep close watch over the Red Shirts' activities in the provinces as ISOC's spokesperson Lieutenant General Ditthaporn Sasasamit openly told the press (*Kom Chad Luek*, 20 December 2010).

Within two years of assuming office, Abhisit issued four such orders: 29 August–1 September 2009; 18–22 September 2009, 15–25 October 2009, and 24 February–25 March 2011 (*Royal Gazette*, 21 September 2009, p. 87, 26 October 2009, p. 113, 21 December 2009, p. 89, and 17 March 2011, p. 56). According to Article 15 of the ISA 2008, in the event of an occurrence which threatens internal security but does not yet require a declaration of a state of emergency, the cabinet shall pass a resolution to have ISOC take responsibility for prevention, suppression, and eradication or mitigation of the occurrence within an assigned area and time-period. Article 17 allows the ISOC director to establish a temporary centre or unit to carry out the operations. Lastly, Article 18 authorizes the director, with the cabinet's approval, to issue preventive regulations as follow:

1. To have relevant state officials implement any action, or suspend any action;
2. To prohibit entry or exit at a locality, building, or designated area during its operating hours, except with the permission of a competent official or being an exempted person;
3. To prohibit exit from dwelling places within a designated time;
4. To prohibit the carrying of weapons outside dwelling places;
5. To prohibit the use of routes or vehicles or to prescribe conditions on the use of routes or vehicles;
6. To order persons to perform or suspend any action in connection with electronic equipment in order to guard against danger to life, limb, or property of the people (*Royal Gazette*, 27 February 2008, pp. 33–44).[6]

In addition, Abhisit's government announced a state of emergency in Bangkok and surrounding provinces twice: 11–24 April 2009, and 8 April 2010 to the end of 2010. During the second period of emergency, the government established the Centre for Resolution of Emergency Situation, in which ISOC and the army leaders had important positions. This Centre played a leading role in the violent suppression of the Red Shirts protesters on 10 April and 16–19 May 2010, resulting in the death of 84 civilians and over 2,000 injured (People Information Centre 2012).

Because the Democrat Party depended heavily on the support of the military and the royalist elites to face the Red Shirts' challenge, ISOC's power grew greatly during the Abhisit administration. Thaksin's limited reform of ISOC was easily undone by Abhisit.

THE ELECTORAL DEMOCRACY PERIOD

Experts on Thai politics agree that the objective of the coups in 2006 and 2014 went beyond the simple ousting of elected governments led by Thaksin Shinawatra and his sister Yingluck Shinawatra respectively. The royalist elites have always been extremely distrustful of politicians, rural voters and electoral democracy. This negativity towards politicians and electoral politics is held not only among the elites, but increasingly among the urban middle class as well. Distrust of politicians has grown steadily since the early 1980s with the expansion of elections and participatory politics.

After Prem stepped down from the premiership after the 1988 election, the role of the military and civil servants in politics gradually diminished. Prem's successor, General Chatichai Choonhavan, became the first elected MP to serve as prime minister since 1976. During his two-and-a-half-year term, however, the Chatichai government was ridiculed by the mass media as a highly corrupt "buffet cabinet". When his government was toppled by a military coup in 1991, the public showed little opposition to the military takeover. In the 1990s, several elected governments failed to last a full term because of corruption scandals. Thaksin became the first elected MP to serve his full term as premier since the move from absolute to constitutional monarchy in 1932. Corrupt politicians and widespread vote-buying, especially in the rural northern and northeastern regions, are perceived as a consequence of money politics. Influential public figures and civic groups calling for "clean" politics have been a prominent feature in the people-participatory democracy movements since the 1980s (Thongchai 2008, pp. 24–27).

Several recent studies have argued that the behaviour of provincial voters can no longer adequately be framed within the vote buying/selling paradigm. Voting decisions are complicated and sophisticated, taking into consideration several factors, such as parties' policies and the level of community engagement of politicians (Apichat, Yukti and Niti 2013; Stithorn 2012; Walker 2012). Unfortunately, the discourse of vote-buying has persisted among the establishment and the urban middle-class people and media. This discourse amounts to a devaluation of majoritarian democracy and a justification for toppling elected governments. The persistent popularity of Thaksin among provincial voters and the rise of the Red Shirts movement, a new lower middle-class with strong belief in their political rights, were challenges to the establishment's dominant power. As the reign of King Bhumibol's drew to a close, anxiety about a decline of royal hegemony prompted the royalist elites to take control of politics during the royal succession (Thongchai 2014; Kasian 2016).

This anxiety was explicit in the National Security Policy of 2015–21, and ISOC's Strategic Plans of 2012–16 and 2017–21, which made the security of the monarchical institution the top priority of internal security policy (National Security Council 2015, p. 5; ISOC 2012, 2017). The monarchy had been the subject of more violations and insults as shown in the increasing number of *lèse majesté* cases and the shutdown of websites, particularly after the 2006 coup. The second most urgent threat was the deep divide among the population. Protection of the monarchy was also a policy priority of the military's development and mass organization programmes (see Chapters 3 and 5). The conservative elite's deep worry over the colour-coded political polarization and the strong loyalty the Red Shirts had for Thaksin and his parties clearly shaped the security policies and plans.

The old powers, nevertheless, could not deny the people participatory politics forever. Both the military juntas, the Council for National Security of the 2006 coup and the NCPO of the 2014 coup, promised they would hold general elections soon after they seized power from elected governments. Despite this promise and despite the increasingly adamant demand for elections, the NCPO clung to power longer than it had originally promised. Coups have always been an opportunity for the conservative elite to rewrite the rules of politics. The Constitutions of 2007 and 2017 were clearly attempts to diminish the importance of electoral politics and elected governments in order to pave the way for the old elites to exert control (Thongchai 2014; Puangthong 2015; Kasian 2016; Prajak and Veerayooth 2018).

The attempt to impose a new authoritarian order over the democratic system was transparent after the 2014 coup. During almost five years under the NCPO rule, military power was entrenched through several means: the 2017 Constitution, the Twenty-Year National Strategy, and the empowerment of independent organizations (Election Commission, Constitutional Court, Anti-Corruption Commission, Ombudsman, etc.) as veto mechanisms against a future elected government. A new electoral system was devised to prevent any future government from gaining a strong majority. The NCPO launched a grassroots development policy, termed *Pracharat*, to compete with Thaksin's populist schemes (Prajak and Veerayooth 2018).

The NCPO introduced several measures to counter the continued popularity and influence of Thaksin. The 2006 military junta had not understood the extreme popularity of Thaksin Shinawatra among rural voters, which soon gave rise to the Red Shirts movement and led to victories by Thaksinite parties, Phalang Prachachon in 2007 and Phuea Thai in 2011 (Puangthong 2015). The junta introduced the 2007 Constitution which put restrictions on electoral democracy, such as having half the Senate selected by members of courts and independent organizations, allowing politicians to switch political parties at any time, limiting a prime minister to two terms in office, and making it easier to launch a no-confidence debate against a prime minister. But these measures were not enough to prevent the return of Thaksinite governments. These events persuaded the NCPO and its allies that they must install a comprehensive superstructure of authoritarian power over electoral politics.

The Internal Security Act of 2008

Pro-democracy studies of recent Thai politics have tended to focus on the military-backed Constitutions of 2007 and 2017 as means to entrench the power of the military and its conservative allies while keeping political parties under control (see Prajak and Veerayooth 2018). These studies have tended to overlooked the importance of the Internal Security Act of 2008 (Royal Gazette, 27 February 2008, pp. 33–44), which focuses on the power and role of ISOC. The 2008 ISA shows the importance of the Cold War apparatus, which has been employed extensively since the act.

After the coup on 19 September 2006, the junta leader, army commander General Sonthi Boonyaratglin appointed General Surayud Chulanont, a retired army commander and a member of King Bhumibol's Privy Council, as prime minister. A top priority of the Surayud administration was the ISA of 2008. The first draft was approved by the Surayud cabinet in June 2007. The final version was passed by the junta-appointed National Legislative Assembly on 20 December 2007, only three days prior to the general elections, which elevated Yingluck Shinawatra as prime minister. The act, which came into force on 28 February 2008, strengthened the power of ISOC more than ever.

The 2008 ISA elevated ISOC's legal status to a new level. Since its creation, ISOC's authority had been based on administrative orders. In 1965, Praphas issued an order to create CSOC/ISOC and appointed himself its director. Prem's Prime Ministerial Order Nos. 66/2523 and 65/2525 granted ISOC a new mission, extending its purpose beyond the limiting remits of the dwindling Cold War. On 1 April 2000, the cabinet of Chuan Leekpai repealed the Anti-Communist Act, which would have ended the life of ISOC had not Chuan a month earlier issued the Prime Ministerial Order No. 187/2542 legally extending ISOC's life. In May 2002, Thaksin issued Prime Ministerial Order No. 158/2545 to extend ISOC's anti-drug responsibility and make changes to the organizational structure of ISOC. Thaksin's order replaced that of Chuan, showing that ISOC's existence was always dependent on administrative orders, and that a government could always change or terminate ISOC by simply issuing a Prime Ministerial Order and gaining cabinet's approval. The ISA 2008 for the first time constituted ISOC by legislation. Amending or repealing an act is more difficult than issuing an administrative order as it requires approval of the House of Representatives and the Senate. In the near future, if an elected government wishes to place the agency under civilian control, reforming the 2008 ISA will present an uphill challenge, especially during the term of the NCPO-nominated Senate. The conservative elites could also deploy the Constitutional Court as obstruction. The military's authority over internal security affairs is thus now well protected.

This legislative grounding appeared to fulfil a long-term dream of General Saiyud Kerdphol. In a secret memo to Prime Minister Seni Pramoj in 1976, Saiyud expressed his worry about the temporary and insecure status of ISOC and tried to persuade Seni to pass an act for ISOC. Saiyud claimed that the government's capacity to fight the increasingly powerful CPT would improve if ISOC was given more power over other state agencies. Saiyud reiterated that he had proposed the idea to governments a long time before but they did not act on his proposal (TUA, So.bo.9.7.2/147). As ISOC gained public notoriety in the aftermath of the democratic uprising in 1973 it became difficult for subsequent elected governments to empower the infamous agency without provoking a public backlash. Saiyud had to wait for the return of a military government in 2006 to fulfil his dream of securing the legal status required to making ISOC a permanent fixture. Saiyud was very active in the anti-Yingluck movement. After the 2014 coup, he urged the drafters of a new constitution to allow the king to intervene in politics (*Khaosod English*, 6 January 2015).

When ISOC was still an organization formed by an administrative order, the Bureau of the Budget did not allocate an annual budget directly to the agency. Article 11 of Prime Ministerial Order 158/2545 required ISOC to prepare projects with estimated annual expenditures and submit them through the relevant agencies that it planned to work with. With the ISA now in place, ISOC receives an annual budget directly from the Revenue Department; see Table 2.3.

To put ISOC's 10 billion baht budget for 2018 into perspective, the parallel budgets for the NSC and the National Intelligence Agency, Thailand's two core national security organizations, were only 304.9 million baht and 760.1 million baht respectively (Bureau of the Budget 2018, p. 1).

The true budget for ISOC's activities was much higher than the above figure. When ISOC sends orders to other agencies, those agencies have to use their own budget, even when carrying out ISOC-supervised activities. For example, when students were mobilized to attend ISOC's educational programme on the king's sufficiency economy philosophy, these activities fell on the Ministry of Education's budget, while ISOC was responsible only for providing a team of speakers and trainers.

Under ISA 2008, ISOC remains under the Office of the Prime Minister, with the prime minister still acting as its ex-officio director. But unlike

TABLE 2.3
Budgets of ISOC, 2009–18

Year	Value (baht)
2009	8,222,878,800
2010	8,240,272,500
2011	8,306,068,400
2012	6,915,923,000
2013	7,980,125,500
2014	8,201,570,700
2015	8,906,478,600
2016	10,200,971,600
2017	6,357,934,200
2018	10,049,512,900

Source: Budget Bureau, Thailand, *Expenditure Budgets of Fiscal Years 2009–2018* (electronic documents), http://www.bb.go.th/bbweb/?page_id=604 (accessed 21 February 2018).

Thaksin's Prime Ministerial Order No. 158/2545, which allowed a prime minister to delegate his ISOC duty and power to any cabinet member, the ISA 2008 stipulates that a prime minister who is unable to perform his duty may only delegate this duty to a deputy director, the army commander. The already limited civilian involvement in internal security matters is thus further slimmed down. Military domination over ISOC became definite—particularly after the coup in 2014, when junta leader General Prayut appointed himself prime minister and thus director of ISOC.

The 2008 ISA also grants ISOC officers impunity in the event of any wrongdoing committed during its operations. The Act has two main parts. Part 1 lays out ISOC's authority to monitor, examine and assess situations and then proposes action plans for the cabinet's approval. All state agencies must abide by the plans and guidelines under ISOC's supervision and cooperation. Section 7(4) requires ISOC to strengthen (1) public awareness of its duty to defend the nation, religion and monarchy; and (2) public participation in solving problems affecting national security and social order. This section unequivocally refers to ISOC's activities on mass mobilization and organization.

When the country's security is in crisis, the cabinet may invoke Part 2 section 16(10) of the Internal Security Act, which provides ISOC with broad power to "prevent, suppress, suspend, inhibit, mitigate and solve" the situation. These terms are not well defined and thus allow for arbitrary interpretation, as happened under the military regime of Prayut. "To prevent" can mean to detain and charge political opponents and stop their peaceful activities completely. With approval from the cabinet, ISOC's director has the power to issue a wide range of orders to the public—to stop people entering or leaving any locations, to impose a curfew, to block transportation, and to inhibit people by using electronic devices. According to section 16(1) and (2), ISOC officers have the authority to monitor, pursue, coordinate and expedite the work of relevant state agencies. If the personnel of any state agency obstructs their operations, ISOC can order them to leave the area and report them to their superior, who will then dismiss them. Worse, section 19 provides ISOC officers and anyone designated by its director with the power to participate in criminal investigations. Under Prayut's regime, the military has often been involved in the arrest and charging of anti-junta activists. The ISA thus allows the military to interfere in criminal investigation, blurring the division of powers.

The ISA strips the Administrative Courts of jurisdictional power in disputes between a citizen and a state agency arising from operations overseen by ISOC. Section 23 stipulates that any order or action under Part 2 of the Act falls within the jurisdiction of the Courts of Justice only. That means people who are affected by state orders or misconduct arising from operations overseen by ISOC cannot file charge with the Administrative Courts. The Administrative Courts can review an order or terminate official actions at any time, even before their full impact is felt. But the Courts of Justice have jurisdiction only over a single case after a person has suffered some form of harm. The Administrative Courts are the only courts that can revoke unlawful acts, including those committed under ISA. The Administrative Courts also have discretionary power to subpoena evidence while the Courts of Justice do not (International Commission of Jurists 2010, p. 10). The design of the 2008 ISA cleverly protects its oppressive mechanism from judicial intervention.

The 2008 ISA also restores the authority of the military over other civilian state agencies to ISOC. Under the revised Anti-Communist Activities Act of 1969, the ISOC provincial director, an ex-officio provincial governor, reported to the ISOC regional director, who was the commander of the army region. ISOC established branches in all seventy-seven provinces, including Bangkok, since the Thaksin administration. Each of the commanders of the four army regions oversaw a selection of the provincial ISOC branches.[7] Thaksin, however, shifted the ISOC provincial directors under the command of the ISOC director, the prime minister, effectively under Thaksin himself. The 2008 ISA restored the previous ISOC structure, which placed the provincial directors under the commanders of the army regions.

The ISA provides ISOC power and authority over the National Security Council (NSC). In the past, according to Article 5.2 of Prem's Prime Ministerial Order No. 66/2523, the NSC advised the cabinet on internal security policy while ISOC was in charge of operations. In Thaksin's Order No. 158/2545, Article 3 stated that ISOC carried out policy and strategy as formulated by the NSC, while Article 11 required ISOC to submit its plans, strategies and annual budget to the NSC for consideration and approval. The 2008 ISA freed ISOC of these obligations. ISOC's policy and plans are approved by the cabinet, and other agencies must follow them. The NSC has more civilians than military officers. ISOC's independence from the NSC means that internal security matters, from the evaluation of threats to the formulation and implementation of policy and strategy, are now largely controlled by the army. During Prayut's government, the NSC has been silent while ISOC appears on the news constantly.

Last but not the least, under the regime of Prayut, who is also ISOC's ex-officio director, the agency's role moved up one notch. Prayut appeared to favour the service of ISOC so much that he often entrusted the agency with important political tasks. Soon after the 2014 coup, when opponents of the coup were being detained, Prayut ordered ISOC to set up reconciliation centres in every province (Reuters, 30 May 2014). In early 2016, when presiding over the ISOC's annual meeting, Prayut assigned the agency to find an urgent solution to the colour-divided politics that had consumed the nation (Channel 3 News, 10 February 2016). In January 2017, the NCPO junta again revealed a plan to mitigate conflict and promote national reconciliation. Ironically, the press reported that ISOC officers prohibited people at public hearings from taking notes in order to prevent them from reporting it to the public later (*Prachatai*, 7 March 2017). Furthermore, ISOC was given the task of drafting a plan of comprehensive national reforms and a twenty-year national strategic plan (2017–36) (*Matichon*, 6 February 2017).

Conclusion

The concept of development for security in Thailand during the Cold War period has been known for several decades. Development policies and projects were designed to support the US containment policy in Southeast Asia and its operations in the Vietnam War. A large part of US economic assistance to Thailand was allocated to infrastructure development. This study, however, examines how the policy of development for security benefited the military and its traditional allies, allowing them to establish and expand political control over society. In this project, legal and political legitimacy was essential.

Development for security was an important part of the political offensive approach of counterinsurgency. The CPM operations allowed state agencies to connect with and utilize the population for their security goal. This approach evolved over five decades from the 1960s to the present day. It did not originate from Prem's Prime Ministerial Orders Nos. 66/2523 and 65/2525, which were not simply a policy to combat the CPT, but had bigger and longer-term objectives of expanding the role of the military in the civilian sphere and strengthening the democratic regime with the monarch as the head of the state.

Through the programmes of economic development, mass organization, indoctrination, and psychological warfare in the counterinsurgency, the Thai military acquired enormous ability to establish its control over society.

As the socio-political situation shifted, the military redefined what could be considered a threat to internal security, and interpreted internal security so broadly that the military role in the socio-economic and political sphere became almost boundless by the advent of the twenty-first century, and the power of ISOC, its political arm, expanded enormously. All branches of the armed forces became actively involved in internal security affairs. The military's authority in matters of internal security affairs extended across all civilian governmental agencies. These changes were watched and handled with care by the conservative ruling elites who discreetly and wisely provided legal and political legitimacy for the military's expansion. The monarchy was the most important source of political legitimacy for the military's expansive role. Members of the institution played a leading role in the development of security strategy from the beginning.

Since the counterinsurgency period, the Thai military has not only claimed the duty and legitimacy to engage in socio-political and economic development for reasons of national security, but has demanded a leading role in those operations. ISOC thus acquired the authority to command other civilian agencies and civil society. This ambition was achieved smoothly when the country was under a series of military governments.

During the Prem government all branches of the armed forces became involved in internal security operations via their civil affairs departments. As the threat of the CPT waned, they devised a strategy to justify the continuation of the military's internal security activities. For five decades, the military's role in civil affairs has been guaranteed in numerous constitutions, national development plans, executive orders and laws.

The acquisition by ISOC of such massive and unaccountable power occurred with little awareness among politicians and civil society and virtually no civil oversight. By the time elected politicians acquired more influence from the 1980s, they may not have understood the political implication of the military's civil projects because internal security affairs had long been dominated solely by the military. They continued to support projects and expand the military's role into new areas. Elected politicians relied on ISOC's suppressive apparatus to quell their political opponents, as in Thaksin's use of ISOC in the war on drugs and the three southernmost provinces, and the Abhisit government's repression of the Red Shirts in 2009 and 2011.

In the eyes of civilians, the military's development work and royalist indoctrination projects seemed apolitical and posed no danger to democracy in normal times. No civilian government, even that of Thaksin, made anything more than very limited reform of the armed forces. When the alliance of the old powers derailed democracy through the coups of 2006 and 2014, ISOC was quickly equipped with more power. The internal security apparatus has served as a political asset for the old power against its internal political enemies. At the same time, internal security affairs have been highly militarized as I will elaborate in the following chapters.

Notes

1. In ISOC's current organizational structure, according to the Internal Security Act of 2008, the Department of Civil Affairs no longer appears. Its mission appears to have been distributed to new departments and centres.
2. https://www.facebook.com/pg/doca.thaiarmy/posts/ and www.ryt9.com/tag/กรมกิจการพลเรือนทหาร; https://www.facebook.com/navalcivil/; https://www.facebook.com/navalcivil/; https://j5.rtarf.mi.th/web/index.php
3. https://www.facebook.com/ArmyCyberCenter/
4. See www.isoc.go.th
5. ARD was merged with the Department of Rural Roads under the Ministry of Transport.
6. Translation by the International Commission of Jurists, https://www.icj.org/wp-content/uploads/2012/12/Thailand-Internal-Security-Act-2008-eng.pdf (accessed 8 January 2020).
7. The First Army is in charge of twenty-six provinces in the central, eastern, western regions and in Bangkok, the Second Army is in charge of twenty provinces in the northeastern region, the Third Army is in charge of seventeen provinces in the northern region, and the Fourth Army is in charge of fourteen provinces in the southern region.

3

The Making of the Development Military

In Chapter 1, I raised the question of how natural resources management became one of the military junta's top priorities. The military forcibly evicted thousands of families from forest reserve areas immediately after the coup d'état of 22 May 2014. The eviction was soon followed by a master plan to reclaim forest land nationwide. This chapter seeks to explain the military's development role and development projects from the counterinsurgency period to the present day, showing how the concept of development for security shifted and expanded, and the implications of these changes.

In Chapter 2, I explained how the term "development for security" or *kan phatthana phuea khwam mankhong/yuttha-phatthana* was coined to justify the military role in socio-economic and political programmes, and how legal legitimation was secured for this role. This chapter will focus on the political factors and key players in the advancement and expansion of the military's development role into new areas in the post-counterinsurgency period. King Bhumibol and his royal development projects were a leading force against communism. Over two thousand royal development projects and the king's visits to the poor in remote areas undoubtedly won the hearts and mind of people nationwide. The active participation of the monarchy in this area, together with the promotion of the public image of a devoted king, was a core strategy in the Thai state's struggle to triumph over communism. As the monarchy and the military worked closely together, it is necessary to address the role of monarchy in the making of *thahan nak phatthana*, the development military.

While thousands of development projects advanced the image of *kasat nak phatthana*, (the development monarch) for King Bhumibol, the military adopted the term *thahan nak phatthana*, the development military, in a bid to secure the same public appeal. The higher the moral authority of King Bhumibol, the more the military relied on royal legitimacy to expand its role in the socio-economic sphere. This institutional relationship allowed the whole armed forces, not just individual military leaders, to expand their role into the socio-political area.

The military's policy of development for security has been dynamic from the counterinsurgency period to the present. Although the policy began as part of the Thai state's political offensive against the communist movement, it continued long after the demise of the CPT, expanding enormously into new issues and into the urban areas. As a result, after the coups in 2006 and 2014 the military could move swiftly into various socio-political and economic areas.

The issue of land use has been prominent in the military's policy of development for security. Conflict over land use and natural resources has continued for decades. Rural voters and civic groups pressed elected governments to allow local people to participate in the management of local resources on grounds of their way of life, the history of their land use, their culture and their needs. Land is a sensitive and complicated issue involving the livelihoods of many thousands of people, yet the military has been inclined to employ strong and decisive measures to achieve fast results. Putting the military in charge of the matter ensures that the security angle takes precedence over other issues. In the military's ideology, small-scale peasants are the enemy of the country's national environment while big-scale plantation firms are beneficial to the national economy and environment. When the military is allowed to have power over socio-economic issues, in the name of defending the nation's internal security, the livelihoods of ordinary people are not its priority, and are thus at risk.

THE DEVELOPMENT MONARCH

From early in his reign, King Bhumibol took a special interest in rural development and insurgent problems in the rural and hill areas. Visits to rural areas and development projects were among his priorities. The military served as a loyal assistant in this matter. Not only did this strengthen the relationship between military and monarchy but also lent legitimacy to the military's activity in this area.

The royal development projects were purportedly designed to fill the gap created by the government's development plans, which emphasized macroeconomic growth but left behind the people in the rural areas, putting them at risk of communist recruitment (Chanida 2007, pp. 125, 130–31). The king emphasized the use of development, rather than force, to counter communist expansion (Connors 2007, p. 67). The royal projects' impact on poverty, however, was never scientifically evaluated. Their scale was smaller than projects operated by the government, but their psychological impact was far greater and spread beyond the area where the projects were located. Visual images of the king's rural visits were constantly reproduced, even after he had passed away, as testament to the monarch's care and devotion for the people. The hearts and minds of several generations of Thai people succumbed to his royal kindness. King Bhumibol's image as a righteous monarch was indisputable. This image was the foundation of hyper-royalism, the intense and excessive royalist culture and ideology which has appeared since around 2000 (Thongchai 2016).

Rural visits also provided opportunities for members of the royal family to show their moral support, care and concern for the defenders of the nation. Meetings with soldiers and the BPP stationed in the frontlines demonstrated how royal family members were willing to sacrifice their comfortable lifestyle and to face risks alongside the loyal fighters. During these visits, the king and his family members often wore military uniforms as an explicit form of identification, associating the royals with the armed forces (Chanida 2007, pp. 183–96).

Some royal development projects demonstrated King Bhumibol's attention to small details concerning the safety of the frontline fighters. For example, the king initiated a series of projects to improve the small arms used by the BPP and soldiers in their fight against the insurgents. These included: having an aide attach an automatic weapon to a police helicopter for defence against being shot down by insurgents; having weapons repaired for the soldiers; providing wireless transmitters for direct communication with military commanders; and donating money for purchasing weaponry. The royal family members also paid visits to injured soldiers in hospital. Whenever there was a news report of a serious battle resulting in many fatalities and panic among the local people, the king would quickly pay a visit to boost morale (Chanida 2007, pp. 180–82). The palace's care and concern for the well-being and safety of soldiers was often recorded in the media.

King Bhumibol also involved himself in strategic planning and advised the military and police to establish state control over areas seized from the insurgents. The armed forces carried out the king's advice as their duty. The king often advised the military and state agencies on the idea of socio-economic development for security as a means to fight the insurgents, and monitored the progress, or lack thereof, in the field. The governments, the military and related state agencies adopted his advice as the nation's development strategy for security (Chanida 2007, pp. 184–85).

King Bhumibol gained the status of a champion of the rural poor while the military undertook the role of loyal assistant to the noble cause, proudly and obediently following the royal guidance.

The Khek River basin royal project in Khao Kho district, Phetchabun province, is often cited by the armed forces as an example of His Majesty's wisdom as well as the military's duty as a loyal servant under His Majesty's command. The mountainous Khao Kho area was well known as the most difficult stronghold of the CPT for the army to seize. Many soldiers lost their lives fighting there, particularly in a six-week battle in 1976. Though the army was eventually able to seize the area in that year, King Bhumibol saw that military measures alone were insufficient to consolidate the state's power over the area. He advised the Third Army Region to set up a strategic development village (*muban yutthasat phatthana*) and provided the funding. A year later, the army populated the new village with landless members from ISOC's mass organizations. The villagers were given land, economic assistance, arms training and a royal-nationalist indoctrination programme. The army refers to the Khek River royal project as a model for its development programmes (Usani 1999, p. 92; Chanida 2007, p. 185).

When the army's *Isan Khiao* or Green Northeast project was launched in 1988, a publication quoted several of King Bhumibol's ideas on development for security as a guideline: "His majesty the king has awakened the armed forces to be aware of one of their important duties, which was inscribed so clearly in the Constitution's Article 56 that '*the Armed Forces shall be used for development of the country*'" (Samnakphim 1989, pp. 21–25, emphasis from the original text). The *Isan Khiao* project was created in the post-counterinsurgency period, when the monarchy continued to lend royal legitimacy to the armed forces. I will return to this issue later in this chapter.

Participating in the royal development projects has been a matter of pride for the armed forces down to the present day. The military's publications and websites emphasize the military's role as the trusted servant of the monarchy, its long history as defenders of the nation, its usefulness for Thai society, and its legitimate duty to pursue socio-economic development (e.g., Usani 1999 and the Armed Forces Development Command's website).[1]

Beginning of Development for Security

In the wake of the 1973 popular uprising, the political opening, and the increasing strength of the left-leaning student movement and the CPT forces, the army was given more authority and scope. The Constitution of 1974 allowed the military to participate in the wider socio-political and economic development of the country. Development for security has featured in all constitutions since then.

By the early 1970s, the concept of development for security appeared widely in official documents regarding the struggle against communist expansion. As a counterinsurgency programme, development for security was designed to be comprehensive, with political, psychological and ideological projects (TUA, So.bo.9.7.2/46; So.bo.9.7.2/70; so.bo.9.7.2/147), and the involvement of several civilian state agencies and the mass organizations that had grown nationwide during the counterinsurgency period.

Development for security was declared the primary objective of the fourth National Economic and Social Development Plan for 1977–81. Sumet Tantiwetchakun, a technocrat at the National Economic and Social Development Board (NESDB) and a prominent figure in the royal development projects, explained that the fight against communism would be effective only when the principle of development for security was integrated into the national development plan, and the allocation of resources followed three principles:

1. The allocation of budgets for the military and economic development must be coordinated in accordance with changing circumstances. The aim is to enhance the economic sustainability and the military's capability in response to national security threats.
2. The goals of social and economic development must be established in line with the goal of national defence by speeding development of key economic sectors and improving human resources to support the national defence system.
3. The areas with security problem must receive special attention in the national plan, injecting socio-economic development programmes to support military operations (Sumet 1988, pp. 114–15).

The above principles were carried over to subsequent national economic and social development plans (NESDB, 1987–91).

Apart from the armed forces, the Ministry of Interior (MOI) played an active role in the development for security programme. Connors has shown that the work of the Local Administration Department (LAD) between the 1960s and 1980s was overwhelmingly concerned with internal security. LAD also took part in the counterinsurgency operations, including in the area of mass organization, and became virtually an administrative and civil wing of the military (Connors 2007, pp. 111–12). Other units in MOI involved in these areas were the Community Development Department, Accelerated Rural Development, and Public Welfare Department.

Several other units of the armed forces also engaged in the programme. The Central Command of National Security, *Kong amnuaikan raksa khwam plotphai haeng chat*, under the Supreme Command Headquarters (now the Royal Thai Armed Forces, or RTAF), was the first unit in charge of the military's development programme. It was established in 1962 by the Thanom government (*Daily News*, 23 December 2018), and renamed as the Armed Forces Development Command (ARDC) or *Nuai banchakan thahan phatthana* in 1997. Currently the ARDC has five regional branches covering every province, including Bangkok.[2] ARDC and its commanders often call themselves *thahan nak phatthana*, the development military, and the media also use the phrase. Apart from the ARDC, the army, air force, and navy have their own development units.

With the appearance of ARDC, ISOC might seem redundant, but ISOC had a much broader role encompassing strategic planning, commanding, monitoring, supporting other state agencies involved in the counterinsurgency operations, and implementing mass organization, psychological warfare and indoctrination programmes.

The Village for Development and Self-Defence Volunteers (VDSV) or *Muban a-sa phatthana lae pongkan ton-eng* (*O.pho.po.*) was a programme established in 1975 as a brainchild of Saiyud when he was ISOC deputy director (TUA, So.bo.9.7.2/147). The programme became prominent in ISOC's strategy. Each regional VDSD group had a Village Security Unit or *Cho.ro.bo* of ten armed men to protect the area. The army provided training in arms use, self-defence and intelligence gathering to some fifty to a hundred able-bodied men in each village, while the village was also treated to programmes in agricultural techniques, marketing, vocational training, leadership, public health and indoctrination (Santi 1990, p. 37). VDSD now falls under the jurisdiction of the Department of Provincial Administration of the MOI. I will discuss mass organizations at length in Chapters 4 and 5.

Development for Security in the Post-Counterinsurgency Period

In 1982, the army established a new department called *Kong kitchakan phonlaruean* or Directorate of Civil Affairs, later emulated by the supreme command, navy and air force. The term *kitchakan phonlaruean*, meaning civil affairs or civil activities, makes the military's activities sound less politically intrusive. The objectives of civil affairs units are to maintain internal security and order and to promote and protect the three pillars of the Thai nation (Rakrat 2016). Suchit and Kanala (1987, pp. 30–32) argue that the true objective of the military's *kitchakan phonlaruean* was to maintain and expand the military's role in the socio-economic and political sphere in the post-counterinsurgency period. The military believed that they must have a role in development to protect the country from any emerging threat. They could not leave the country's fate to self-serving politicians.

Currently, their civil work is in line with the extended definition of the military's development mission. It includes socio-economic development, natural resources and environment protection, improvement of agricultural methods, community services, disaster relief operations, promotion of the sufficiency economy philosophy of King Bhumibol, and protection and promotion of the Democratic Regime with the King as the Head of the State (*Manager Online*, 15 April 2006; the Armed Forced Development Command's website).

The ties between the monarchy and the military in the area of development for security continued into the post-counterinsurgency period. Participating in the royal projects remained a top priority. Several civil affairs projects of the RTAF, army, air force, and navy were royal-initiated projects. According to the Office of the Royal Development Projects Board, there were 4,741 royal development projects between 1952 and 2017, falling into eight categories (ORDPB 2017, pp. 2–5):

1. development of water resources;
2. agricultural development;
3. environmental protection;
4. occupational promotion;
5. public health;
6. transportation and communication;
7. social welfare and education; and
8. comprehensive development.

The development projects of the military have a similar range, as can be seen from their websites.[3] As of 2018, the army had 127 royal development projects, the largest number among the four branches of the military civil projects (www.สปรมน.com).

Apart from its own Directorate of Civil Affairs, the army also established the Office of the Royal Initiatives Projects and Security Co-ordination. Most of the army's projects are devised and operated by the development divisions located in each of the four army regions (Chanida 2007, pp. 128–29). The Second Army Region, covering twenty provinces in the northeast region, has the highest number of projects (Usani 1999, pp. 3–5).

Before 2019, ISOC had a Centre for Coordination of Royal Initiatives Projects and its own Directorate of Civil Affairs (Suchit and Kanala 1987, pp. 38–39), both of which no longer exist. Civil works are carried out by several departments within ISOC, such as the Office of the Mass Affair and General Information, Office of Intelligence, Centre for Digital for Security, and Office of Policy and Security Strategy (see www.isoc.go.th). ISOC's continues to act as the coordinator and supervisor of the internal security affairs of the armed forces, police, and civilian state agencies.

New Mission: Fighting Poverty

The special bond between the monarchy and the military forged in the Cold War formed the basis for several new development-related projects of the military in the post-counterinsurgency period, when the military quietly expanded into new socio-economic issues.

In December 1995 at the annual *Chaichalemphon* ceremony of conferring flags on regiments and soldiers who in return swear allegiance to the throne, King Bhumibol spoke as follows:

> The principle duty of the military is to defend the nation and to protect the nation's sovereignty with military strength. Besides, there are other duties, which are equally important. They are alleviation of the people's hardship and development for peaceful progress of the country and the people. These duties may seem unnecessary. But if one considers them carefully, the country's security and safety mean peaceful existence and free of dangers and economic suffering. Since these are necessary, the military must be ready both physically and mentally at all time so that you can perform your duties efficiently (quoted in Usani 1999, p. 32).

This speech was made long after the demise of the CPT, and was printed in a book *Phrabatsomdet phrachaoyuhua kap kongthap thai nai khrongkan-annueang ma chak phraratchadamri* [The King and the Thai Armed Forces in the Royal Initiated Projects] to commemorate his 72nd birthday in 1999. The military no doubt embraced this message. All five commanders of the armed forces, including the police chief, praised King Bhumibol's devotion and wisdom. They vowed that the armed forces would diligently follow his majesty's direction (Usani 1999, n.p.).

The message gave a clear justification for the military to remain active in the socio-political sphere in the post counterinsurgency period. The definition of development for security in the king's speech slipped from defeating communism to eradicating poverty. The war on communism metamorphosed to "a war on poverty". Yet poverty posed more danger to the nation than communism because it was boundless, the battlefields were everywhere, and the causes were varied. The fight against poverty had a political dimension, hence it was necessary for the military to engage in democratization (Usani 1999, pp. 32–35; see also Bunklom et al. 1991, p. 172; Directorate of Civil Affairs, the Army 2002).

The military's extended mission was translated into several large-scale and controversial public projects from the mid-1990s to the present day. These projects include: the *Isan Khiao* or the Green Isan/Northeast project; the *kho.cho.ko.* Land Distribution Programme for the Poor Living in Degraded National Forest Reserves in the Northeast of Thailand; the Five Provinces Bordering Forest Preservation Foundation; and the NCPO's *Pracharat* and *Prachatipatai thai niyom* or the State-People and Thai-ism Democracy project.

Isan Khiao

The *Isan Khiao* Project, begun in 1987, was the first large-scale military-cum-royal development project in the post-counterinsurgency period. Its official name is the "Project of the King's Royal Kindness to Develop the Northeast".

According to General Chavalit Yongchaiyudh, then army commander and a key person in the Democratic Soldiers, the project began on 25 March 1987 at the royal-sponsored cremation for frontline soldiers, when King Bhumibol asked Chavalit to help the people facing drought in the five northeastern provinces of Chaiyaphum, Nakhon Ratchasima, Buriram, Roi-et and Maha Sarakham. Chavalit held a press conference, telling the public of the king's wish and his command for the army's assistance. Seventy-two hours later, the army drove 100–200 water trucks to the five provinces to ease the people's suffering. At another audience with the king in June 1987, Chavalit reported what the army had accomplished, and the king asked the army to find a long-term solution to the drought problem in the northeast. Chavalit soon announced the *Isan Khiao* project to the public, emphasizing the trust that the king bestowed upon the army, which retained overall control of the project, coordinating the work of state agencies, private sector stakeholders and the people (Bunklom et al. 1991, p. 172; Samnakphim 1989, pp. 13–25).

In his speech on Thai Armed Forces Day a year later, Chavalit praised the king: "as our Supreme Commander of the Thai Armed Forces, His Majesty has great vision and wisdom that he has discovered another crucial national threat. That is poverty. His Majesty has tirelessly worked and devoted his life to battle against it all along" (quoted in Samnakphim 1989, p. 22). The *Isan Khiao* project, Chavalit proudly said, was therefore "the big battleground of a war on poverty. The Thai armed forces, working side by side with the people and all state agencies, have mobilized all their powers to combat poverty seriously and continuously" (quoted in Samnakphim 1989, p. 25).

Since the project had received the king's approval, it was elevated to the top of the national agenda and gained full support from the government. Prime Minister Prem, in his capacity of director of ISOC, took up the chairmanship of the project's executive committee while Chavalit was the deputy chairman. ISOC became the coordinating authority (Theeraphat 1991, p. 17). The project also garnered financial supports from the private sector and international bodies. By 1991, eighty state agencies from ten ministries, along with private enterprises and universities, were involved in various sub-projects, while the government budget allocated to the project increased rapidly between 1988 and 1991 (see Table 3.1). The British government also pledged financial support (Pye 2005, p. 96).

The project soon grew beyond solving drought problems and extended to cover all seventeen provinces in the northeast. It had three major programmes:

TABLE 3.1
Budgets for *Isan Khiao* Project, 1988–91

Year	Budget (million baht)
1988	2,883.83
1989	4,154.55
1990	8,058.4922
1991	10,403.399

Source: Theeraphat Serirangsan. *Thasanakhati khong phunam chumchon phak i-san kap kanphattana khong tahan tam khrongkan i-san khiao* [Attitudes of the I-san Community Leaders towards the Military's Development in The Green Isan Project]. Research report submitted to the Administrative Centre of Royal Development Projects for the Northeast of Thailand, 1991, p. 49.

1. Development and restoration of the natural environment: reforestation, improvement of soil quality, building dams and reservoirs, rain making, and construction of water tanks.
2. Generation of income and employment: promotion of rubber plantation, eucalyptus plantation for paper pulp and sustainable energy, tapioca farming for alcohol making, cattle farming, silkworm farming and fresh-water fish farming.
3. Improvement of life quality: issues of public health and nutrition, education, religion and culture (Theeraphat 1991, pp. 21–25).

The Green Isan's huge funding and scope not only placed the military in charge of significant development projects again, but also became a resource for Chavalit to build up his popular base in the northeast region. McCargo (2002, pp. 62–63) points out that Chavalit, who was planning to enter electoral politics, channelled the funds through a network of local village headmen and subdistrict heads in order to build a base of popular political support.

Although King Bhumibol's wish to alleviate poverty and protect the natural environment in the country's poorest region was sincere, the involvement of the military imported the security mindset and coercive power, resulting in conflict and misery for small-scale northeastern peasants. The demise of the CPT had opened the doors for the logging industry to exploit the forests. Since the military had long entrenched its territorial control and influence in the area through counterinsurgency operations, it quickly established itself as a powerful stakeholder in the rural development and forestry programmes. As Oliver Pye (2005, Chs 5–6) shows, the *Isan Khiao* project appeared in the context of growing demand for wood pulp in Thailand on the one hand, and a national agenda of reforestation on the other. In 1985, the Prem cabinet assigned the Royal Forestry Department (RFD) to formulate plans for creating 30,000 square kilometres of private tree plantations as part of the reforestation policy. Many foreign and Thai companies expressed their interest in investing. Some applied for promotional privileges from the Board of Investment. Some applied for use of governmental land. However, much of the allocated land was already occupied by poor peasants. Lacking the coercive power of the military, the RFD was unable to drive people off the land until the army launched the *Isan Khiao* project. The military thus became involved in the conflict over natural resources.

The reforestation programme in *Isan Khiao* included halting illegal logging, promoting forest plantations, and accelerating a Forest Village

Programme, which aimed to reorganize existing villages into new, grid-like settlements. ISOC took part in enforcing the programme. The plan was to plant 3.4 million *rai* of economic forest and forcibly move 30,000 households, who had allegedly encroached on the national reserve forest, out of 2.1 million *rai* of the national reserve forest and into fifty-three newly created forest villages. Another part of the plan promoted eucalyptus plantations to supply the pulp-and-paper industry. By claiming royal endorsement and governmental support, the *Isan Khiao* project attracted great interest from private investors in eucalyptus plantations and the paper industry. However peasants living in the forest areas protested against the eucalyptus scheme. Under an earlier counterinsurgency programme, government had granted many of these peasants limited land rights to live in the reserve forest. Government now wished to withdraw these rights and grant the land as concessions for private plantations. The peasants were now vilified as forest encroachers in the eyes of the authorities (Pye 2005).

Amid the protest, a scandalous incident fuelled the protest. Suan Kitti Corporation[4] was a eucalyptus plantation firm owned by Kitti Damnoenchanwanit, one of the biggest rice exporters who had strong connections with many politicians. After the company had been given a concession to grow eucalyptus plantation on degraded forest, some 156 of its employees were caught cutting down 3,000 *rai* of pristine forest so that the company could apply for a concession to "reforest" a degraded forest area. The incident exposed the corrupt connections between high-ranking politicians, the RFD and private interests, which lay behind environmental damage carried out in the name of reforestation. In 1990, the government of Chatichai Choonhavan issued a ban on large-scale commercial plantations. The *Isan Khiao* reforestation programme lost momentum. After General Chavalit resigned from the army in the same year, the *Isan Khiao* project faded away (Pye 2005, pp. 97–106).

Without the communist threat, development for security projects in the post-counterinsurgency period were heavily influenced by commercial interests. Development under military management turned into a war against poor peasants, whose hearts and minds the military had once wooed.

Kho.cho.ko.

Elected governments continued to utilize the army and ISOC in plans for eradicating poverty and protecting forests in rural areas. Possibly these governments were under the impression that the army had sufficient manpower and experience to coordinate complex operations across various state agencies, along with experience of operating in rural areas for decades.

In April 1990, the elected government of Chatichai Choonhavan assigned ISOC to coordinate a major development project for the northeast. Three months later, ISOC submitted the "Land Distribution Programme for the Poor Living in Degraded National Forest Reserves in the Northeast of Thailand", abbreviated in Thai as *Kho.cho.ko* (or *Kho.Jor.Kor*). ISOC claimed that the plan aimed to distribute degraded forest areas to poor peasants and to begin reforestation in the northeast. *Kho.cho.ko.* was a continuation of the Forest Village programme under the *Isan Khiao* project. King Bhumibol's statement was again used to advertise the benevolence of the project (Pye 2005, p. 119).

In June, the cabinet appointed a board, chaired by General Suchinda Kraprayoon, the army commander and deputy director of ISOC, and appointed ISOC assistant director, General Issaraphong Nunphakdi as the project director. The two generals were leaders of the junta, the National Peace-Keeping Council (NPKC), which seized power from the Chatichai government on 23 February 1991 (Pye 2005, p. 113). The NPKC leader was General Sunthorn Kongsompong, who was also actively involved in the *Isan Khiao* project.

The junta not only embraced the project started by the government it had overthrown, but vastly increased its scale, aiming to reorganize land use in all of Thailand's 1,253 national forest reserves, where thousands of families lived and made their livelihoods. As Pye has shown, the project was clearly under the control of the leading figures in the NPKC junta, ISOC and forestry officials. After the coup, the budget for the project shot up from 270 million baht to over 1 billion baht, with the largest shares going to the Defence Ministry and ISOC. The project also gave the military a route to enter the lucrative forest plantations industry. The junta was accused of serving the pulp and paper companies rather than improving the livelihood of the poor or protecting natural resources. The project faced massive resistance from several thousand affected peasants. In May 1992, the NPKC bloodily suppressed a popular uprising, resulting in an outcry that forced the military to retreat from politics. Immediately afterwards, sustained protests in the northeast and Bangkok brought an end to the *Kho.cho.ko.* project (Pye 2005, Ch 6).

The Five Provinces Bordering Forest Preservation Foundation

Although the NPKC and its *Kho.cho.ko* project were overthrown in the 1992 uprising, the army and ISOC continued their mission of protecting natural resources and the environment. The showcase of the army's forest protection came in the form of the *Mulnithi anurak pa roi to 5 changwat*, the Five Provinces Bordering Forest Preservation Foundation (FPBFPF). Although the foundation is not well known to the public, its activities are intriguing. It became a platform for the NCPO and army leaders to build ties with big corporates in the name of protecting natural resources and the environment.

The forest in question covers an area of over 1.2 million *rai* (474,442 acres) in five eastern provinces of Chachoengsao, Sa Kaeo, Chanthaburi, Chonburi, and Rayong. The foundation's activities include preservation and restoration of forest areas, protection of wildlife, improvement of the livelihood of people in the communities, and promotion of public awareness on environmental issues. According to its website, the area was originally under the authority of the Royal Forestry Department and the army's ranger forces.[5]

After the 1992 violent crackdown shattered its political legitimacy, the army focused its civil work on protection of natural resources with a focus on the royal development projects. The FPBFPF project received Queen Sirikit's royal patronage in 1993 and became part of the royal development projects. The army became the key agency taking care of the project. Its website and monthly magazines often emphasized Her Majesty's deep concern for the deterioration of forest areas and natural resources. The army set up a fund for the project and had it registered as a foundation in 2006.

Since the area covered by the FPBFPF is in the eastern region, it was overseen by the 21st Infantry Regiment (the Queen's Guard), 2nd Infantry Division which has its headquarters in Prachin Buri province. The regiment is known as the base of the *Burapha phayak* or Eastern Tiger faction, which dominated the army and the ruling juntas after the 2006 coup. General Prawit Wongsuwan, deputy prime minister and defence minister in the Prayut government, has been president of the FPBFPF since 2006.

Prawit is known as the most influential figure in the Prayut government and the NCPO junta. He was at the centre of a public scandal after people on social media noticed that he wore many luxury watches but none appeared in his asset declaration submitted to the National Anti-Corruption Commission (NACC). An amateur investigation conducted by netizens on social media concluded that he had at least twenty-five watches worth almost 40 million baht (*GM Live*, 18 January 2018). Prawit claimed that the watches were loans from a close friend, who had deceased. Although the partisan NACC cleared Prawit, this incident added further damage to the already fragile legitimacy of the military government, which had claimed that ending corruption by the Yingluck government was one reason for the coup. Corruption clearly worsened under military rule (*Bangkok Post*, 29 January 2019).

Patthawat Suksiwong, who was named by Prawit as the true owner of the twenty-five luxury watches, was a member of the FPBFPF. He was a founder of Com-Link, a telecommunication company which reportedly thrived on strong connections with leading state authorities (*Isra News*, 24 December 2018). Another committee member and honorary advisor is Charoen Sirivadhanabhakdi, president of the Thai Beverage Public Company.

As of February 2019, the majority of committee members are also members of the Eastern Tiger faction, including General Prayut Chan-o-cha, General Anupong Paochinda, General Udomdet Sitabutr, General Khanit Saphithak, General Thirachai Nakwanit, General Walit Rotchanaphakdi and General Wit Thephasadin na Ayutthaya. Other committee members were close associates of Prawit, such as M.R. Pridiyatorn Devakul na Ayutthaya, General Noppadon Inthapanya, General Phatthana Phutthananon, General Loetrit Wetsawan, General Kittiphong Ketkowit, and General Nat Intharacharoen. Nine of the twenty-four committee members were appointed to the NCPO's National Legislative Assembly and some held positions in the cabinet (*Isra News*, 26 December 2017). Prawit has apparently been deeply involved in the foundation's works as his photo appears often on the website.

Although FPBFPF originated as a royal-initiated project of Queen Sirikit, the ORDPB, the coordinating organization for the royal development projects, is absent from the FPBFPF activities. The royal development status still gives the project prestige. FPBFPF has attracted large sums in donations from big corporates, detailed on the Foundation's website and Facebook page, ranging from several hundred thousand to over 1 million baht. For example, after the foundation had announced that it wanted to produce a theatrical play in honour of Queen Sirikit in August 2015, it received 9,500,999 baht from donors including King Power International, Thai Beverage Public Company, True Corporation Public Company, PTT

Public Company, and Siam Commercial and Electronics. In addition, Thai Beverage donated 2,000,000 baht in August 2012; the Singha Beer Corporate gave 4,000,000 baht in September 2015; and Samart Corporation Public Company gave 3,000,000 baht in February 2019 (Facebook and website of the FPBFPF). Many of these companies are known to enjoy privileges and concessions in doing business under the NCPO government's *Pracharat* project (Prajak and Veerayooth 2018).

The Forest Master Plan

Conservation of forest land and natural resources has been prominent among the NCPO's policy priorities. The joint forces of military, police, civil servants and paramilitary launched their operations immediately after NCPO had seized power on 22 May 2014. Despite being two decades apart, the NCPO's approach was similar to that of the NPKC in the 1990s.

On 14 June 2014, General Prayut Chan-ocha issued NCPO Order No. 64/2014 regarding the encroachment on and destruction of forest resources. The order directs related state agencies to arrest people who encroach on, seize, possess, destroy, or act in ways that cause damage to forests. It authorizes state agencies to remove any encroachers on national reserve land (*Prachatai*, 15 June 2014). ISOC and the Ministry of Natural Resources and Environment (MONRE) were assigned to formulate a strategy and road map for implementing this order. Three months later they unveiled a master plan to resolve problems of forest destruction, with the objective of increasing forest cover from 31.57 per cent of the country's area to 40 per cent within ten years, adding more than 26 million *rai* to the existing forest area (ISOC and MONRE 2014). ISOC's Fourth Centre for Operations Coordination, which is responsible for matters of natural resources, environment, energy and food security, has taken a leading role in coordinating with ISOC Region Headquarters, the police, the MOI, and paramilitary forces, to implement the plan.[6]

The NCPO order indicated that the primary targets would be the capitalists or large-scale encroachers. The poor and landless, and people who were living in the forest area before it was declared as forest reserve were not to be affected by the order (*Prachatai*, 17 December 2014). However, in April 2015, the Office of Thai National Police proudly announced that in the first six months of implementation 1,622 people had been charged in 2,758 cases of destroying forest, 235 people had been charged in 265 cases of sale of prohibited wild animals or forest products, 110 people had been charged in 108 cases of destroying natural resources and the environment, and 602 people had been charged in 1,920 cases of encroaching on forest and public land (*Prachatai*, 25 April 2015). The order had been enforced in several provinces, particularly in Buriram, Chaiyaphum, Nan, Roi-et, Kalasin, Sakon Nakhon, Nong Bua Lamphu, Chanthaburi, Surat Thani and Mae Hong Son. A majority of these areas were sites of disputes between villagers and state agencies prior to the coup. For example, the first villages which faced eviction in 2014 were in Dong Yai national forest reserve, the same area where the military junta had been evicting villagers in 1991 under the *Kho.cho.ko.* project (*Bangkok Post*, 26 June 2014).

Representatives of small-scale peasants and the Thai Lawyers for Human Rights argued that those who have been arrested, prosecuted and forcibly displaced from their homes and communities were mainly poor people who had been dwelling in the areas involved before they were declared forest areas, and people whose way of life had long depended on forest resources, including peasants operating small-scale agricultural businesses or landless peasants. Moreover, in order to prevent people from returning to their land, authorities had demolished many houses, uprooted and destroyed trees, and cut down tens of thousands of rubber trees, allegedly to solve the oversupply of rubber that caused low prices for rubber in the world market. The protest was much smaller than that against the *Kho.cho.ko* project, thanks to the junta's firm suppression of its political opponents since it came to power. Still, the military began surveillance of the villagers' campaigns, meetings and seminars on natural resources management. Many participants were summoned and forced to sign agreements that they would not carry out any further activity. The NCPO showed no interest in examining the land rights of communities or their histories and traditions (Thai Lawyers for Human Rights 2015; *Prachatai*, 20 May 2015).

The military's harsh approach stemmed from its perception that small-scale farmers have been the principal cause of environmental degradation and deforestation. Such was the long-held dominant perception among related state agencies (Forsyth and Walker 2012, p. 57). The military believed that the problem had worsened because the past governments had been too weak to settle the issue. The concentration of power of the ruling junta was an opportunity for the military to carry out its mission. Although the NCPO tried to show the public that it targeted rich commercial investors, such as owners of resorts and rubber plantations (Nation TV, 30 April 2017), poor farmers bore the heaviest impact of the policy.

The dubious aspect of the NCPO's forest policy was its reforestation programme, which shared some similarity to those of the *Isan Khiao* and

Kho.cho.ko. projects. It invited private firms to become involved in the reclaimed forest areas. High-ranking officials of the RFD admitted that reforestation of the reclaimed 27 million *rai* of land must include plantations of high-demand and valuable trees such as palm oil, rubber, teak, and rosewood. Ironically, at the beginning of the operations to reclaim forest land, small-scale rubber farmers were severely affected as the authorities destroyed their plantation quickly. But the reforestation programme allowed big corporates to plant rubber and other trees to supply the furniture and bio-fuel industries. Furniture entrepreneurs had long complained that forest policy had caused shortages of teak and rosewood and a trend of decline in export value (*Prachachat Thurakit*, 10 March 2018).

To facilitate the involvement of private corporate interests, General Prayut used the supreme power granted him under Article 44 of the 2014 interim constitution to amend the National Forest Act of 1941 to allow private companies to harvest and transport presumably privately grown trees without going through normal oversight and examination procedures (*Royal Gazette*, 30 July 2014). While the junta preached on the protection of natural resources and environment, it went out of its way to assist private corporates at the expense of small-scale farmers.

The junta did not hesitate to facilitate projects that caused environmental damage. For example, villagers in Ban Namun, Khon Kaen province had long opposed a petroleum drilling survey by Apiko Company. After the coup, the company began moving drilling equipment into the area but faced obstruction from villagers. Apiko soon secured assistance from the government and a joint operation of military-police-paramilitary helped guard and facilitate the transport of equipment. The military even threatened villagers with the use of martial law if they caused obstruction (Thawisak Koedphoka 2015).

The same happened to the protesters against potash mines in the northeastern provinces of Sakon Nakhon and Udon Thani. In January 2015, the Prayut government gave permission to the Chinese state-owned China Ming Ta Potash Corporation to explore 120,000 *rai* of land in Sakon Nakhon, bypassing the obligatory process of environmental impact assessment. In the same month, the government suspended the work of a joint committee between the Udon Thani Environmental Conservation Group and the Department of Primary Industry and Mining, effectively ending the participation of local people in an investigation into the social and environmental effects of potash mining. While the corporates' businesses were well facilitated, protesters in the two areas faced intimidation and charges by state authorities (*Prachatai*, 5 March 2015; 28 March 2017).

During the NCPO's five-year rule, its cabinet approved at least six projects, which reduced the forest reserve areas by 6,243 *rai* of land (1,000 hectares) (*Prachatai*, 8 March 2019; TCIJ, 19 September 2015; Manager Online, 9 September 2016):

1. On 15 May 2015, Prayut executed Article 44, issuing an order to remove national reserved forest status from the Masamao forest in Mae Sot district, Tak province. The area of 2,182 *rai* (349 hectares) was to be utilized for the junta's new special economic border zone in Tak province.
2. On the same day, Prayut revoked the same protection status from a 716-*rai* community forest in Chaiya village in Nong Khai province. A community forest in Thailand is a common resource area used by specific rural communities. Its condition is crucial for the livelihoods of people in the community who have protected and managed the area to maintain their sustainable livelihood. For over two decades, rural people and advocates have fought for legal recognition of community forests nationwide (Anan 2000). The RFD had endorsed the legal status of the Chaiya village's community forest in November 2008. The revocation was completed swiftly and without community consultation.
3. In June 2016, General Anupong Paochinda, Minister of Interior, granted a subsidiary of the Red Bull Public Company a right to utilize the 31-*rai* Huai Mek community forest in Khon Kaen province. The company had been purchasing land around the community forest since 2013 and wanted to expand its operation to the adjacent forest. The ensuing public outcry, however, pressured the company to withdraw its plan.
4. The influential Siam Cement Group, in which the biggest shareholder is the Crown Property Bureau, obtained a concession to use land in the Tab Kwang and Muak Lek Forest Reserve in Saraburi province for mining operations until 2036. The total size of the land granted to the company was 3,311 *rai* (approximately 530 hectares). The protected area contains a large and ecologically rich Watershed Class 1A zone, which is usually restricted from human activity, including commercial use.

In February 2020, ISOC's 4th Centre for Operation Coordination proudly announced its accomplishments since 2014. For the year 2019 alone, there were twenty-six cases related to conflict over natural resources and forest land (The Fourth Centre for Operations Coordination, ISOC, 2019).

The Development Military in New Areas

In February 1991, the NPKC used corruption among politicians as a pretext for toppling the elected government of Chatichai and promised to return Thailand to democracy soon. Its legitimacy was questioned when its intention to hold on to power became transparent. Anti-military protests began to gain momentum in May 1992, ending with a bloody crackdown on 17–19 May 1992, in which at least thirty-nine people were killed and thousands of protesters were arrested. The NPKC was accused of using excessive force against unarmed civilians (Physicians for Human Rights 1992). General Suchinda Kraprayoon resigned as prime minister after King Bhumibol intervened to end the turmoil. The army lost legitimacy and popularity. Its leaders pledged to stop interfering in politics and all NPKC leaders have kept a low profile ever since. The army, the perennial favourite of King Bhumibol, was called to assist with the royal development projects. In the post-counterinsurgency era, these projects were no longer concentrated in the security-sensitive remote rural areas. Following the 1992 crackdown, the military developed a role in new security issues and urban-related problems with support from the monarchy.

Though civilian governments wanted the military out of politics, they did not see the need to end the military's engagement in the socio-economic sphere or to cut down its civil affairs projects. In 1992, Prime Minister Chuan Leekpai established and chaired a National Committee for Rural Development and Distribution of Prosperity in the Rural Areas. A year later, the committee assigned the Ministry of Defence to coordinate plans for development for security in thirty provinces along the borders. The army even engaged in preparing the master plan for the Eighth National Social and Economic Plan (Usani 1999, p. 38).

The Monkey Cheeks Project

Management of water resources in rural areas was one of King Bhumibol's keen interests. In the post-counterinsurgency period, water management extended to flood prevention in urban areas. The most prominent project was named the *kaemling* or monkey cheeks project. Though it has spread to many provinces, it began as a solution to the floods that affected Bangkok almost every year during the rainy season. The first agency the king called to assist on this pilot project was the military.

Rainwater deposited on northern Thailand has to pass Bangkok on its way to the sea. During September–October the flow peaks from monsoon rains and high tides in the Gulf block the outflow into the sea. The king came up with the idea of "monkey cheeks", based on his observation of the behaviour of monkeys which like to munch on bananas but retain some in their cheeks to swallow later. The idea was translated into construction of reservoirs around Bangkok along with canals, dykes, and water gates to divert excess water flowing from the north into these monkey cheeks to be released later when the sea level dropped below the level of canals. In addition to mitigating the risk of flooding, the retained water in the monkey cheeks could be used for irrigation during the dry season.

The king's idea could have been implemented by an elected government and civilian agencies. However, at an audience on 17 November 1998, the king gave advice on the idea of money cheeks to General Mongkhon Amphonphisit, then supreme commander of the armed forces. The next day, General Mongkhon ordered his troops to survey the canals and drainage in the provinces around Bangkok. He then set up a working committee for a flood prevention project including the Supreme Command Office, Bureau of the Royal Household, Royal Irrigation Department, Bangkok Metropolitan Administration, Provincial Administration of Samut Prakan Province, Office of the Royal Development Projects Board, Armed Forces Development Command, Royal Thai Survey Department, Department of Highways, State Railway of Thailand and Port Authority (Usani 1999, pp. 48–49).

With royally bestowed legitimacy, the army occupied the leading and coordinating positions on this new project. Under the NCPO, the army is still engaged in digging and maintaining many monkey cheeks projects nationwide, sometimes independently, sometimes in conjunction with other state agencies (*Manager Online*, 13 January 2016). Even though some have questioned the effectiveness of monkey cheeks, the official status as a royal development project overrides any complaints (*The Isaan Record*, 11 September 2017).

Suppressing Illicit Drugs

Suppressing illicit drugs is another new security area in which the Thai military has become involved since at least the 1990s. It is inscribed as part of the armed forces' mission and policy. The military role became prominent during an influx of methamphetamine, known colloquially as *ya ba* (the crazy drug), in the late 1990s and early 2000s. In October 2000, King Bhumibol granted an audience to General Samphao Chusi, then supreme commander, at the Klai Kangwon Palace in Hua Hin. According to General Samphao at the press conference, the king was deeply worried about the rise of drug problems and told him to have the army, the BPP and Village Scouts participate in the prevention and suppression of illicit drugs (*Matichon*, 17 October 2000). The royal concern put pressure on the government to pay serious attention to the matter. In February 2001, less than a month after he was elected prime minister, Thaksin declared that he would "wage a war on drugs" as illicit drugs were enemies of the state. This campaign immediately became a top priority of his administration (*Matichon*, 4 and 6 March 2001). In early 2003 then Thaksin launched a three-month campaign which resulted in the extrajudicial killing of over 2,500 people (Puangthong 2015).

The army and the BPP had taken part in anti-drug operations before King Bhumibol's advice to General Samphao as most drug trafficking took place along the borders. With the demise of communism, the interception of drug traffickers on the border became a priority of the armed forces. The North Star Operation, launched in 1997, was a coordinating office for agents of the Office of the Narcotic Control Board (ONCB), the police, and the army. The Operation set up border stations and checkpoints for searching targeted individuals and residences, as well as conducting intelligence operations along the borders of northern Thailand. The following year, the "Bunchusi Plan 1998" was established to conduct intelligence operations in the northern region with cooperation among staff of the ONCB, the BPP, Provincial Police Region V and VI, First Army Region, and Internal Security Operations Command Region III. The "Strategic Plan on the Prevention and Suppression of Illicit Drugs in Northern Border B.E. 2542–2544 (1999–2001)" further extended these operations (ONCB 2002, pp. 29–40).

The army played a central role in those operations because it already had intelligence infrastructure and manpower in the border areas. The deputy commissioner of the Immigration Bureau even proposed that the government should bring in ISOC to assist in the operation and declare martial law to deal with cross-border crimes including drug trafficking, illegal immigration and illegal logging (*Matichon*, 18 August 2000). The king's direct advice to the army leader gave higher priority to the problem and granted legitimacy for the army to engage in narcotics suppression outside the border areas.

The army's mission extended to public health aspects of the drug issue, including using military barracks for drug treatment and rehabilitation. The army proposed to incorporate a drugs combating programme in the training for reserve officers and to double high school student trainees to

300,000 per year (*Matichon*, 26 October 2000). These proposals were later included in Thaksin's anti-drugs plans (*Matichon*, 27 November 2000). Leading military figures, such as General Prem Tinsulanonda, often voiced support for the armed forces' role (*Siamrath* daily, 30 March 2001). His famous catchphrase "drug dealers are traitors" was often recounted in media coverage and displayed on banners in public spaces nationwide.

From this point onward, the anti-drugs campaign has become increasingly militarized (Puangthong 2015). This is the problem when the armed forces becomes the key institution to address a new security problems which is socio-economic in origin.

Sufficiency Economy and Sufficiency Democracy

King Bhumibol's sufficiency economy philosophy (*setthakit phophiang*) emerged in the midst of the economic crisis in 1997. It was proposed as an economic behaviour model for Thai people to avoid a similar economic catastrophe in the future. It was soon adopted as the core principle of the national social and economic development plans. The promotion of this royal idea was more political than economic, particularly after the coup in 2006. The sufficiency economy principle became a buzzword for the military junta to disguise its political agenda. King Bhumibol's economic ideas, wisdom, and virtues were core subjects in an ISOC-designed learning programme for recruits. The NCPO brought the Cold War's development for security strategy back to life in full.

In the throes of the financial crisis in 1997, King Bhumibol devoted his customary birthday speech to the sufficiency economy. He not only gave advice on coping with economic hardship, but also criticized the greed of capitalism, excessive attention on economic growth, overconsumption and overexploitation of natural resources. His message was interpreted as a critique of the agenda that Thai policymakers and politicians had pursued for decades. The royalists claimed that the king's idea had been conceived as early as 1974, when he gave a speech to students at Kasetsart University, warning of the possible impact of rapid economic development. When Thailand was hit by economic crisis three decades later, it confirmed how visionary and wise the monarch was. Therefore, the royalists claimed, Thai people should attentively follow the greatest monarch's guidance. The sufficiency economy philosophy thus had two sides. On one side, it heightened the moral and political power of the monarchy. From that time onwards, King Bhumibol was portrayed as the role model of a frugal man despite being one of the world's richest monarchs. An image of his squeezed-out tube of toothpaste went viral on the press and social media. Several hundred books, articles, and research papers were produced on the king-guided sufficiency economy.[7] On the other side, the sufficiency idea implicitly criticized short-sighted policymakers and politicians (Ivarsson and Isager 2010, p. 226; Krittian 2010, p. 215).

The hyper-royalist atmosphere obliged governments and bureaucratic elites to adopt the king's philosophy, including as the guiding principle of the Ninth National Social and Economic Development Plan (2002–6) during Thaksin's government even though Thaksin only half-heartedly embraced the idea and pursued neoliberal economic policies that clearly ran contrary to the philosophy promulgated by the king. Yet once an idea is granted royal status, it can only be promoted, never removed. The sufficiency economy philosophy was vigorously promoted after the emergence of the anti-Thaksin Yellow Shirts movement in 2005. Soon after General Surayud Chulanont became prime minister in October 2006, he announced that his government would adopt the idea as the foremost principle of economic policy. Several anti-Thaksin royalists publicly supported the idea and criticized Thaksin's globalist and populist policies (Krittian 2010, p. 216). General Prayut also announced that the king's idea was the core principle of the country's Twenty-Year National Strategy (2017–36) (National News Bureau of Thailand, 24 November 2017).

The traditional elites were concerned over Thaksin's popularity among the majority of the rural people, and over his followers' discourse of being *ta sawang*, "open-eyed", disillusioned and awakened about the monarchy's political interference. The alleged involvement of members of the palace and the palace entourage in several contentious political incidents against Thaksin and his faction after 2006 undermined the moral authority of the monarchy (Thongchai 2010). The promotion of the sufficiency economy became more specifically targeted against Thaksin's popular neoliberal policies as part of an attempt to restore the people's loyalty to the monarchy, particularly in regions where the Red Shirts movement was strong (Rossi 2012). Even though King Bhumibol passed away in October 2016, the royalists, and especially the military government under Prayut, still relied heavily on the late king's legacy to defend the monarchy and legitimize the military regime.

In September 2015, the Prayut government launched a gigantic flagship project entitled *Pracharat*, meaning the people state or state and people. Several hundred billion baht were injected into programmes for low-cost housing, community convenience stores, schools and Internet connectivity, support for small and medium enterprise start-ups and agricultural products (*The Nation*, 19 October 2015). In addition, the junta introduced a Twenty-year National Strategy, a device for the military and its conservative allies to control elected governments and the country's socio-economic development into the future. Prayut's government reiterated that both *Pracharat* and the national strategy were derived from King Bhumibol's sufficiency economy (National Bureau of Thailand, 24 November 2017). The junta established learning centres for the sufficiency economy philosophy in over 83,000 villages nationwide. Political and ideological indoctrination was an integral part of the *Pracharat* programme. In January 2018, General Prayut unveiled the idea of *Thai niyom yangyuen*, literally sustainable Thai-ism. He explained that *Pracharat* and *Thai niyom yangyuen* were interrelated. *Pracharat* was for economic development and *thai niyom yangyuen* focused on instilling good values (*Post Today*, 26 January 2018).

A month later, General Anupong Paochinda, Minister of Interior, kicked off the *Thai niyom* campaign in the presence of provincial governors and district chiefs. The campaign was organized on four levels:

1. the national level chaired by Prime Minister Prayut;
2. the provincial level chaired by a provincial governor or the permanent-secretary of the Bangkok Metropolitan Authority;
3. the district level and Bangkok's communities chaired by a district chief or Bangkok's district director; and
4. the subdistrict and Bangkok's community level.

At the subdistrict level, the district chief in the provinces or district director in Bangkok had to set up an operational unit of seven to twelve people including civil servants, security officers, a local wise man (*prat chaoban* or local philosopher), and members of the volunteer/mass organizations in the area (*Khom Chad Luek*, 3 November 2016). The *Thai niyom* programme emphasized *kan op-rom*, educational training or indoctrination. ISOC, which was the main organization in charge of the learning centres, formed a hundred instructor teams (*Prachachat*, 15 February 2018; Ministry of Interior 2018, p. 2). Many of the people recruited to the training programmes under the *Pracharat* and *Thai niyom* flags appeared to be members of ISOC's mass organizations.

In 2018 the Ministry of Interior produced a 66-page "Manual for National Development in Line with the Sustainable Thai-ism Project", providing instructions on how to operate training courses, how to persuade people, and what issues should be emphasized. Predictably, this indoctrination relied largely on the late king's legacy. For example, the manual suggests instructors begin the information sessions with *withi thai pho-phiang*, the Thai way of life of sufficiency, by letting people watch a video clip titled, literally *We will be strong for King Rama 9* (Ministry of Interior 2018, p. 32). The highly sentimental six-minute video clip, produced by a private advertising firm Box Wedding and released to the public at the end of October 2016, begins with scenes of the night of the king's decease, 13 October 2016, showing the deep sorrow and great sense of loss among Thai people. It ends with the message that Thais will always stand together for King Rama 9.[8]

In essence, *Thai niyom* reflects the anxiety of the conservative elites over societal polarization, corrupt politicians, majoritarian politics, people's free choice of politicians, and the influence of Western democracy, which, they claim, is not compatible with Thainess. The solutions to such problem are to change people's mindset on their way of life; to persuade them to practise the king's sufficiency economy; to persuade them not to sell their votes and to educate them on the importance of voting for *khon di* (a good person) and *khon keng* (a capable person); to educate people on the attributes of *khon di*; to keep watch of politicians' use of the national budget; to take care of the poor who register in the junta's social security programme; to promote Thainess; to educate people on the flaws of Western democracy and the importance of *prachathipatai thai niyom* or Thai-ism democracy; and to respect the rule of law (Ministry of Interior 2018).

These concerns were emphasized at the launch of the *Thai niyom* campaign by General Anupong. He did not try to hide the perception of the conservative elites that Thai people aspired to have the wrong kind of democracy and voted for the wrong people, hence government had a duty to teach people about the right version of democracy. He instructed his Interior Ministry officials that they must work hard with the people in their localities, telling them to "not behave like a boss anymore". Otherwise, he claimed, they would lose the battle (*Prachachat*, 15 February 2018).

Since its appearance as a reaction to the 1997 economic crisis, the sufficiency economy philosophy has been transformed over time by the conservative elites. It was elevated to the foremost guiding principle for socio-economic development, confirming the image of King Bhumibol as a visionary development monarch and thus denying the legitimacy of politicians. Though King Bhumibol passed away on 13 October 2016, the NCPO still had to rely on his moral authority. The military junta claimed the sufficiency economy lay at the core of its political and economic schemes, thus warning against any criticism of something with such royal status.

However the cloak with which the junta attempted to mask *Pracharat* and *Thai niyom* was too transparent to hide their populist policies and political aims.

Conclusion

The monarchy and the military worked closely together on a strategy of development for security during the time of counter-communist operations. The military continued to employ such strategic planning, even after the fall of communism. With the palace's constant support, the military extended its development role in the post-counterinsurgency period, claiming that the military was better equipped and more trustworthy than civilian politicians for this task. The objective of development for security during the counterinsurgency period shifted from counterinsurgency to the eradication of poverty and the response to new security threats which widened the scope of security.

The royal hegemony of King Bhumibol was essential for the expansion of the military's socio-politico-economic role after the counterinsurgency period. The royal association guaranteed legitimacy, ensured government's budget support and blocked criticism, especially when many of the military's development projects were under royal patronage. The armed forces enthusiastically embraced this new role. As the royal development projects expanded into new areas, the role of the military extended into all areas of society. The military's civil works became institutionalized. Although at certain time particular military leaders or cliques faced political opposition, the military's civil works continued to be embedded in society. Development works created an image of the military as being development oriented, benign, apolitical, and useful to the people. When the army faced popular pressure to retreat from politics, it could turn to focus on development. The hierarchical relationship between the monarchy and the military continued in the new sphere of development.

The military's civil works ramified into new socio-economic concerns, and spread beyond the remote and rural parts of the country affected by the insurgency to encompass the whole country, including the urban areas. The media regularly carried news on the military's engagement in various activities, such as mitigation of natural or man-made disasters, combatting human trafficking, suppressing drug trafficking, and protecting natural resources. The public and media were not troubled by this military engagement in civil affairs. They became so used to the military presence that they failed to question the limits of the military's responsibility. Particularly at times when the military takes control of government, the military's involvement in all sorts of activities, even those that are traditionally delegated to other branches of government, has come to seem natural.

Elected civilian governments appeared unaware of the complexity of the military's civil affairs projects. They have invited the military to assist in various socio-economic problems on the naïve perception that the armed forces' manpower and infrastructure throughout the country can help improve the efficiency of government actions.

The management of natural resources and land usage involves many interests including poor communities, big corporates, and political organizations. The problems are often complex, yet the military tends to apply tough and swift measures, rather than a participatory process, often resulting in widespread grievances and violations of basic human rights. The military tends to blame the poor for destroying the natural reserve forest, while facilitating the schemes of big corporates. Development for security, while claiming to protect natural resources, gave arise to conflicts of interest and corruption scandals. Under the NCPO from 2014 onwards, the relations between the military leaders and the major corporates, both in the *Pracharat* schemes and in the FPBFPF project to enlarge the area under forest cover, became especially close and open. The military government did not bother to hide the cordial relationship with the big corporates.

The increasing polarization of Thai society, the unfaltering popularity of politician like Thaksin, and the looming royal succession caused anxiety among the conservative elites. Protection of the monarchy became the main mission of the armed forces, with the NCPO relying greatly on King Bhumibol's legacy for their own legitimacy. The promotion of the sufficiency economy philosophy was intended to undermine the legitimacy of politicians and electoral politics and simultaneously reiterate the benevolence of the sacred institution. The NCPO continued to exploit the late king's ideas for its entry into electoral politics, competing in the general elections in March 2019 via its party, Phalang Pracharat. Although the Prayut government's economic policies were populist in nature, the junta leaders projected the sufficiency economy philosophy as a critique of Thaksin's populist policy. They appeared to hope that this royal idea could win the hearts and minds of rural voters. However, the late King Bhumibol's legacy is waning and King Vajiralongkorn's moral authority has not yet measured up to his father's. Besides, no figure of moral authority could save the junta leaders from their own cronyism, corruption scandals and oppressive politics. The charm of King Bhumibol's legacy will not last forever.

Notes

1. http://afdc-ict.rtarf.mi.th/afdcintra/stories/Mission/mission.html
2. Ibid.
3. The Army's Directorate of Civil Affairs, http://doca.rta.mi.th/; The Navy's Directorate of Civil Affairs: shorturl.at/mqtDV; The Air Force's Directorate of Civil Affairs, shorturl.at/gstBH; The Royal Thai Armed Forces, http://www.rtarf.mi.th/index.php/th/
4. The Suan Kitti Co. Ltd was a subsidiary of the Soon Hua Seng Corporation, a giant agro-industry company.
5. http://www.5provincesforest.com
6. http://4occ.isoc.go.th/
7. A search on Chulalongkorn University's online library with the key word *Setthakit phophiang* (sufficiency economy) on 11 May 2018 yielded 1,016 items.
8. https://www.youtube.com/watch?v=q-F_i-X1Y4I

Establishing State-Dominated Mass Organizations

Mass control was one of the most important components of the Thai state's counterinsurgency operations from the early 1960s. Building a loyal citizen base was the aim of state-sponsored mass organizations and popular mobilization. A solid popular base could not only be used against enemies of the state, but could serve as proof of *khwam samakkhi*, unity, mass support for the state against the alien communists. The sheer number of people and their royal nationalist activities confirmed the legitimacy of the state and the existing social order.

This chapter begins by tracing the operations of state-supported mass organizations during the anti-communist period from the 1960s to early 1980s, when several right-wing movements appeared. Some had good ties with ISOC and were involved in the massacre of students and activists at Thammasat University on 6 October 1976. Their activities and names gradually disappeared from public view after 1976. People tended to assume that the military and its rightist allies had ended the operation of mass organizations, and that the semi-democratic regimes of General Kriangsak Chamanan (October 1977–March 1980) and his successor General Prem Tinsulanonda (March 1980–August 1988) gave no importance to these organizations. Quite the opposite was true.

Despite the appalling reputation of the military-supported rightist militias as a result of the Thammasat massacre, the conservative elites never abandoned the mass control programme as it was still needed to perpetuate their political power. On the one hand, the establishment understood that the state had to retreat from an ultra-rightist position, which would only strengthen its leftist enemy. On the other hand, mass organizations took on new importance after the re-emergence of parliamentary politics from the late 1970s. The military embraced democratization as a new mission, but still saw popular control programmes as an essential element of protecting the country's internal security. This brilliant plan was shaped by the semi-democratic regimes of Kriangsak and Prem, without any awareness on the part of politicians, elected governments, and civil society.

This chapter evaluates the limitations or failures of the military's political offensive during the intense period of counter-communist warfare between the 1960s and the late 1970s. This assessment is important for my argument against the long-held praise of the landmark Prime Ministerial Order No. 66/2523, which is seen as bringing the Thai state a swift victory over the CPT.

THE PEOPLE'S COOPERATION

The creation of mass organizations, as discussed in Chapter 1, was based on the concept of civilian-police-military joint operations (CPM), which was part of the state's political offensive approach. The cooperation of local people with state forces was seen as indispensable for the defeat of the communist movement.

Under the CDM principle, civil servants, police and military work together with local people. The role of each branch is based on its specific expertise. For example, police took care of day-to-day safety within remote communist-infiltrated areas; soldiers provided arms training to militias; soldiers, police and village strong men formed village defence units; police and soldiers took part in special offensive forces, patrolling and defending the areas with local militias; and civil servants carried out socio-economic development and indoctrination programmes. In practice, their roles could overlap. For example, the army and the BPP both participated in economic development and indoctrination programmes. Ideally, people would be satisfied with the improvement in living standards that arose as a result of these programmes, while state propaganda and royal-nationalist indoctrination would enhance their loyalty, turning them into a mechanism for popular defence, state surveillance, and propaganda (TUA, So.bo.9.7.2/65; So.bo.9.7.2/70; Tanham 1974, p. 136).

Some groups had a small unit of armed paramilitaries attached to them, such as the Village for Development and Self-Defence Volunteers (VDSV) programme or *Muban a-sa phatthana lae pongkan ton-eng* (*O.pho.po*), but not all mass organizations were given arms training. Some were permanent groups with the legal standing while others were ad hoc groups that lacked any legal basis. The one activity that every group had in common was royalist indoctrination. Royal patronage or symbolic royal recognition—flags, emblems, audience with members of the palace—was crucial for attracting popular participation (Hyun 2014, pp. 363–64). Such practices continue until the present day (website of the Royal Thai Armed Forces, 24 July 2018).

Village development projects were created in order to improve the living standards of people in communist influenced areas. These development projects ranged across construction of local infrastructure, improvement of agricultural methods, public education, and public health facilities and knowledge. Civilian state agencies, together with the army and ISOC, also undertook so-called "information programmes" and psychological operations, such as producing leaflets and broadcasting radio programmes. Mobile information units were established to visit the remote areas and inform local people of government policy and promises (Tanham 1974, pp. 75–77).

From a defence perspective, the objective of CPM was for state agencies to provide safety and security for villagers living in areas sensitive to communist infiltration. The strategists believed that, on the one hand, support from people living in these areas was essential for establishing state defence operations, while on the other hand, people would not cooperate if the authorities failed to ensure long-term safety and security for them, and would quickly shift their allegiance to the communists, who promised them a better future. State surveillance over the remote areas would never be effective unless the government could recruit loyal villagers who had a comprehensive knowledge of the local area and could keep a constant watch over their neighbours in a way that outside authorities could not. Arming local people would enhance the tie and trust between the people and state authorities, making them feel authoritative and proud to be part of the powers that be. ISOC headed these operations with personnel support from the police, the BPP and army (Saiyud 1986, pp. 41–47; Tanham 1974, pp. 78–84). Lately, the NCPO's forced eviction of small-scale farmers from the forest reserve areas heavily employed CPM in the operations. Many pictures are posted on the Internet.[1]

ORGANIZATIONS OF THE COLD WAR POPULAR DEFENCE

During the counterinsurgency period, the well-known right-wing militias were the Village Scouts, Red Guars, and *Nawaphon* (New Strength), but there were many more. Several state-organized paramilitary and civilian organizations mushroomed in the 1960s and 1970s.

According to the ISOC director, General Saiyud Kerdphol (1986), there were at least twenty different state-supported paramilitary and civilian groups in the 1970s, including: VDC, *A-sa phatthana lae pongkan ton-eng* (Volunteers for Development and Self-Defence, or VDSD); *A-sa samak pongkan phai fai phonlaruen* (Civil Defence Volunteers, or CDV); *Ratsadon raksa khwam sa-ngop lae phatthana muban* (People for Peace Keeping and Village Development); *Chut patibatkan chuai-luea prachachon* (Emergency Response Team); *Thai a-sa pongkan ton-eng* (Thai Self-defence Volunteers); *Ratsadon a-sa samak phatthana thongthin lae pongkan prap-pram atchayakam* (Volunteers for Community Development and Crime Suppression); *Ratsadon a-sa lae pongkan ton-eng* (People Volunteers and Self-defence); *Kong kamlang tit a-wut* (Armed Group); *Klum siang chaoban* (Voice of the People Group); *Klum bang rachan* (Bang Rachan Group); *Chaoban phithak thin* (Homeland Defenders); *Ratsadon samakkhi* (United People), *Ratsadon a-sa samak pongkan chai-daen* (Volunteers for Borders Defence); *Ratsadon a-sa samak pongkan phu ko kan rai* (Volunteers for Counterinsurgency); and *A-sa pongkan atchayakam lae a-sa samak banthao satharanaphai* (Volunteers for Crime Prevention and Disaster Mitigation) (Saiyud 1986, p. 82; ISOC 2012, pp. 2–3).

The proliferation of these civilian and armed militia groups was partly a result of competition among related state agencies. Colonel Han Phongsitanon (1975, p. 176), an ISOC veteran, pointed out that the higher the number of mass organizations related agencies claimed to have created, the more success they could claim. Han doubted the efficacy of many of these groups. His experience working in ISOC led him to believe that government officers at the ground level did not take their task seriously enough.

The following section provides basic information on state-sponsored mass organizations: their origins and specific objectives, and estimated sizes of the groups which were created during the counterinsurgency period. Most of them are still active today.

1. Volunteer Defence Corps (VDC) or A-sa raksa dindaen (O.So.)

The Volunteer Defence Corps (VDC), commonly known in Thai as *A-sa raksa dindaen* or *O.So.*, was established under the Phibun administration by the Volunteer Defence Corps Act of 1954. Ball and Mathieson (2007, pp. 25–27, 92) have provided excellent information about the VDC, one of the first paramilitary groups created at the beginning of counterinsurgency operations with assistance from the US government.

Their primary duty was to assist the BPP, also founded with support from the US, in the hill and border areas that were under strong communist influence. As their members were recruited from people living in the localities, their knowledge of the areas and the people were beneficial to the state forces. VDC's duties cover a wide range of areas: to protect the country's borders from incursion and illegal transgression; to provide security to villagers; to combat communism; to help with natural disasters and security emergencies; to protect ethnic people in the hills; to maintain security in the refugee shelters; and to promote nationalism and royalism.

Although the VDC has been under the authority of the MOI and its minister is the ex-officio commander in chief, VDC is the most militarized among the state-backed paramilitary groups. Its members received military training from the army, wear military-like camouflage uniforms, and are allowed to carry heavy weapons such as rifles and semi-automatic pistols. The VDC is the only one of these organizations whose members carry official ranks. The titles of their ranks are rather unique and the members are proud of them as they were given by King Bhumibol. They are similar to ranks used in the Ayutthayan period: *Nai kong yai, Nai kong ek, Nai kong tho, Nai kong tri, Nai muat ek, Nai muat tho* and *Nai muat tri*. Their status, however, is subordinate to the police and the military. They function as assistant to the latter.

The number of VDC units grew rapidly during the Vietnam War. By 1980, VDC claimed to have around 52,000 members. Most of them were based in the northeastern provinces. VDC members and activities declined after the fall of the CPT. Their roles gradually shifted towards the areas of new security threats and maintaining law and order along the borders, in village and urban areas, including drugs suppression, maintenance of security in the refugee camps along the Thai-Myanmar borders, disaster relief, combatting illegal activities, illegal logging, road checkpoints, and protecting and guiding tourists. VDC membership surged with the development of the conflict in the three southernmost provinces, increasing from 15,373 personnel in 2004 (Ball and Mathieson 2007, p. 74) to 25,925 in 2018 (*News1*, 10 July 2018).

2. Village Protection Unit (VPU)

The first paramilitary organization created by CSOC/ISOC in 1966–67 with support from the United States Operations Mission (USOM) was the Village Protection Unit (VPU) or *Chut khumkhrong muban*. The VPU was established by the "Strategic Plan 09/10" of ISOC. At the same time, USOM created the VDC to work with VPU.

A VPU consisted of a combination of ten to twenty VDC personnel with two to three local policemen. The VPUs were stationed in villages and their main duties were to protect villagers, implement psychological programmes, survey the villagers' needs, and interrupt communication between the CPT and its moles in the villages. If a unit faced a heavy armed strike from the insurgents, a strike platoon stationed nearby the area would move in to help. A platoon consisted of the military, the BPP, police, and the VDC. According to the CSOC/ISOC's internal evaluation in 1972, the VPU programme failed to help achieve the primary objective of establishing a sustainable political offensive at the village level. Ideally, the VPU was supposed to establish peace and security in a village as a precondition for government to implement other political offensive measures, such as village development and political programmes. However, after several years had passed, the insurgents became stronger and were able to occupy more areas. Although the number of VPUs increased in response to the CPT's increasing strength, the strategy failed to achieve peace and security in the remote areas. As a result, military measures continued to dominate counterinsurgency operations (ISOC 1972, pp. 2-14–2-15). The most fearsome part of the counterinsurgency operations, however, seemed to be the mobile assassination unit under the charge of the army, which targeted the CPT leaders (TUA, So.bo.9.7.2/70. pp. 2-15–2-40).

3. Village for Development and Self-Defence Volunteers Programme (VDSV) and Village Security Unit (VSU)

The VDSV (*Muban a-sa phatthana lae pongkan ton-eng* or *O.pho.po.*), initially under ISOC command, was established in 1975. Now it is under the jurisdiction of the Department of Provincial Administration (DOPA) of the MOI. Currently, VDSV is governed by the Village for Volunteers Development and Self-Defence Act B.E.2522 (1979). Its members are called Volunteers for Development and Self-Defence (VDSD or *A-sa phatthana lae pongkan ton-eng* or *O.pho.po.*).

Each VDSD has ten armed men protecting the area. They are named as the Village Security Unit (VSU) or *Chut raksa khwam plotphai muban* (*Cho.ro.bo.*). The army and VDC provided training in arms use, self-defence and intelligence gathering to fifty to a hundred able-bodied men of each village. Villagers in general received various socio-economic development and training programmes on such subjects as agricultural techniques, marketing, vocational training, leadership, public health and indoctrination (Santi 1990, p. 37). The programme involved various government agencies, such as those of Ministries of Interior, Education, Agriculture, and Public Health, to engage in the counterinsurgency operations. Village development programmes were intended to motivate people to cooperate with the state.

The programme was the brainchild of Saiyud when he was the deputy director of ISOC. In light of the increasing strength of the communist movements regionally and domestically, he wrote a secret memo, dated 7 July 1976, to Prime Minister M.R. Seni Pramoj. The memo urged Seni to give priority to the expansion of VDSV and to enforce organizational efficiency. Saiyud indicated that VDSV was the only programme representing the true meaning of development for security since it combined political-economic-psychological measures with military measures (TUA, So.bo.9.7.2/147).

Many years later, VDSV attracted the attention of the Office of the National Economic and Social Development Board. In 1982, a research team, led by Sumet Tantiwetchakun, who later became a key person in the royal development projects, assessed the effectiveness of the programme in strengthening national security through a survey conducted in forty-two villages in nine provinces. The research concluded that the performance was not satisfactory as both the government officers and local people lacked direction, vision, long-term planning and inter-agency coordination. Additionally, VDSV failed to draw active participation from the people (NESDB 1982).

In 1976, there were about a thousand VDSV units in thirty-eight provinces (Santi 1990, pp. 41–42). Both the fourth and fifth national economic and social development plans (1977–81 and 1982–86) aimed to add another 4,000 villages (NESDB 1982). The number of VDSV units continued to increase and expanded to every province, except Bangkok, in the post-Cold War period. This expansion was due to several factors: tensions along the Thai-Myanmar borders, the flow of illicit drugs from Myanmar, the re-emergence of violence in the three southern Muslim provinces and the colour-coded political polarization. There were more than 75,700 volunteers in 1999 (Ball and Mathieson 2007, pp. 95–96).

4. Village Head Assistant for Peace Keeping Programme
The Village Head Assistant for Peace Keeping Programme or *Khrongkan phu chuai phuyaiban raksa khwam sa-ngop* was created in the mid-1960s. Three to eight able-bodied men in a village were chosen and sent to the district office for arms training. Upon their return, these men were given the task to train another 200 men in their villages, who in turn would then

assist with the VPU's defence activity. People living in the highly sensitive areas, also known as "red zones", were often recruited into Information Gathering Units and received training in espionage that lasted from three day to two weeks (TUA, So.bo.9.7.2/70. pp. 2-15-2-40). The programme has expanded nationwide and continues until the present day.[2]

5. People Development and Peace Keeping Unit

In 1969, CSOC/ISOC launched a programme of People Development and Peace Keeping Unit or *Nuai ratsadon phatthana lae raksa khwam sa-ngop muban*. This unit claimed to recruit 400 people for armed and espionage training. They were divided into groups of twelve to live in a village. Six of them took care of village development, which included providing assistance to villagers, while another six were in charge of security matters. All of them simultaneously worked as spies for ISOC. By 1972, 4,000 people went through the programme (TUA, So.bo.9.7.2/70. pp. 2-15-2-40). This programme has ceased to exist today.

6. The Thai National Defence Volunteers (TNDV)

The Thai National Defence Volunteers was established by the military government of Kriangsak in 1978. It was intended to be an umbrella organization for several militia groups which had appeared in the rural areas during the anti-communist period and which were now brought into a single organization to establish efficient management and command as well as to reduce the budget burden (ISOC 2012). TNDV has been under the direct authority of ISOC since its establishment. The army and the MOI have also been involved in the programme. One unit consists of ten able-bodied men chosen from the village. TNDV works closely with a district chief (*nai amphoe*), who is under the provincial governor. As the ex-officio ISOC provincial director, all governors must report TNDV activities to the regional directors or army Region Commanders.

According to a 1978 Regulation of the Prime Minister's Office, TNDV's responsibility covers a wide range of issues, including preventing and countering communist threats, suppressing riots and other disturbances, undertaking surveillance for intelligence gathering, providing security for the villages, helping in disaster relief, helping suppress crimes and developing the village. The recruits are required to participate in a ten-day training programme, including the use of light weapons. They are allowed to carry arms when they are called to assist in state operations, with permission from the director of the TNDV district or the district chief. Initially, the TNDV units were established only in communist-infiltrated villages but they soon spread to urban areas, including Bangkok (ISOC 2012, p. 5 and Appendix; Ball and Mathieson 2007, p. 43).

According to Ball and Mathieson (2007, pp. 44 and 218–19), the TNDV were disliked and distrusted by local people for their corrupt practices over the use of local development funds. Their influential leaders were known for turning innocent people over to state authorities. They thus failed to achieve their task of collecting intelligence for state authorities. In the post-counterinsurgency period, the group was exploited to serve the personal interest or political orientation of military leaders. In 1983, General Arthit Kamlang-ek, then army commander and a contender to replace Prime Minister Prem, reportedly mobilized the TNDV to support the army's push for constitutional amendments, which would prolong the army's control over the parliament and government. The TNDV members were also used as canvassers for army-supported candidates during elections. They assisted minimally with security operations in the three southernmost provinces. TNDV are currently divided into four categories:

1. The self-defence TNDVs serve in the danger zones or the border areas, such as the three southernmost Muslim provinces. Their duties include countering and preventing terrorism and all forms of threat, and keeping security in their villages. Members of this group are allowed to carry weapons and receive armed training.
2. The "development and protection" TNDV units serve in villages or municipal areas. They focus on disaster relief, crime prevention and suppression, and village development.
3. The disaster prevention and mitigation TNDVs serve in the urban areas.
4. The marine TNDVs consist of fishermen or workers in the fishing industry in twenty-two coastal provinces. They assist the navy in maintaining law and order over coastal activities. This group is under the navy's command.

7. *The Reservists for National Security (RNS)*
The Reservists for National Security (RNS) or *Kong-nun phuea khwam mankhong haeng chat* (*Ko.no.cho*) was a product of Prem's administration, established in 1981 and placed under the authority of the army as Prem held the positions of premier and army commander concurrently. In 1986 RNS was moved to fall under the authority of ISOC. Currently, its existence is supported by Prime Ministerial Order No. 288/2534 (1991 CE). Since the majority of the military reservists came from either the peasant or working

classes, who were also the popular base of the CPT, Prem believed that the state should recruit these people. His government planned to train fifty to seventy classes of 100–200 reservists per year, making a total of around 5,000–14,000 people every year. Since it was Prem's initiative, the programme grew steadily. Between 1982 and 1992, the programme trained 658,915 reservists and established 504 Reservist Villages in 72 provinces. Their experience in national service makes them useful to the state as defence in their villages. In addition, the reservist have to undertake political and psychological programmes, such as the Democracy Pavilion programme which focused on promoting the notion of a Democratic Regime with the King as the Head of the State (ISOC 1992, pp. 1, 7. 22).

8. *The Civil Defence Volunteers (CDV)*
The Civil Defence Volunteers (CDV) or *Asa samak pongkan phai fai phonlaruean* was created under the Disaster Prevention and Mitigation Act 1979, which was later replaced by an Act of 2007. CDV was originally under the Department of Local Administration but now is under the Department of Disaster Prevention and Mitigation (DDPM) of MOI. Its primary mission is to establish a civil defence system throughout the country. The units assist state agencies in prevention, monitoring and mitigation of crimes, man-made and natural disasters, providing rescue and relief operations for the affected, maintaining surveillance in local neighbourhoods, guarding government premises, facilitating road traffic, and joining royalist and religious ceremonies (DDPM n.d.).

9. *Village Health Volunteers (VHV)*
The Village Health Volunteers (VHV) or *Asa samak satharanasuk pracham muban* (*O.so.mo*) belong to the Ministry of Public Health (MOPH) and are supported by the MOPH regulations, dated 2011. Their main activities are to provide primary healthcare, to communicate health information to people, to promote a healthy lifestyle, and to prevent contagion in a community. Each village can have one VHV per ten people. The majority of the volunteers are women, especially housewives. In return for their service, volunteers are entitled to several privileges, such as healthcare coverage for themselves and family members, daily wage and compensation, monthly allowance, royal insignia, and quota seats for their children to study in the MOPH's programmes (Department of Health Promotion 2011, pp. 23–25).

A study by Kauffman and Myers (1997) indicates that the majority of people in a northeastern village did not know the VHVs in their community and few had used their services. Besides, the increasing urbanization of villages reduced the significance of the VHV as the point of entry in the healthcare system. The guidebook for VHVs published by the MoPH in 2011 shows that the programme has been modernized to meet new public health risks. For example, it emphasizes support for the elderly, pregnant women, the disabled and chronic patients. It also pays attention to preventive measures against diseases in the urbanized villages related to modern lifestyle, such as diabetes, cancer and hypertension (Department of Health Promotion 2011).

A recent study by Sitthipon Ketchoi (2017) found a high-level of performance by 200 VHVs Non Thon subdistrict, Khon Kaen province. They are able to build good links between the government and the population, and local people have been very receptive to the VHVs' work. The introduction of the 30 baht universal health coverage by the Thaksin administration appeared to make people, especially the urban poor and rural people, pay more attention to health issues. Before the 2006 coup, there is no evidence showing ISOC's attempt to exploit members of VHV for political purpose. But their political usefulness emerged after the 2014 coup, as I will show in Chapter 5.

10. The Village Scouts
The Village Scouts or *Luksuea chaoban* were founded in 1971 under the BPP. It was the most successful state-organized mass movement in the latter half of the 1970s. Within a few years of its establishment, the movement became urban-based and its membership grew to 5 million. The activities of the Village Scouts went into rapid decline following the Thammasat massacre in October 1976 (Bowie 1997; see further detail below).

Proliferation of the Ad Hoc Groups, 1973–76

The above groups carried official status, and their work was concentrated in the remote security-sensitive areas. There were several other temporary right-wing civilian groups which emerged during the contentious period of 1973–76. Their main mission was to counter the rise of the radicalized student movement in the capital.

The ruling elites saw mobilization of the people as increasingly urgent after the 1973 popular uprising and the rise of leftist movements domestically and regionally. At the same time, the US was withdrawing troops from the Vietnam War and from Thailand. A report signed by Saiyud in his capacity as deputy director of the CSOC/ISOC in August 1976 reflected this anxiety. Saiyud urged the government of M.R. Seni Pramoj to support his plan for the expansion of the VDSD. He believed that locally based mass organizations would be the decisive factor for the fate of Thailand. He urged his superior to pool the resources of the armed forces and the MOI into a comprehensive expansion plan. General Saiyud's intention was to have the VDSD branch out to all levels: national, regional, provincial, district, subdistrict and village (TUA, So.bo.9.7.2/148). Between 1975 and 1976, ISOC created VDSD units in around a thousand villages nationwide (Santi 1990, p. 37).

Apart from the infamous Red Guars or *Krathing daeng* and *Nawaphon*, there were many other ad hoc groups, including: *Chomrom achiwa seri* (Free Vocational Students Club), *Phet thai* (Thai Diamond), *Chang dam* (Black Elephant), *Phithak thai* (Protection of Thainess), *Sahaphan nak sueksa khru haeng prathet thai* (Federation of Teacher College Students of Thailand), *Naeo-ruam rak chat* (League of Patriots), *Prachachon phu rak chat* (Nation-Loving People), *Naeo-ruam to-tan phadetkan thuk rup-baep* (League Opposing All Forms of Dictatorship), *Khabuankan patirup haeng chat* (National Reform Movement), *Sahaphan khru a-chiwa* (Federation of Vocational Teachers), *Kammakon seri* (Free Labour), *Khang-khao thai* (Thai Bats), *Kluai-mai thai* (Thai Orchids), *Wihok saifa* (Lightning Birds), *Sahaphap raeng-ngan ekachon* (Union of Private Enterprise Labour), *Chomrom mae ban* (Housewives Club), and *Nawaphon* (Suthachai 2008, pp. 154–56).

Many of these groups were well known to the 1973–76 students and activists for their royal-nationalist campaigns and participation in the 6 October massacre. All of them gradually faded from the public eye and eventually ceased to exist after 1976.

ISOC's Mass Operations

How various right-wing groups in the 1970s operated and coordinated among themselves is not clear as information is scarce. Apart from the book on the Village Scouts by Bowie (1997), research on the right-wing movements is limited. There has been no serious study on *Nawaphon*, the unofficial but most powerful right-wing group of this period, despite being often mentioned by scholars (such as Morell and Chai-anan 1981; Suthachai 2008, pp. 154–56).

ISOC has often been referred to as the creator and sponsor of right-wing groups in 1973–76. The largest and most powerful of these groups was believed to be *Nawaphon*, founded in 1974, which allegedly took part in the killings and lynching of students at Thammasat University. Its leader and public face was Watthana Khieowimon, who claimed that his group had over one million members with local cells and networks across the country. Some people believed that it had assassination units. Such claims were credible partly because some prominent public figures openly admitted that they were members or supporters of *Nawaphon*, including Thanin Kraivichien, then Supreme Court judge, later prime minister after the 1976 massacre and King Bhumibol's privy councillor, and General Samran Phaetthayakun, then commander of the army Region One and Region Three and King's Bhumibol's privy councillor. A few other army and police generals were ostensibly involved (Suthachai 2008, pp. 155–56).

Thongchai Winichakul (2020, pp. 43-44), however, points out that in his search for the rightist thugs involved in the anti-student campaigns and Thammasat massacre, he was unable to find anyone identifying themselves as a member of *Nawaphon*. Apart from Watthana's bragging, there was no evidence to support the estimates of *Nawaphon*'s size. The biggest gathering in the name of *Nawaphon* was only around ten thousand people and most of them were local civil servants. Thongchai argues that its powerful image was a rumour that has been recycled among scholars, none of whom had produced any substantial evidence to support the claim. Research on US documents by Eugene Ford (2017, p. 259) also casts doubt on Watthana's claim that *Nawaphon* maintained good connections within the CIA and senior levels of the US government. It appears that the powerful image of *Nawaphon* may simply have stemmed from Watthana's aggressive and boastful exclamations. In my documentary research at Thammasat University Archives, *Nawaphon* did not appear in any ISOC confidential documents and reports, even those discussing the expansion of mass organizations. For example, in July 1976, Saiyud wrote a report to Prime Minister Seni about the urgent need for the government to expand the mass organizations nationwide rapidly. He did not mention *Nawaphon* at all. Instead, the VDSV was his main focus (TUA, So.bo.9.7.2/147). Moreover, *Nawaphon* disappeared from public view not long after the Thammasat massacre. If *Nawaphon* had had such a gigantic mass base, ISOC would have used the group and would not have abandoned it quickly and casually. I will show later in this chapter that the ruling elites systematized the operation of mass control even after the demise of the CPT. The ISOC's neglect and abandonment of *Nawaphon* makes no sense.

Thongchai offers a hypothesis that *Nawaphon* was probably phantom organization created by the rightist elites. They intentionally inflated the image of a massive rightist movement in order to intimidate the students. Possibly *Nawaphon* did not have its own separate popular base but used local cells belonging to several other state-organized mass organizations, both the permanent and temporary ones listed above. It is highly likely that, when a situation arose, ISOC would use its authority to coordinate state agencies to mobilize members of various groups for Watthana, who then claimed that ISOC's masses were members of his *Nawaphon*. ISOC contributed to the exaggerated image of *Nawaphon* (Thongchai 2020, p. 44). Members of the state-supported mass organizations can change their hats according to the state's demands. This strategy was remarkably effective in contributing to an image of the Thai state's solid popular support. This is also true for the case of the *Chit-a-sa* or the Volunteer Spirit programme, discussed in Chapter 5.

ISOC's operation manual, dated 1972, indicates the existence of assassination units run by the army and ISOC. The units were usually stationed in the red zones with the task of executing key communist suspects or spies operating covertly in localities in order to cut ties and support between the insurgents and villagers. The killings carried out by these assassination units were intended to send a message to villagers that the state forces had an upper hand over the insurgents and that villagers should not cooperate with them (TUA, So.bo.9.7.2/70, pp. 2–40). General Panlop Pinmanee, former ISOC deputy commander, confirmed this when he openly bragged that he led the army's assassination unit based in the northeast in the 1970s.[3] *Nawaphon*'s assassination units likely belonged to the army.

Assessment of the Military's Political Offensive

The torture, lynching and desecration of corpses at the Thammasat massacre on 6 October 1976 were carried out mainly by rightist civilians (Puangthong and Thongchai 2017). The massacre revealed the success achieved in turning the royalist mass into a deadly political weapon. However, the massacre should not be the only criterion to assess the Thai military's political offensive during the counterinsurgency period. The strategy must be assessed against its primary objective, which was to win the loyalty and cooperation of people living in the communist-influenced areas. Government policy since the 1960s emphasized the use of political measures over military ones (Saiyud 1986; Chai-anan, Kusuma and Suchit 1990, p. 67). However, right through the end of the ultra-rightist government of Thanin Kraivichien in October 1977, the military's use of force still dominated counterinsurgency operations while the mission of winning over the hearts and minds of the people was far from being achieved. Here, I aim to provide some evidence of the limitations, if not the failure, of the military-led political offensive.

On 29 February 1968, Saiyud, then director of the Operations and Coordination Centre of ISOC, boasted in a speech at the Foreign Correspondents Club of Thailand about the impressive achievement of the military-led political offensive. He claimed that communist attacks and sabotage were in decline while the government received positive cooperation from villagers, including an increasing number of intelligence reports from the people. He added that the number of communist defectors to the government side continued to increase. One of the successful programmes Saiyud mentioned in his speech was the 09/10 plan (Saiyud 1986, pp. 27–28). Unfortunately, a few years later, an ISOC internal classified report from 1972 gave a contrasting picture. The report made a comprehensive assessment of several strategic plans launched since 1967, and reported disappointment with the lack of progress, including on the 09/10 plan (TUA, So.bo.9.7.2/70).

The objective of the 09/10 plan was to reclaim remote rural areas under communist influence. To achieve this objective, government had to first establish security and stability for villagers in the areas, as the most effective way to persuade people to side with the state. The plan was designed to provide arms and security training to villagers, and to establish the civilian-police-military joint operation. The state-sponsored paramilitary force, the Village Protection Units (VPU), was formed under this plan. The plan was for the combined forces of paramilitary, military and police to first eliminate the communist influence in the affected areas, and only when security and stability was achieved would they be able to implement programmes of village development, ideological indoctrination and psychological warfare. ISOC began this experiment in eleven sites. Five years later, the report concluded that little had been achieved. None of the initial eleven sites had been declared a communist-free zone. Instead, the number of critical areas had shot up to sixty-seven. This goes to show that one should not confuse the increase in paramilitary units with success. ISOC's report stated that the increasing number of paramilitary units was a response to the CPT's increasing strength, and was causing an unwelcome budgetary burden on the government (TUA, So.bo.9.7.2/70). By 1974, the government forces were facing an increasing number of insurgent attacks in every region. The red zones expanded quickly (TUA, So.bo.9.7.2/88).

The report also disclosed ISOC's frustration that the increase in armed conflict against the insurgents prevented members of ISOC's mass organizations carrying out rural development programmes. Both villagers and paramilitary forces were too scared to cooperate with government agencies. As the insurgents attained more strength, the use of force continued to dominate counterinsurgency operations. The government was deeply concerned about the increasing loss of life by members of state and paramilitary forces. As a result of the failure to establish security in red zones, it was impossible to implement the civil activities and psychological programmes effectively. In the six years leading up to 1972, the agencies involved in counterinsurgency operations were only able to respond to communist actions. They lacked strategic thrust while the insurgents held advantageous positions in many areas. Besides, state authorities did not have the enthusiasm nor seriousness needed to successfully carry out counterinsurgency operations. The same evaluation applied to ISOC's many other strategic plans, including 110, 111, 111-ko, 112, 113, 114, and 115 (TUA, So.bo.9.7.2/70, pp. 2-63-2-65).

By mid-1976 Saiyud admitted failure. His frustration is evident in his confidential report, dated 7 July 1976, to Prime Minister Seni Pramoj. In his own words:

> All projects of the prevention and suppression of the insurgency are outdated, ineffective, and unable to achieve the goals. In other words, they failed to keep up with the increasing threats because they lacked coordination, power, appropriate direction and control (TUA, So.bo.9/7/2/147).

In the 1960s and 1970s, state forces regularly used violence against villagers in the sensitive areas, resulting in distrust and suspicion. ISOC's name was often mentioned in cases of human rights violations, leading to calls for the abolition of ISOC after the 1973 popular uprising. ISOC was so notorious that its chief architect, Saiyud, requested Prime Minister Kukrit Pramoj in 1974 to approve his request to change the name of the organization from Communist Suppression Operations Command to the softer-sounding Internal Security Operations Command (Saiyud 1986, pp. 14–15).

One of the best-known cases of mass violence conducted by the military and ISOC was the so-called Red Drums massacre in 1971–72 in the southern provinces of Phatthalung, Trang, Nakhon Si Thammarat and Surat Thani. People were rounded up on grounds of engaging in communist activities or providing support for them. Many were tortured. Some were released. The most unfortunate were killed in a brutal way, placed inside empty 200-litre petrol drums, doused with petrol and burned alive. It was estimated that around 3,000 people were killed. This incident became known to the public after the Thanom-Praphas government was toppled by the popular uprising in October 1973 (Haberkorn 2017, pp. 79–82; Chulalak 2016).

The abuse of state power worsened during the polarization of 1973–76. The case of Ban Na Sai village in Nong Khai province in the northeast in January 1974 showed how state forces and the ISOC's paramilitary forces were involved in a large-scale violation of human rights against people suspected of being or supporting communists. Eyewitnesses testified that the operation was carried out by the BPP officers, counterinsurgency officers and members of the VDVs. More than a hundred houses were burned along with their newly harvested crops and belongings. A family of three, including a young child, who refused to leave their house, were killed in the burning house. Accounts of the two massacres show how ISOC and other state forces employed extreme violence against people in sensitive areas. Even though the two incidents hit the national news headlines, the authorities reacted to the public and media inquiry with arrogant denial and contempt. The lack of accountability was possible because state forces were often protected by impunity (Haberkorn 2017, pp. 80–108). These were the two biggest incidents of mass violence perpetrated by the military and ISOC that became known to the public. It is highly likely that there were many small-scale cases of human rights violations that went unreported.[4]

The Thammasat massacre was the ultimate proof that the use of violence had trumped the political offensive. The brutal attack on students and activists at Thammasat University was evidently orchestrated by state forces, right-wing politicians, royalists, military leaders, press and media along with members of state-supported mass organizations (Thongchai 2020).

The evidence of state violence shows the military's failure to favour the political offensive over the use of violence, hence deepening political and armed conflict. The stronger the radical movements were, the more military measures appeared to dominate the counterinsurgency operations. The lack of knowledge and enthusiasm to pursue political means had been a cause of concern among the chief architects of the military's political offensive approach since the beginning of the counterinsurgency operations.

Since 1961, Somchai Rakwichit (1961), CSOC's top strategist, trained by the CIA in psychological warfare, complained about the lack of progress because the authorities in the localities did not give priority to the counterinsurgency operations. Somchai was critical of the ground officers for the lack of cooperation among themselves as well as their disinterest in learning and understanding the local cultures. In 1971, a similar concern appears in a confidential CSOC document signed by Praphas, then CSOC director, to Prime Minister Thanom. Praphas referred to the previous Prime Ministerial Order No. 110 of 1969, which had ordered all related state agencies to give utmost importance and cooperation to the government's anti-communist policy and adhere to the use of political offensive over military measures. But there was no progress two years later. Praphas then urged Thanom to dispatch an order to all related agencies to emphasise that they must give priority to the anti-communist policy and plans (TUA, So.bo.9.7.2/65).

In his memoir, Colonel Han Phongsitanon (1975, pp. 168–86) showed that most state authorities had neither the competence nor commitment to carry out the political offensive. Han spent nine years as ISOC's chief of intelligence. He criticized the mainstream perception that the communists were an external threat, the lackeys of a foreign enemy or terrorist, and argued that this perception not only led to abuse of state power, but caused the counterinsurgency operations to lose cohesion and direction. Han even questioned the use of village spies within ISOC's mass organizations. He believed that most ordinary villagers were safe because the CPT was trying to recruit them, not kill them. But many spies worked for their personal interests and were disliked by their neighbours. They often provided false information to the authorities in exchange for rewards. The authorities tended to suspect or distrust villagers who refused to work for them. Instead of understanding the possible repercussion villagers might face from the communists, the authorities' suspicion led to suffering or suppression of the people in the communities, which ultimately proved to be counterproductive to the counterinsurgency operations.

The attempt to create local defence groups took its toll on the local militias and spies. Partly because they were not professionally trained and carried less sophisticated weapons, partly because they lived in the affected areas and were known to be working as militias or spies for the government, they were vulnerable to being attacked (Han 1975, pp. 168–86; Ball and Mathieson 2007, p. 36).

A military-centric approach still dominated the counterinsurgency operations until the late 1970s. Those who advocated political means, such as General Chavalit and Colonel Han, were often accused of being communists. Colonel Han was forced to resign in 1975 because of such accusation (Chai-anan, Kusuma and Suchit 1990, pp. 144–45).

Success of Royalism

Despite the domination of military methods in the counterinsurgency operations, one political offensive measure began to show a promising sign: the propagation of royalism and the monarchical role. As Bowie's research shows, the Village Scouts became the most powerful state-organized mass organization to counter the radicals during 1973–76, thanks to the explicit support from the monarchy. The palace's interest in the movement stemmed from dissatisfaction with the incompetence of the army-led counterinsurgency operations. King Bhumibol was concerned about the military's heavy use of armed force and about unjust actions that exacerbated people's distrust and resentment towards the government. On multiple occasions, he publicly expressed his concern about the military's hostility towards villagers and hill peoples. Bowie argues that, despite the existence of twenty paramilitary groups, by the early 1970s there was no strong state-organized mass movement until the king and members of the royal family became engage openly with the Village Scouts (Bowie 1997).

The Village Scouts movement was founded in 1971 by officers of the BPP, Somkhuan Harikul and Charoenrit Chamrasromrun. In 1972, King Bhumibol expressed interest in the movement by offering his patronage and donating 100,000 baht. In addition, he provided a symbol of royal connection to members of the movement in the form of maroon scarves that every Village Scout received upon initiation. The king and his family members frequently visited Village Scout units to bless them with scarves and flags, fostering ties and loyalty. This royal patronage helped the expansion of the movement in important ways. First, it gained cooperation from various bureaucratic agencies to organize the initiation ceremonies. In 1976 alone, the movement conducted 2,387 initiation sessions involving almost 2 million new members. As the movement grew, it had to gain more cooperation and support from various bureaucratic agencies. Second, the royal patronage attracted financial support from both the government and the private sector. Third, it generated popular support from people of all classes for the Village Scouts movement as well as for other right-wing groups, which demonstrated their loyalty to the monarchy. The palace's engagement with the Village Scouts movement became more conspicuous after 1975, following the growing radical movements in Thailand and the fall of Laos, Cambodia and Vietnam to the communists, which exacerbated the anxiety that Thailand would be the next domino to fall. At its peak in 1976, about 2 million Thais or 10 per cent of the adult population were Village Scouts members (Bowie 1997, pp. 85–111).

State forces, mainly various branches of the police, were involved in the storming, shooting and killing of students in the Thammasat massacre, but the torture, lynching and desecration of corpses on that morning were carried out by the hysterical mob, many of them wearing Village Scouts symbols. These brutalities were well recorded in the press and film clips, later available on the internet (Puangthong and Thongchai 2018). The cruelty visited on the students, who were accused of being communists and disloyal to the pillars of the nation, exhibited the success of the royal nationalist ideology.

The involvement of ordinary people allowed the rightist elites to evade accountability. A booklet published by the National Reform Council (NRC) (1976) reveals that the military junta who staged a coup in the afternoon of 6 October 1976 were not reluctant to exploit the right-wing mass for the elite's benefit. It explained that the violence at Thammasat University took place because of repeated provocations by the radical students, who were trying to turn Thailand into a communist country. It claimed that one incident in particular, in which drama students performed a mock hanging, outraged ordinary Thais because the students made the hanged man looked like Crown Prince Vajiralongkorn, thereby insulting the monarchy and committing a grave offence.[5]

The NRC further accused the students of carrying heavy weapons and initiating the attacks against authorities. The patriots, *phu rak chat*, finally lost patience and wanted to teach the students a lesson. The booklet claims that the authorities were trying to control the situation but were outnumbered by the fiery patriots who loved the nation so much that they were willing to protect the nation's sacred institution with their lives; state forces were unable to prevent a hundred thousand angry patriots from attacking students. In the official narrative, the rightist perpetrators were honoured as patriots while the students were accused of being treasonous and un-Thai. A similar narrative can be found in the court testimonies of police and rightist witnesses.[6]

Violence committed by anonymous ordinary citizens was invoked to shield state forces and the establishment from responsibility, to substantiate the rightist elites' claim that the majority of Thai people supported them, and to justify the atrocities at Thammasat University.

Of course, the rightist thugs responsible for the Thammasat massacre were mostly drawn from the organizations formed by ISOC, and were inspired by a heavy dose of royal-nationalism. The massacre successfully ended radical movements in urban areas, but it did not end the people's war. On the contrary, it strengthened the CPT, which welcomed thousands of fleeing students, peasants and union workers into its ranks. As a result, the armed struggle in the hills and rural areas intensified. The military-led political offensive through mass organizations had failed to achieve its primary objective—to establish security, loyalty and the Thai state's domination in the rural areas. This requires a reassessment of the Prime Ministerial Order Nos. 66/2523 and 65/2525.[7]

Reassessment of Order Nos. 66/2523 and 65/2525

In April 1980, one month after Prem took over the premiership, he issued a landmark order, the Prime Ministerial Order No. 66/2523, titled "Policy to Win over Communism". In 1982, he issued another Prime Ministerial Order No. 65/2525, titled "Plan for Political Offensive to Win over Communism". The two orders have often been hailed by the military and scholars as the origins of a successful army-led political offensive and an appropriate approach to defeating the communist movement (Chai-anan, Kusuma and Suchit 1990, pp. 8–9; Marks 1994, pp. 196–205). The army often boasts these two orders as the military's brilliant strategy to defend the Thai nation from the evil communists and the successful establishment of reconciliation and stability. Testimonies by army officers and official publications have often referred to these orders as the principal framework of the internal security strategy (Sahai Chuang and Banchon 2003, pp. 159–62). The latest reference was made in January 2017 when the Prayut government claimed that a reconciliation plan imposed on political parties followed the principles of Order No. 66/2523 (ThaiPBS News, 24 January 2017).

These commentators note the failure of the military's political offensive right before the implementation of Prem's two orders, and recognize that two important factors contributed to the CPT's defeat, namely the Sino-Vietnam conflict and divisions within the CPT (Chai-anan, Kusuma and Suchit 1990; Sahai Chuang and Banchon 2003). Yet they treat the two orders like magic spells that brought the Thai state victory over the CPT in a very short period of time. I argue that, although these orders were intended to defeat communism, they were issued in the wake of serious internal disarray within the CPT. There is no proof that the army was successful in enforcing its political offensive at the ground level at all. The success of the two orders has been exaggerated and their perceived success has been exploited to legitimize the military's expansive role in the socio-political arena in the post-counterinsurgency period.

When Prem announced Order No. 66/2523 in April 1980, the problems inside the CPT were already evident. Two factors were decisive in bringing about the defeat of the CPT. The first factor was triggered by the Vietnamese invasion of Cambodia in order to topple the Khmer Rouge regime in January 1979. China immediately launched fierce attacks on Vietnamese border towns. The Sino-Vietnamese conflict was disastrous for the CPT's armed struggles. The China-dominated CPT soon issued a statement condemning Vietnam and the Soviet Union, which immediately ruptured the CPT's relations with Vietnam and with Laos, a close ally of Vietnam and Soviet Union. The CPT's main supply route from China via Laos was terminated and its bases in Vietnam and Laos were closed down. The situation worsened when China agreed with the Kriangsak government to end its arms and logistic support to the CPT so that the two countries could form an alliance against Vietnam. In July 1979, China shut down the CPT's Voice of the Thai People radio station based in southern China, the only communication the CPT had with the outside world (Suthachai 2019, pp. 437–39). In exchange for China ending its support to the CPT, Thailand allowed use of its borders to convey arms and strategic supplies from China and Western countries to the anti-Vietnam forces along the Thai-Cambodian borders (Puangthong 2005).

The second factor was the conflict inside the CPT between the China-dominated leaders and the students. The CPT's political and military strength reached its peak after about three thousand students and activists fled to join their bases in the aftermath of the Thammasat massacre. However, it lost this newfound strength very soon afterwards due to conflicts between the students and the pro-China CPT leaders. News about student leaders quitting the CPT bases began to appear as early as October 1978 (*Matichon*, 14 October 1978 and 21 May 1979). Kriangsak's amnesty in 1978 and later Prem's Order No. 66/2523 no doubt, helped speed the outflow (Morell and Chai-anan 1981, pp. 304–5).

Without the Sino-Vietnam conflict and the CPT's internal conflict, it would have been difficult for the Thai military to defeat the CPT so quickly. By the time that Order No. 65/2525 was issued, the CPT was already in shambles, and the Thai elite's anxiety that Thailand would be the next domino to fall had already subsided. The army's attempts to seize the CPT headquarters and principal base area in the Khao Kho mountain range along the borders of Phetchabun and Phitsanulok provinces had earlier failed. But in 1982, just two years after the issuance of Order No. 66/2523, the army was able to capture it completely (Marks 1994, p. 204). In October 1983, ISOC reported to the government that all major strongholds of the insurgents had been destroyed, and the military soon declared a total victory over the CPT (Ball and Mathieson 2007, p. 101). This was a major military victory, not a political one.

The significant implication of the two orders which has been overlooked is that Prem laid the foundations for the military to continue its political intrusions into society in the post-counterinsurgency period.

INSTITUTIONALIZATION OF MASS ORGANIZATIONS

After the coups on 6 October 1976, the Thanin government (October 1976 to October 1977) bolstered the activities of the Village Scouts to mobilize the royalist popular base, counter the increasing CPT strength in the countryside, and support his increasingly unpopular government. After the Thanin government was removed by a coup on 20 October 1977, the new NRC junta withdrew support from the Village Scouts. As Bowie (1997) noted, by the mid-1980s the movement had lost its vitality.

This does not mean that the NRC and the ruling elites saw no use in mass control and wanted to terminate this machine. On the contrary, they still saw the benefit of building a broad base of royalist support and continued to draw on the patronage and symbolism of the monarchy. The royal family continued to attend Village Scouts training sessions and other events after the 1976 coup and into the present. Queen Sirikit hosted twenty-three exclusive banquets for the Village Scout members of all regions between 1994 and 2004 (Hyun 2014, pp. 363–64). However, the military leaders were intent on keeping these movements under state control to ensure they did not become a threat to the ruling regime. Once the communist threat was in decline, there was no further need for mass organizations to be ferocious and confrontational.

The semi-democratic governments of Kriangsak and Prem began reorganizing the state-sponsored mass organizations through several laws and orders. The Village Scouts movement fell under the MOI and was prone to political exploitation. Its leaders had no close link with the NRC junta, but were allied with a rival faction in the military. In addition, the NRC junta received only half-hearted support from the monarchy. Its power was, therefore, insecure. Meanwhile, the media and general public grew bolder in criticizing the aggressive and unruly behaviour of the movement's members and the political ambitions of its leaders. The movement's association with the Thammasat massacre risked tarnishing the image of the monarchy. The NRC, therefore, needed to rein in the Village Scouts movement and prevent it being manipulated by rival politicians and interest groups. In April 1979, Kriangsak issued a Prime Ministerial Order to establish the Village Scouts Operational Centre under His Majesty's patronage (VSOC or *Sun patibatkan luksuea chaoban nai phraboromrachanukhro*). The VSOC was placed under the more neutral organization of the Boy Scouts (Bowie 1997, pp. 270–73).

The Kriangsak administration also reorganized other militia groups. In September 1978, Kriangsak issued the "Regulation of the Prime Ministerial Office" to set up a new mass organization entitled the "Thai National Defence Volunteers" (TNDV or *Thai a-sa pongkan chat*). The purpose was to bring together several village-level militia groups, which had created by various government agencies during the counterinsurgency period. Many were now redundant but the various agencies competed for budget to support their particular group. The establishment of TNDV dissolved other groups and integrated their members into a unified structure under the command of ISOC. Only the Village Scouts, the VCD and the VDSD remained as separate organizations. The TNDV regulation set out a command structure from the national to village level, rules of recruitment, objectives, physical and ideological training programmes, budgets, badges and membership cards (ISOC 2012). Through this formal structure ISOC could keep tabs on the members and remobilize them when the situation required.

Prem's two orders, Nos. 66/2523 and 65/2525, not only provided legitimacy for the continuation of the military's political strategy in the post-counterinsurgency period, but discreetly expanded the objective of the military's political offensive from counter communism to establishing "Thai style democracy" or the "Democratic Regime with the Monarch as the Head of the State".

Order No. 66/2523 stipulated that to win the final war over communism and all forms of authoritarianism, it was essential for the military to have a role in democratization. Order No. 65/2525 fleshed this proposition out. At this critical point, there was a need for instilling a sense of belonging and loyalty to the nation into every Thai, eliminating injustice and corruption in state agencies at all levels, promoting popular participation in politics and democratic movements, treating communist defectors as fellow countrymen, fighting the communist movement infiltrating the urban areas, enhancing information operations, and pushing the psychological programme. All these projects had to be implemented through mass organizations. To quote the Order No. 66/2523:

> 4.4 The ability of people of all professions to govern themselves and the opportunity for their political participation must be promoted. Ways and means must be laid out to ascertain the people's problems and the latter's wishes must be considered the foremost factor in planning operational guideline to fulfil those wishes.
> 4.5 Organization of all existing democratic movements must be promoted, based on consideration of the rights and interests of such groups and on vigilance against confusion between democratic movements and communist movements which hid behind the banner of democracy.

Mass control is more explicit in Order No. 65/2525:

> 4. *Strategy*: To create a unified agency comprising bureaucrats and people who believe in the ideals of democracy as the core leaders and to struggle to win over communism within a short period of time.
> 5. *Tactics*: To use this organizational unit as an instrument to establish democracy.
> 6. *Operational Framework*: The organizational unit is to be responsible for safeguarding the people's interests, creating true democracy and fulfilling the basic needs and desires of the people.

Both orders described at length how state agencies should work with several civic groups, including student groups, the business sector, former leftists, communist defectors, mass media and the general public. The variety of target groups showed that the ruling elites wished to expand their domination over civil society beyond the rural areas. During the counterinsurgency period, villagers in the remote rural and hill areas with strong communist influence were the main target of state-supported mass organizations. But in the post-counterinsurgency period, the target was much broader. Popular control was necessary for entrenching the Democratic Regime with the Monarch as the Head of the State. As Montesano (2019) has pointed out, while the two orders emphasized the role of the military and bureaucracy in democratization, they did not mention the parliament or politicians at all. The royalist elites wished to limit the role of parliamentary politics and politicians in internal security affairs.

Governments continued to expand community-based mass organizations. The Prem administration planned to establish another 4,000 VDSVs throughout the country. The VDSV programme was integrated into the Fifth National Economic and Social Development Plan 1982–86 so that it was entitled to government budget (NESDB 1982). In 1982, the Prem administration approved a plan for a new mass organization, the Reservists for National Security (RNS) or *Kong nun phuea khwam mankhong haeng chat* under ISOC. Prem recognized that most reservists came from the peasant and working classes, which formed the popular base of the CPT. Prem believed the government should recruit these people for security activities before the insurgents did. The ambitious plan was to establish at least one reservist unit per district (ISOC 1992, p. 7).

"People participation" was a key concept of the counterinsurgency operations, becoming a cliché in official documents (ISOC 2002, pp. 8–9). But people participation did not mean citizens participating of their own free-will. Prem's two orders portrayed the people as being too ignorant and easily misled by dangerous organizations or self-serving politicians; their participation had to be guided by state-approved activities and ideology. While the second order talks of promoting democratic movements, it urges government agencies to be vigilant because people might be confused between democratic and communist movements, as the latter may hide behind the banner of democracy. This idea persists in ISOC's present-day operations.

Suchit and Kanara (1987, pp. 43–50), who evaluated the effectiveness of ISOC's various mass organization programmes, concluded that, despite the official rhetoric, these programmes failed to promote democratic awareness and participation among the rural population, but rather emphasized security, discipline and surveillance.

Conclusion

The state-sponsored mass organizations originated in the Thai state's battle with the CPT. The idea was to have citizens function as a civilian force, which included vigilantes, patriots, intelligence gathering hands, an acting bridge between the central power and the remote localities, a propaganda machine, and agents of development. The indoctrination programmes aimed to strengthen the power of the monarchy and royal nationalist ideology. In other words, people were the state's popular defence in both military and political terms. The end of the anti-communist war did not bring an end to the mass organizations. The ruling elites continued to see the importance of controlling the popular conscience and dominating all important civil groups in both rural and urban areas. Hence the military's framework of mass organization and mobilization has remained until the present day, as I will show in the next chapter. Ironically, mass control is carried out in the name of democratization, and democratization became a new mission of the military's internal security operations.

The political offensive of the counterinsurgency operations had limits and flaws. The approach was initiated from the mid-1960s to attract the people to the state's side. But by the late 1970s, even the architects of the approach were deeply worried about its failure, evident from the CPT's growing strength, and about the massive violations of human rights exemplified by the Thammasat massacre. In this context, the significance of Prem's two orders needs to be reassessed. How far were they responsible for the defeat of the communist movement?

The two orders were the military leaders' prompt response to the changing situation. The governments of Kriangsak and Prem offered conciliation and accommodation for the mass defection of students and activists in a timely manner. But without the Sino-Vietnamese conflict and divisions with the CPT, it is doubtful that the state could have achieved victory in such a short period of time. The narrative about the successful role of these two orders not only draws a veil over the limits of the military's counterinsurgency operations, but provides justification for the military to pursue its prominent role in the nation's internal security affairs after the demise of communism.

While the image of state-dominated mass organizations was badly tarnished by their brutal engagement at the Thammasat massacre, the so-called reformist governments of Kriangsak and Prem gave priority to reorganizing and institutionalizing their mass control system. As Prem positioned the two orders at the top of the national agenda, they helped facilitate the military's political operations and their importance remained long after the fall of the CPT. They prepared the way for the military's political role in the post-counterinsurgency period. They laid out a vision of democratization spearheaded by the military with no role for parliament and politicians. In the next chapter, I will discuss how the legacy of the Cold War period has lived on and in fact gained new relevance following the deep divide in Thai politics after the coup in 2006.

Notes
1. https://www.isoc.go.th/?s=ทวงคืนผืนป่า
2. Mass Affair Division, MOI, https://multi.dopa.go.th/mad/main/web_index
3. Interview with Pallop Pinmanee, Bangkok, 5 December 2017.
4. During my five-day trip in the northeast in December 2017, I met several former

cadres of the CPT from a peasant background. They recounted how state violence in their villages forced them to join the maquis.

5. This is the propaganda by the military media and rightist newspaper, *Dao Sayam*. The students' staging of a mock hanging at Thammasat University referred to the public hanging of two activists in Nakhon Pathom on 24 September 1976, a day after the activists had put up posters, protesting against the return of Field Marshal Thanom Kittikhachon to Thailand. The mock hanging was intended to show the ongoing brutality of the state authorities towards activists.

6. For example, Salang Bunnag, see Museum of the Office of the Attorney General, "Ekkasan khamhaikan phayan fai jot 078 Phantamruattho Salang Bunnak" [Testimony of Witness for Prosecution No. 078 Police Major Colonel Salang Bunnag], 21 October 1976, downloaded from Documentation of October 6 Online Archives, https://doct6.com/archives/1647 (accessed 1 February 2019).

7. Both Orders were published in Chalermphon Som-in, ed., *Phraratchabanyat pongkan kankratham an-pencommunit pho.so.2495* [The Anti-Communist Activities Act, 1952 CE] (n.p.: n.d.).

Remobilization of the Royalist Mass Since 2006

Chapter 4 has outlined the original idea and objective of state-dominated mass organizations from the counter-communist period until the semi-democracy period. This chapter will focus on the remobilization of the royalist mass since the toppling of the elected government of Thaksin Shinawatra by the 2006 coup. I will discuss the reinvigoration of the remnant organizations from the Cold War era, the creation of new groups and programme, their targets, the ruling elites' objectives and the reasons for joining state-sponsored mass organizations.

The policy of the semi-democracy regime to maintain the military-dominated mass organizations, despite the fall of the CPT, proved beneficial to the conservative elites when they faced new political threats. They could switch on the mass control programme immediately. The moves to remobilize, expand and strengthen their popular base began after the coup in 2006. They targeted a wide range of people from villagers to urban professionals, business and religious groups, the old and the young. Royal-nationalist ideology remained the central theme for cementing people into a state apparatus, along with many material benefits for members of the mass organizations. The effectiveness of these organizations is doubtful. There are many official reports, news pieces, announcements, video clips, and pictures about activities of the military-dominated mass organizations posted on the websites, Facebook and YouTube accounts of ISOC, the army, ISOC provincial offices and of various mass organizations. Materials collected from these sources have proven to be very useful for this chapter.

Objectives

Since the coup in 2006, the establishment has faced a series of challenges: the unbeatable popularity of the exiled Thaksin Shinawatra and his parties;

the emergence of the Red Shirts movement and polarized colour-coded politics; a proliferation of critical messages towards the monarchy online; the end of the reign of King Bhumibol; the crisis of royal succession; and anti-military movements. The claims that Thailand is a unified country and the monarchy is universally respected have become fiercely contested. Despite military coups in 2006 and 2014 and numerous judicial measures, the Thaksin faction continued to win elections. All these issues caused anxiety about a decline of royal hegemony and the effect on the power and privileges of the conservative ruling elites.

The foremost objective of the revival of mass organizations and mobilization since the coup in 2006 is to protect the monarchy, the royal hegemony and status quo of the establishment by strengthening and expanding the network of royalist citizens. Members of the networks are meant to function as defenders and promoters of state ideology and institutions, and the ears and eyes of the state. ISOC's Office of Mass Affairs and General Information announced on its website a plan to establish a nationwide mass surveillance networks by loyal citizens.[1] Although there are many threats to national security in the post-Cold War era, including terrorism, illicit drugs, human trafficking, and violence in the three southernmost Muslim-dominated provinces, these threats are subordinate to the threat to the power of the conservative elites. The main purpose of mass surveillance is to keep watch over anti-monarchy and anti-military activities in both the actual and cyber worlds.

This anxiety is evident in the National Security Policy of 2015–21 and ISOC's Strategic Plans of 2012–16 and 2017–21. Threats to the monarchical institution and cultural and ideological differences among the population were prioritized as the leading threats to national security that state agencies had to address urgently. The authors of these security policies attribute these deviations to lack of education and ignorance resulting from the ordinary people's poverty. They claim that uneducated lower income citizens are easily deceived by subversive political groups and the media (National Security Council 2015, p. 5; ISOC 2012; ISOC 2017, p. 25).

ISOC's publication on *Thai asa pongkan chat* or the Thai National Defence Volunteers (TNDV) describes the royalist elites' plans to revive the Cold War-era mass organizations. The preface reproduces a letter signed by General Prayut, then army Commander and ISOC deputy director, dated 31 August 2012, addressed to the personal secretary of Queen Sirikit, requesting her to convey the letter and the content of the report to Her Majesty the Queen. The letter also mentions that General Naphon Bunthap, then deputy chief aide-de-camp general to the late King Bhumibol,[2] had earlier suggested that ISOC should strengthen TNDV and other mass organizations under its command. His advice was well heeded (ISOC 2012, pp. 1–2). The palace clearly paid special attention to this revival of Cold War measures.

The report of twenty-four pages plus an appendix explains that ISOC's role and TNDV's activities diminished after the lapse of the Anti-Communist Activities Act in 2000. Members of TNDV had, nevertheless, remained loyal to the nation and the monarchy because ISOC had continued to engage with them, particularly in organizing annual monarchy-related events. The report adds that, since the country is facing new security problems, it is vital to integrate the works of all state agencies and mobilize the people's participation.

The report's introduction shows that Prayut ordered publication of the report so that all state agencies would learn the history of TNDV's courageous devotion to the people, and would ensure that members of mass organizations continue to uphold patriotic ideology as part of their responsibilities. This patriotic ideology includes being loyal to the monarchy, knowing their duties and being ready to protect and honour the monarchy at all times. Prayut emphasized that:

> [ISOC] must try to revive the Thai National Defence Volunteers, make it strong and expand its networks nationwide with fast and effective outcome. In addition, all the mass organizations under ISOC must give first priority to the protection and respect of the monarchy while other objectives are second. (ISOC 2012, p. 9)

This message was reiterated at a meeting of ISOC officers after Prayut, then the ISOC director, had become the prime minister (*Matichon*, 6 February 2017). The report also reveals that in recent years other state and private agencies have begun revitalizing other civil organizations, such as the Village Health Volunteers, the Civil Defence Volunteers, and the Forest Protection Volunteers.[3] ISOC has tried to integrate these group into TNDV's activities (ISOC 2012, introduction, pp. 6–9).

The curriculum of the royalist indoctrination programme can be found in three books: *Kan hai khwam samkan kap sathaban phramahakasat lae kan thoetthun sathaban* [Giving Importance and Respect to the Monarchy], *Kan songsoem pratchaya setthakit pho-phiang* [Promotion of the Sufficiency Economy Philosophy], and *Kan pok-khrong rabop prachatipatai* [Democratic Government]. All three were produced by the Faculty of Education, Kasetsart University and the Office of Policy and Security Strategy of ISOC (2010a,

2010b, 2010c). They serve as guidebooks for ISOC's trainers, indicating the issues that the trainers should emphasize during the training sessions. Most of their content stresses the importance of the monarchy, including the royal-nationalist history of the Thai kingdom, King Bhumibol and the ten virtues or the Rajadhamma, King Bhumibol's wisdom and devotion, royal development projects, growing royalist consciousness among the people, the importance of unity as well as teaching people how to protect the institution and to express their gratitude to the king. Similar content appears in the guidebook of the *Pracharat* and *Prachathipatai thai niyom* project (Ministry of Interior 2018), the NCPO's populist policy described in Chapter 3.

In the guidelines for the reinvigorated TNDV, members and community leaders had to go through three-day training programmes. Even the old members had to receive retraining. Those belonging to the ad hoc groups received only a half day to one day training session. According to video recordings, training activities include games, group singing, acting performances, cooking, parachute jumping and bonfire parties (Phonchai Sae Tang 2016; Phonthep Sae Tang 2016). They look like the initiation rituals for the Village Scouts in the 1970s (Bowie 1997, Ch 6), albeit with less emotional intensity.

The following sections provide a broad picture of the currently active mass organizations—the old groups, the newly created ones and the new recruitment programmes.

Old Groups

Membership of the Volunteer Defence Corps (VDC) surged after the revival of conflict in the three southernmost provinces from January 2004 and the increased role of ISOC and the military in the area. VDC's major duties in the provinces include assisting the police and military, providing security protection to government facilities and personnel, manning roadblocks and checkpoints, and training Village Security Units or *Cho.ro.bo*. Some volunteers were involved in the abuse of power and violations of rights against Myanmar refugees and Muslim citizens in the three southernmost provinces. Local people saw these volunteers as incompetent and lacking in discipline. Some were involved in illegal activities together with soldiers, police and civil servants, such as human trafficking, trafficking of illicit drugs, arms smuggling, extortion and bribery. Some worked as armed thugs or hitmen for influential corrupt officials and politicians (Ball and Mathieson 2007, Ch 7; Srisomphop 2013, pp. 558–61). The number of VDC personnel grew from in 2004 to 25,925 in 2018 (Ball and Mathieson 2007, p. 74; *News1*, 10 July 2018).

Since the coup in 2014, VDC members in camouflaged uniforms have been seen in Bangkok, often working as guards or traffic facilitators at official or private functions and at sport events. On 15 February 2020, the birthday of my own workplace, the Faculty of Political Science at Chulalongkorn University, VDC members were present to provide such services, probably because many alumni of the Faculty hold high positions at the MOI which oversees the VDC.

The number of Thai National Defence Volunteers (TNDV) declined in the post-counterinsurgency period but has since revived. As of 2011, TNDV had 217,238 members with the highest number in the northern region. In 2012 ISOC set a goal of recruiting 5,600 new members every year. Former members were summoned for a one-day retraining programme while new recruits were trained over three days and two nights, and unit leaders over five days and four nights (ISOC 2012, pp. 7, 10). An Internet search on *Thai asa pongkan chat* (in Thai) throws up numerous video clips about its recent activities on YouTube. The same is true for other groups. These video clips show that ISOC provincial branches throughout the country have been busy reviving, recruiting and training members of TNDV.

By 2017, ISOC reported that it had established the Village for Development and Self-Defence Volunteers (VDSV) programme in 14,328 villages in seventy-six provinces. Only Bangkok does not have a unit. The size of each *Cho.ro.bo*, an armed paramilitary unit attached to the VDSV, increased from ten to thirty men. Although VDSV is under the MOI, ISOC is in charge of the selection of villages for the programme (National New Bureau of Thailand, 13 March 2017; DOPA, n.d.).

The Prem administration planned to establish at least one Reservist Village in every district nationwide, but gave priority to villages which were not part of the VDSV programme. That condition has since been dropped. ISOC advertisements in the press in 2014 show that the Army was trying to expand the size of the Reservists for National Security (RNS) regardless of their locality. Any reservists were eligible to apply for membership at the ISOC Headquarters. The plan was to recruit 3,900 new members per year (*Banmueang*, 3 June 2014).

The Civil Defence Volunteers (CDV) have appeared in several recent ISOC activities, particularly mass surveillance training programme (*Thairath*, 27 August 2016). A video clip of ISOC's training programme for the CDV in Laem-ngop district, Trat province, in 2016, shows that the training focused on handling unrest and mass control. The curriculum seems to be a response to the colour-coded demonstrations and popular uprisings (Hansuek Chimphali 2016).

The Village Health Volunteers (VHV) have become another channel for the ruling elites to control the population. Soon after the 2014 coup, ISOC chaired a meeting with more than a thousand VHVs based in Nonthaburi province, where the Red Shirts movement was strong. Evidently many VHVs in Nonthaburi were members of the Red Shirts movement. ISOC demanded that the VHVs sign an undertaking to cooperate with the NCPO's reconciliation plan, and that the Red Shirts leaders end all political activities, tell their supporters to follow the NCPO's orders, and support the Democratic Regime of Government with the King as Head of the State (*Manager Online*, 26 June 2014). ISOC tried to turn the VHVs in other provinces into a network of surveillance (*Manager Online*, 26 July 2017).

The Village Scouts' activities re-emerged after the 2014 coup. The Facebook account of the "Information Centre of Village Scouts under Royal Patronage" shows they have been revived in several provinces, although they are no longer a prominent mass organization.[4] They still wear the crimson-colour scarves but the original initiation ritual is not required. They too were recruited into ISOC's training programme.

New Groups

Several new groups and programmes have been created by ISOC and managed by its Department of Mass Affairs and General Information, but have an ad hoc status and seem to be loosely organized. The groupings are based on a common background, such as business people, students, and those who share similar hobbies. They are a mix of social classes both in the urban and rural areas.

1. Professional and Community Groups
- The Association of Business People for National Security
- The Association of Catholics for Internal Security
- The Association of Muslim Community Leaders for Internal Security
- The Association of Thai-Sikh Business People for Internal Security
- The Association of Thai-Indian Business People for Internal Security

According to the website of ISOC's Mass Affair and General Information Department (www.betamassisoc.isoc.go.th/), all of these groups were established in the mid-1990s. Their group names show that ISOC was involved in their creation. Members must go through ideological training programmes. The Association of the Business People for National Security, which claims to have 2,422 permanent members, seems to be the biggest among the five groups. As of 2017 the group had organized sixty-five training classes for 10,141 people. Their main activities consist of organizing royalist ceremonies, such as the birthdays of palace members, charities, and promoting "Thai-style democracy".

2. Diamonds in the Mud Programme
Diamonds in the Mud, founded in 1984, is ISOC's scholarship programme for children of people living in villages with active Village of Development and Self-Defence programmes or from the three southernmost provinces. Forty-five scholarships are awarded every year for study at the Faculty of Education, Srinakharinwirot University. After graduation, the recipients must return to their localities and work as teachers. The scheme guarantees them teaching positions in the public schools. This is a privilege over other graduates since they do not have to go through the highly competitive application process with several ten thousand applicants. The aim of this initiative is to produce good royalist teachers and to reward members of the VDSD.

3. Thai Big Bikes Love the Nation ISOC Club and Thai Offroaders Love the Nation
Thai Big Bikes Love the Nation ISOC Club (*Chomrom bik bai thai chai rak phaendin ko.o.ro.mo.no.*) and Thai Offroaders Love the Nation (*Thai of-rot rak phaendin*) are new social groups under ISOC management, with their Facebook pages and banners displaying the ISOC logo. Both began their activities in 2014 and try to recruit new members every year. All new members have to go through the ISOC indoctrination programme. A 30-minute video clip of a meeting between top ISOC officers and representatives of the Big Bikers, posted on YouTube, shows that ISOC wanted these people to act as the state's ears and eyes on crime and unwanted political activities (Billy Airforcerider 2014). Their involvement in annual royal ceremonies sends a message to the public that even people of these new trendy groups with a freedom-loving or rebellious character are loyal to the ancient institution of the monarchy.[5]

4. The People's Participation Programme
The People's Participation programme or *Khrongkan prachachon mi suan ruam* is possibly the broadest but loosest of these organizations. Its target

covers business people, civil servants, teachers, students, journalists, new social groups and ordinary folks.

High school and college students are one of the main targets. Since the 2014 coup, ISOC appears to give great importance to youth. Using its coordinating power, ISOC provincial branches can order the Ministry of Education to mobilize students for the programme. In February 2017, the Office of the Private Education Commission signed a Memorandum of Understanding to cooperate with ISOC in promoting the security of national institutions. They planned to organize seminars with the administrators of private schools in all four regions and Bangkok (Website of Office of the Private Education Commission 2017). The same year, the Ministry of Education's Non-Formal Education Department signed an MOU with ISOC, promising that its 7,400 Learning Centres nationwide will promote the sufficiency economy philosophy of the late King Bhumibol (INN News, 9 October 2017). One of ISOC's favourite royalist speakers was Miss Oraphim Raksaphon, nicknamed Best, whose sensational style caused controversy in late 2016 (see Chapter 1).

An interview with a vocational college student in Kanchanaburi province gives an insight into ISOC's modern psychological programme. He said that every year a teacher would choose a hundred students to attend an ISOC-coordinated programme entitled "Expansion of the Mass Network Based on the Mass Mobilization Project" at an army camp in the province. His senior friends attended this programme in 2017 and his turn came in 2018. The course lasted three hours. Apart from the compulsory content of being loyal to the monarchy, the course covered national security threats, particularly computer crimes, illicit drugs, and the corrupt and self-serving behaviour of politicians. He said the instructor told the students that "politicians are corrupt. Don't believe them or share what they say on social media. Don't share illegal messages, meaning challenging the power of the establishment. Even if you delete them later, you are still guilty because they are recorded on the computer already." The instructors also trained students how to observe and remember wrongdoers and how to report them to the authorities. The interviewee said that he enjoyed the training and admired the military very much.[6]

Another interesting mass surveillance project under People's Participation is the *Ro.Do. Cyber* (Territorial Defence Student Cybers). *Ro.Do.* are part of the national reserve forces. The participants are tenth to twelfth graders. Students who complete the three-year military training programme can avoid being drafted into the full-fledged military.[7] Since the 2014 coup, the *Ro.Do.* is the latest group the military has been trying to bring into its net.

In February 2018, General Prawit Wongsuwan, the true leader of the NCPO junta, authorized an order for the Ministry of Defence to recruit 1,000 cyber warriors from the pool of young reservists (General Ritti Intharawut's blog, 3 April 2018).[8]

In June 2019, Major General Prakan Pathawanit, commander of the Territorial Defence Students Unit, announced a plan to modernize the *Ro.Do.* training programme in order to create the *Ro.Do. Cyber* force. The new programme raises the proportion of general education from 30 per cent to 45 per cent of the total time, adding segments on the history of the Thai nation, the monarchy, the military role and security, primary care provision, civil defence, leadership, and volunteer spirit. The *Ro.Do.* cyberists have a mission to promote the monarchy, understanding of the NCPO junta and its government, and national reconciliation. As of 2019, there were over 300,000 *Ro.Do.* students nationwide, of whom about 95,000 have to participate in King Vajiralongkorn's Volunteer Spirits programme, described below (Thai PBS, 19 June 2019; 16 October 2019).

Other mass surveillance projects under the People's Participation umbrella are *Khrongkan ta sapparot* (Pineapple Eyes project), *Laksut khayai khrueakhai muanchon ko.o.ro.mo.no.* (Programme of Expansion of ISOC's Mass Network), and *Khrueakhai khao prachachon fao rawang pai* (Network of People's News and Surveillance).[9] The image of Pineapple Eyes captures the ruling elites' wish to create a system of surveillance which sees everywhere in all directions like the many eyes of a pineapple. Members of these projects are drawn from various groups such as students, journalists, civil servants, urban and village people.

Estimated Size

Although I provide the number of members of some mass organizations above, it is difficult to offer exact numbers. Many people have been through a one-day or three-day training programme but are not permanent members of any organization. Still, it is worth reproducing the figures that are available.

In 2011, the governor of Trang province, in his capacity as the provincial ISOC director, mobilized people to show their loyalty and respect to the monarchy on the occasion of King Bhumibol's 84th birthday. The event took place in February even though the King's birthday was in December. As the celebration was presided over by General Prayut, then army commander, the army tried to assess the size of the mass membership. ISOC reportedly claimed that Trang province alone had around 13,000 members belonging to various groups: VDC, VDSV, TNDV, CDV, VPH, VSU, Village Scouts, and many other unregistered groups (*Manager Online*, 4 February 2011). As of March 2019, there were reportedly 1,024,407 VHVs nationwide (*Prachatai*, 19 March 2019).

According to an ISOC Powerpoint presentation analysing its performance between 1 October 2014 and 31 March 2015, the total number of its organized mass as of March 2015 was 236,419 (see Table 5.1). This number did not include several groups such as the Volunteers Defence Corps, the Village Development and Self-Defence, and the Civil Defence Volunteers, which are officially under the authority of the MOI and MOPH.

In May 2016, ISOC's spokesperson told the press that ISOC would mobilize over 500,000 people to assist with the referendum campaign for the NCPO's draft constitution (*Post Today*, 7 May 2016). This figure likely reflects the true number of people it thought it could mobilize when necessary. The figure will be bigger at the time of the writing given the consolidation of ISOC's power under the NCPO.

TABLE 5.1
Partial Number of ISOC's Mass in March 2012

Name of Group	No. of Members
Thai National Defence Volunteers	116,711
The Reservists for National Security	37,172
Diamond in the Mud (29 classes)	914
People's Participation Programme	26,809
Security Network of Executives (9 classes)	860
700 of Community Radio Stations for Security	42,500
Local Thinkers Love the Nation	200
Big Bikers Love the Nation	495
Off-roaders Love the Nation	514
Cultural Leaders Love the Nation	130
Total	236,419

Note: This comes from an old website, which has ceased to exist.
Source: Department of Mass Affairs and General Information, ISOC, http://www.1374.org/13_download.php (accessed 22 October 2016).

Missions of the Mass

Websites and Facebook accounts run by ISOC and members of its mass organizations are filled with details and photos of group activities on various monarchical and Buddhist ceremonies, such as Chakri Dynasty Day, birthdays of the royal members, Coronation Day, Vesak Day and the royal cremation of the late King Bhumibol. Some activities were televised. The massed crowds habitually wear yellow clothes for ceremonies pertaining to King Bhumibol and King Vajiralongkorn, and light blue for Queen Sirikit (colours originally based on the day-in-week of their birth).[10] The army and ISOC regularly mobilized these coloured crowds to show the strength of royalism (*Manager Online*, 4 February 2011).

The duties of mass surveillance networks vary according to locality and context. Before the 2014 coup, the military had their eyes and ears positioned inside Red Shirt villages. As a result, immediately after the coup, armed soldiers quickly moved to detain, arrest, or summon many Red Shirt leaders in the north and northeast, to warn others against staging any demonstration, and to order the removal of red flags, a symbol of their political identity, from the village entrances. People dared not wear red shirts and were required to ask for permission from the provincial military office if they wanted to travel outside their local area (Head 2016; Prachatai, 1 July 2014). A Red Shirt leaders I interviewed said that he knew that his activities before the coup had been watched by state authorities and Yellow Shirts in the village. However he was not worried because he had believed that the Red Shirts movement was strong enough to counter a coup.[11] He was wrong.

The surveillance of the Red Shirts was especially tight during times of political tension, such as the day of the court verdict on former Prime Minister Yingluck Shinawatra concerning the rice subsidy scheme. Authorities did not want the incident to be an opportunity for the Red Shirts to demonstrate their unwavering support for the Shinawatras, so they tried to stop people's movements. They set up Line groups in the localities for reporting incidents directly to the authorities in charge, including crimes.[12] Many Red Shirts received phone calls from military officers warning them not to travel to Bangkok to show support to Yingluck.[13] The surveillance and intimidation of the local and national Red Shirt leaders effectively prevented any mobilization against the NCPO regime after the coup.

In the meantime, members of the mass organizations were told to promote the monarchy by posting, reposting, and sharing positive messages while reporting to the authorities any posting on social media deemed insulting to the monarchy, and not sharing anything that appeared to be a challenge to the government's authority.[14]

ISOC created hotline accounts on Facebook, Line and Twitter for people to report undesirable political activities. One of them was the *007 Sai khao khwam mankhong* or 007 Security News Line.[15] It has become customary for ISOC to hold annual press conferences to report on the number of websites carrying content against the monarchy that it had shut down (*MThai*, 25 December 2014; *Manager Online*, 7 September 2015).

The combined use of human eyes and ears with cyber technology to counter the enemy of the ruling elites came to light in a parliamentary censure debate against Premier Prayut on 25 February 2020. Wirot Lakkhana-adison, a member of parliament of the now defunct Future Forward Party, which had gained huge support from young voters, accused ISOC of sponsoring a website (pulony.blogspot.com) between 2017 and 2019. The contents of the website were divisive and biased against the Muslim population, perpetuating unrest and conflicts in the three southernmost Muslim provinces. Wirot also found Defence Ministry documents concerning its information operations (IO). The documents provided details of how to create and spread fake news and false accusations against the government's critics, particularly the Future Forward Party, and the rate of compensation for its staff. The IO employed at least three Line chat groups, members of which then created two accounts on Facebook. Many of the members carried military officer rank, while some were non-military. Wirot even publicized the QR code of two Line groups and urged people to add themselves to the group so that they could see for themselves the contents of the group chats. The exposure caused panic among group members, who hurriedly withdrew from the groups. An hour later, the accounts were deleted (*Thairath*, 26 February 2020).

Prayut, as defence minister and ISOC director, simply denied the accusation and the existence of the pulony.blogspot.com website. But a day later, the ISOC spokesperson admitted ISOC ran the website. He even confirmed the authenticity of Wirot's documents but offered a defence that its IO was aimed at creating good understanding in the three southernmost provinces (*Matichon*, 27 February 2020).

By the year 2019, the NCPO and its government faced growing challenges from various civil society groups, including student activists, anti-military groups, NGOs, and those affected by government-supported industrial projects. In reaction, members of paramilitary forces have often been called to assist police and army to suppress local protesters. They have also been employed in the forced eviction of small-scale peasants from reserve forest areas.[16]

The case of a coal-fired power plant in Thepha district, Songkhla province in southern Thailand, shows how the military government was able to exploit local people to support its policy or to counter its opponents. In November 2017, the Prayut cabinet approved a plan for building the coal-fired power plant. The project had faced strong opposition and organized protests from local people in Songkhla and nearby provinces for fear of the serious environmental impact on the communities. Past civilian governments had yielded to local demand and suspended construction. However, under the NCPO government, the project was revived, possibly in a belief that the military's iron fist would be able to suppress the protest. However, people fearlessly organized a demonstration under the banner of the "network of Songkhla-Pattani People against the coal-fired power plant". About 3,000 people planned to walk from Thepha district to the city of Songkhla, where a mobile cabinet was holding a meeting. They wanted to submit a petition to Prime Minister Prayut but the authorities responded with intimidation. At least fifteen people were arrested for violating the NCPO's order against a gathering of more than five people (*Prachatai*, 27 November 2017).

On the same day, the office of the ISOC Fourth Region Forward welcomed a group called the "Network of Thepha People for Sustainable Development", which claimed to represented 67 civil society groups in Songkhla with 50,000 members which supported the plantation project. The leader, Phanawat Phongprayun, claimed that his group represented many more people than those opposed to the project (*Prachatai*, 27 November 2017). Over eighteen months earlier, the Prachatai news website (8 April 2016) had reported that Phanawat and his group organized a public forum promoting the benefit of the plant to local people, and that Colonel Pramot Saengloi, then head of public relations of the ISOC Fourth Region Forward, had been responsible for dispatching information about Phanawat's activity to the media. Phanawat also appeared to be a leaders of the Network of Rubber and Oil Palm Farmers in sixteen southern provinces. This group hit the national news headlines for several days in early 2014, when it blocked roads in the south, demanding the Yingluck government buy rubber at a high price (*Thairath*, 2 March 2014). The group also joined the PDRC demonstration in Bangkok to topple the Yingluck government (*Sanook*, 12 November 2013).

In addition to strengthening the traditional defence infrastructure, the military governments passed two cyber laws to control Internet content deemed threatening to national and monarchical security: the Computer Crime Act passed by the Surayud government in 2007, and the Cybersecurity Act by the Prayut government in 2019. These laws have been widely condemned as violations of basic human rights. The Cybersecurity Act, in particular, was termed a "cyber martial law" by advocates for Internet freedom as it provides authorities with sweeping powers to intrude on citizen's privacy regardless of the rule of law. In an emergency situation or a moment of actual or anticipated cyber threats, authorities can summon individuals for questioning and enter private property without court orders to access computer data and networks, to make copies of information and to seize computers or any devices. Those who refuse to comply can face criminal charges (Reuters, 28 February 2019). Clearly, the Thai establishment believes that tightening control over public activities is a solution to the intransigent political conflict.

On the approach to the general election in March 2019, the NCPO junta eyed the members of mass organizations as potential voters for its proxy party, Phalang Pracharat. The Prayut government increased the monthly honorarium for 1,024,407 VHVs nationwide, timing the first payment just a few days before the polling day (*Prachatai*, 19 March 2019). As it turned out, Phalang Pracharat gained the highest number of popular votes of any party, an extraordinary result beyond general expectation. Certainly many factors contributed to its victory, including alleged vote buying throughout the country, the party's ability to persuade several former MPs of the Phuea Thai party to shift their affiliation, the Election Commission's suspicious vote counting, and the populist policies under the *Pracharat* project. The mobilization of ISOC's mass organizations was deemed necessary at this important political moment.

Incentives and Motivation

Material benefits have been provided to various groups to sustain and expand the royalist popular base. The benefits for members of several mass organizations were increased after the coup in 2006.

Before 2014, the pay for VDCs ranged between 4,470 baht and 8,970 baht per month, plus cost of living allowance for those working outside their residential area. In 2016, the Prayut government raised the pay scales to a maximum of 13,285 baht plus 200 baht per day when on duty (*Matichon*, 3 May 2016). Two years later, the scales were increased again to a range of 8,450 baht to 16,650 baht per month plus 200 baht per day while on duty. This means VDC benefits jumped almost 100 per cent within two years. The VDC also receive pension like other government personnel (*News1*, 10 July 2018).

Members of the VDC and TNDC, who wear uniforms and carry arms, can earn extra income when there is an event such as a sports match, political gathering, or upmarket wedding banquet which requires staff for maintaining safety and orders.[17] Being selected to attend a royal events or to have an audience with members of the palace serves as another kind of reward (ISOC 2012, p. 6).

Although some benefits are relatively small in value, they are significant for low-income earners. The volunteers usually came from a lower stratum of society. Many aspire to have a stable career, which to them means joining the civil service, police or military, but their low education deprives them of economic opportunities. Some are attracted to the official uniforms, which they equate with being more powerful and authoritative. Being members of the state-supported organizations allows them an opportunity to build personal and political connections with people in authority, an advantage in a patronage system such as in Thailand. People of all strata from the poor to business tycoons seek connection with the powers that be.

Even the seemingly social rebels like members of the big motorcycle club desire such connections. A 23-minute video clip uploaded on YouTube (Billy Airforcerider 2014) provides insight into the mentality of this particular group. The clip records a meeting between representatives of the Big Bikers club and the director of ISOC's Office of Mass Affairs and General Information, Major General Phanuwat Nakwong on 9 January 2014 at the ISOC office. One of the bikers, nicknamed Billy, informed ISOC authorities that there were 400 big bikers registered at the Association of Siamese Motorcycles based in Phatthaya, Chonburi province. They lived at various places around the country but gathered for annual meetings. Billy claimed that his group was nonpartisan and had independently organized activities to pay tribute to the king and queen in the last few years. Members of the group always carried a sign "We love the King". He boasted that, with support from ISOC, his group could mobilize up to 100,000 people for future events.

Billy then raised a problem he wished ISOC to help settle for the group. He said that most big motorcycles violated the law because they were assembled and modified to meet the requests of the riders and hence could not be legally registered except at great expense, implying that a big bribe was needed. Not everyone could afford to pay. In addition, the bikers were aware that the public viewed them with suspicion because of their gangster-style dressing. They hoped that receiving training and working with ISOC would help improve their public image and social status. He concluded that "This would certainly be beneficial to the big bikers circle. I have been waiting for so long to see who would be a hero to help us coordinate so that we could jointly do good deeds to the society, in the same way as people from different classes and professions have done before us."

Representatives from two other big bikers groups were present in the meeting. These two groups appeared to be from affluent backgrounds. They claimed to have a few hundred members in their circles, including the famous singer Ad Carabao of the Carabao band. They were ready to mobilize their followers to join ISOC's royalist activities.

In reply, Major General Phanuwat told them that ISOC wished to have members of their groups focus on intelligence work because their non-political appearance was perfect for the job. ISOC would provide them with training to face the new and emerging threats to the nation, such as illicit drugs, illegal migration, deforestation, terrorism and crimes (Billy Airforcerider 2014).

THE ROYALIST COMMUNISTS

Among the people recruited by the army and ISOC, one group is worth special mention: the former communist cadres from rural areas. The name "royalist communists" comes from the Thai abbreviation *Pho.kho.tho.ro.o* in which *Pho.kho.tho* stands for the CPT and *ro.or* means *raksa phra-ong* or royal guards. The term was coined by former comrades who disagreed with their military-dominated political activities. They appeared in the news under the banner of *Kongthap plot-aek prachachon phuea prachathipatai* or the People's Liberation Army for Democracy, later changed to *Kongthap plot-aek prachachon haeng prathet thai* or the People's Liberation Army of Thailand.

After the fall of the CPT, many peasant-class cadres settled together in communities, especially in the north and northeastern regions. Some cadres became local leaders with official status, such as village heads and public health officials. Some groups held annual commemorations at the former CPT base areas to remember and pay respect to their deceased comrades. The relations between groups were loose but cordial. Before the emergence of the colour-coded political conflict, most former cadres favoured Thaksin's party, whose policies were beneficial to their livelihood.

However, intervention by the military resulted in polarization, often quite extreme.[18]

The mobilization of the royalist communists began after the coup in 2006, thanks to the effort of General Surayud Chulanont, whose father, Lieutenant Colonel Phayom Chulanont, was a former army officer who turned communist. After the coup by Sarit in 1957, Phayom decided to leave his family and join the CPT. He was appointed the CPT's military commander and died of heart failure. Surayud made his army career in counterinsurgency operations, which provided him with opportunities to build connections with ex-communists. Those connections became useful when the conservative elites faced challenges from Thaksin and his rural supporters.

After the fall of the CPT, the Prem administration launched a resettlement scheme to assist peasant-class cadres to resume normal lives and reintegrate to mainstream society. Each family received 8–15 *rai* of land (equivalent to 3.2–6 acres). The initial plan in 1985 applied only to former cadres in Mukdahan, Sakon Nakhon and Yasothon, former strongholds of the CPT in the northeast, extended to some other cadres in Phitsanulok, Phayao, and Tak provinces in the north, and over 1985–87 to the south also. Each family received cash of 50,000 baht (equivalent to US$2,000 in 1985). The scheme ended but the demands did not.

Many former cadres, who were left out from the initial phase, demanded equal treatment. In 2002, the Thaksin government promised to provide aid to the poor and landless cadres. As land was not available, the government offered cash of 125,000 baht per family.[19] However Thaksin did not deliver on this promise. Soon after Surayud became prime minister in October 2006, he revised the plan and between January and March 2007 he gave away 125,000 baht to 2,609 ex-communists, a total sum of 263,120,465 baht. The scheme applied to those living in northeastern provinces. Surayud himself presided over the grant giving ceremonies (*Kom Chad Leuk*, 30 April 2017).

After the Surayud government closed the scheme, a new group of ex-communists showed up and demanded financial aid. The government led by Abhisit Vejjajiva assigned deputy prime minister Suthep Thaugsuban, the most powerful figure in the party and government, to handle the matter. He increased the sum of aid to 225,000 baht per family and extended this to former cadres in the north and south. Over 30,000 people applied for the reward. This figure was higher than the estimated strength of the CPT forces at their peak. On 13 May 2020 the cabinet approved payments to 9,181 people. The money was paid only in May 2011, less than three month before a general election, at which the Democrat Party again lost to Thaksin's Phuea Thai party. Those who failed to gain the reward continued to petition the new Yingluck government but met refusal. Their fortune improved after the NCPO coup in 2014. The Prayut cabinet approved payment of a total sum of 1,391,175,000 baht to 6,183 people. ISOC Region 2, in charge of the northeastern region, was authorized to finalize the list of ex-communists and issued instructions for the handout ceremonies to be held at the military barracks with the ISOC regional commander presiding and with exhibitions on the topics such as royal development projects and government activities. The authorities were instructed to treat the former communists well, as if they were warriors who had changed their minds and wanted to begin helping with the development of the country (*Kom Chad Luek*, 30 April 2017).

A royalist communist leader, Pai, a village head, claimed that he had known General Surayud because he had been based in the area where Surayud's father Phayom was in command and had helped take care of Phayom when he was ill. Surayud's resettlement plan was a way to return the favour. He claimed that his network spanned fifteen northeastern provinces. He frankly admitted that he had been working for ISOC for many years because he was the headman of a village which received assistance under the development for security programme. Whenever the village had a problem with government agencies, his military connections could settle matters quickly and efficiently.[20] Pai said that, apart from mobilizing members of his network for the anti-Thaksin protests, his network helped keep watch on their areas for the military (Interview 2 December 2017, Mukdahan).

An official document of ISOC Region 2, published in *Kom Chad Luek* (30 April 2017) instructed all ISOC Regional Offices to think of ways to utilize these ex-communists as their informants or to make them into supporters of the government's activities in the future.

In June 2012, Chaturon Chaisang, a leading member of the Phuea Thai party, criticized the Constitutional Court for its politicization and lack of impartiality. The UDD leaders threatened to organize a popular petition to the parliament to have the Constitutional Court's judges dismissed (*Manager Online*, 23 June 2012; *Kom Chad Luek*, 18 June 2012). Shortly after, around 3,000 self-proclaimed ex-communists from several provinces in the northeast gathered in front of Udon Thani provincial hall and another 2,000 in Khon Kaen province to show their support for the Constitutional Court in retaliation to these comments. In early July, the same group of royalist communists joined hands with ultra-royalists who were fanning the nationalist fire in the dispute with Cambodia over the Phreah Vihear Temple. They called on people to unite to protect the monarchy in face of the Red Shirts movement (*Prachatai*, 6 July 2012). They even encouraged General Prayut, then army chief, to ignore the authority of Yingluck's government. Over one hundred of them travelled to Bangkok to give a bouquet to Prayut and call on the military to fight against the parliamentary dictatorship and monopoly capitalists, who were serious threats to the three pillars of the nation and the armed forces (*MThai News*, 10 July 2013).

The royalist communists were more than simply supporters for activities opposing Thaksin and the Red Shirts movement. They helped the army and ISOC to mount surveillance in the Red Shirts-dominated areas in the north and the northeast, former CPT strongholds. Although in the counterinsurgency period, the army had defeated the CPT in these regions, thirty years later these regions gave their support to Thaksin and the Red Shirts movement. From December 2010, the UDD and the Red Shirts created Red Shirt villages in these two regions, hanging big banners and red flags in front of their villages as a sign of rebellion against the establishment and against Bangkok-centric politics. The royalists saw this as a sign of the nation's division, a secession from the kingdom (i.e. Phichai Rattanadilok na. Phuket 2012; *Thairath*, 20 May 2012).

Many former communists in the northeast joined the Red Shirts because they benefited from Thaksin's policies. Many former cadres, who had received political training under the CPT. were politically active in their villages and natural leaders in their localities. In this context, the royalist communists with their well-established networks were a vital resource for the establishment's project to establish influence in these regions. The royalist communist leaders, however, admitted that it was difficult to combat Thaksin's popularity in the region (Interview with Pai, 2 December 2017, Mukdahan). The ex-communist Red Shirts accused the royalist communists of betraying their ideology for personal benefit. They suggested that many royalist communists had never joined the CPT and the scheme was riddled with corruption (Interview with Wan, 1 December 2016, Mukdahan).

The NCPO used financial rewards to lure many ex-communist Red Shirts. In Nakhon Phanom province in December 2017, I had a meeting with over fifty former cadres demanding fair treatment from the government. The group leader claimed to have a network of ex-communists in fifteen northeastern provinces. He now represented over 1,200 former cadres in Mukdahan, Nakhon Phanom, and Kalasin. These people had received the package offered by the Prem administration and were unhappy that the amount was less than those given by the governments of Surayud, Abhisit, and Prayut. They believed that many of those who enjoyed the bigger rewards were not real ex-communists and claimed that state agencies had helped to fake their identities in return for a share in the benefit.

This group has prepared a petition, demanding that a future government top up their package to equal those given later, and are waiting for the right time to submit this. During my meeting, members of the groups kept repeating that they were politically neutral, not Red nor Yellow Shirt, and took no part in political activities. Perhaps they did not want to prejudice their chances of receiving an additional aid package from the government. They knew that ISOC had been involved in submitting names of ex-communists for past rewards and thus wished to disguise their true political orientation. Thaksinite parties had consistently won elections in Nakhon Phanom. When I asked them about government policies, many voiced their disapproval of Prayut's populist policies, especially the Pracharat's 300 baht voucher for the poor, which tended to benefit the big corporates. By contrast, they obviously approved of the Thaksinite parties' policies (Meeting with the group of Rong, 3 December 2017, Nakhon Phanom). The schemes for resettling ex-communists had turned into a means to divide and rule old comrades, and to discourage their political activity.

The recruitment of the former communists and other groups in the north and northeast shows how desperate the ruling elites have become in their efforts to combat the popularity of Thaksin, and how they have deployed taxpayer money in large amounts.

The Volunteer Spirit Programme

In Thailand, volunteering for public good emerged with the student movement in the early 1970s, when students were increasingly radicalized. One of the most popular student activities was visiting poor villages in rural areas in an effort to learn about their hardship, both physically and structurally, with the aspiration of fighting for a better society for these people. However the student movement was brutally crushed by the Thammasat massacre in 1976. After areas of southern Thailand were devastated by a tsunami in 2005, volunteering for short-term civil activities become popular again amongst the educated urban middle-class. But this revitalized volunteering has been deradicalized. It aims to promote morality among individuals rather than focusing on structural problem and socio-economic injustice. It conveys a notion of cultivating moral values within the volunteers as "good people" for the Thai nation. Volunteering has been appropriated by the politics of "good people" vis-a-vis "bad people" (Nattaka Chaisinthop 2014).

In Thailand, the person who represented the highest moral authority was King Bhumibol. According to the royalist narrative, he volunteered his life for the betterment of Thai people. The Volunteer Spirit or *Chit-a-sa* scheme was created for people to bid farewell and pay their last respects to the beloved king after his death on 13 October 2016. The scheme was reportedly initiated by his son and successor, King Vajiralongkorn. Although the cremation ceremony ended on 29 October 2017, the scheme continued with a slightly different title "*Chit-a-sa 904*", where 904 is a palace communications code number of King Vajiralongkorn that is widely used as his mnemonic.

In preparation for the royal cremation ceremony on 26 October 2017, the Prayut government in mid-2017 invited officials and members of the Thai public to register as volunteers to assist in the historic events under a slogan "Do a good deed for father" (*tham khwam di phuea pho*). The programme aimed to demonstrate the reverence, love and loyalty for King Bhumibol as well as making merit for him. The activities included making cremation flowers, helping with public relations, construction, transportation, public services, medical services, security and traffic. Each volunteer received a special ID card, a blue cap, a yellow scarf, a black polo shirt and an armband. The number of volunteers nationwide reportedly reached four million (*Post Today*, 5 October 2017). David Streckfuss interpreted the programme as an attempt by the king to mobilize people to pledge allegiance to the monarchy, boosting the image of King Vajiralongkorn and creating a popular base that could help ease the transition to his reign (Reuters, 3 September 2018).

During my interview with a village head in a northeastern province, he showed me an official letter from the district office, dated 29 November 2017, sent to *kamnan* (sub-district heads) and *phuyaiban* (village heads) with detailed instructions on how they should implement the Volunteer Spirit Programme. First, the slogan was modified from "Do a good deed for father" (*tham khwam di phuea pho*) to "Do a good deed with heart" (*tham khwam di duai huachai*). The new slogan apparently carries a broader notion, not specifically devoted to King Bhumibol alone. Second, the volunteer had two main duties: to cheer for the king and to do general public works. Third, the village heads and members of the village committee had to select village-level heads of the programme and send their names to the district office for official appointment. Fourth, *kamnan* and *phuyaiban* had to organize at least one volunteering activity a month in their area, and send a report, together with pictures of the activity, to the district office. Lastly, during these activities, the volunteers had to wear a cap, scarf, volunteer ID card, plain-colour top and dark-colour trousers. Students had to wear school uniforms. Later, all the *chit-a-sa* volunteers had to wear yellow shirts during these activities.

Volunteers were seen at the world-captivating rescue operation for twelve young footballers and their coach in Chiang Rai province in the north in June–July 2018. At the rescue site, volunteers and state officials, including cabinet members, were obliged to wear the volunteer uniform. Thanks to King Vajiralongkorn's royal kindness, the international coordinated rescue operation gained full and smooth cooperation from Thai state agencies and the people (ABC News, Australia, 5 July 2018).

As of early 2019, the scheme has been promoted vigorously by state agencies, particularly the armed forces. New members must go through an ideological training programme similar contents to those of ISOC (*Prachatai*, 3 December 2019). Websites and Facebook accounts of the armed forces, ISOC, ministries, and ISOC's mass organizations have carried news and pictures of the volunteering activities, such as planting trees in towns, reforestation, collecting garbage, and cleaning footpaths. Members of the state-sponsored mass organizations were also mobilized for the scheme.[21] According to a district chief in a northern province, after the end of the royal cremation ceremony, the number of people joining the volunteering activities dropped significantly. The MOI and ISOC had to mobilize their networks of mass organizations to maintain the vibrancy of the Volunteer Spirit Programme (Interview on 29 November 2017, Phetchaburi). Civil servants and soldiers have to routinely engage in volunteer activities.

Effectiveness

It is not easy to evaluate the effectiveness of the military's mass control programmes. Since the 2014 coup the military governments have been trying to build up popular support by various means, including coercive measures and populist economic schemes (Prajak and Veerayooth 2018). Some populist programmes have specifically benefited members of mass organizations, and have no doubt contributed to the effectiveness of the mass control and surveillance programmes. But in general the efforts to build up the royalist popular base and mass surveillance have yielded mixed results.

Those recruited to the training programmes do not necessarily absorb and accept the military's indoctrination. Many people in the northern and northeastern provinces, who identified themselves as Red Shirts, had to join the mass mobilization or volunteer in the state-organized programmes, because they did not want to be targeted by authorities for not being subservient. Some of them had been members of the paid paramilitary organizations, such as the VDC, before the emergence of colour-coded politics. They became Red Shirts later but did not withdraw from the VDS because they needed the income.

Some members of the mass organizations in the northeast told me openly that they were Red Shirts at heart and loved Thaksin's pro-poor policies. They had to negotiate between their duties in the organization and their political conscience. They were willing to assist in crime watch in the neighbourhood, but were reluctant to keep watch on their Red Shirt fellows. Although they had to carry out orders from their superiors, they would try not to harm or jeopardize their relationship with their neighbours. For example, if they received an order to report on the movement of Red Shirts in their localities, they would inform the local Red Shirt leaders that they were being watched and should not do anything. People understood the difficult situation their friends were facing (interview Puen, 2 December 2017, Sakon Nakhon).

Some sub-district heads and village heads in the two Red Shirts-dominated regions faced a similar dilemma. Although they were a key channel for the military/ISOC to implement policies and penetrate into the local levels, they sympathized with the Red Shirts' struggle and preferred Thaksin's party. They had to perform their state duties to satisfy their superiors while maintaining relationships and trust with their community members. For example, when Yingluck was facing trial over the rice-pledging scheme, the military government did not want the Red Shirts to gather and show their moral support for Yingluck. The police, soldiers and community leaders were instructed to stop Red Shirt supporters from traveling to Bangkok. While the police and soldiers tended to threaten the people, the Red Shirt sub-district head and village head just asked their community members if they were planning to go to Bangkok on those days, as a way to send a mild warning that they should not go. Most people would listen and not travel in order not to cause trouble to themselves and their leaders, allowing the latter to report to their superiors that they had already checked and warned their people. If some people broke their word and slipped away to Bangkok, it was no longer their problem. They could claim that they had fulfilled their duty (interview Puen, 2 December 2017, Sakon Nakhon).

Despite the Prayut government's populist policies and restrictions on rival parties, the election results of March 2019 showed that the majority of voters in the northeast were still loyal to Thaksin's Phuea Thai party. The party gained 84 out of the 116 seats in the region. However, this was 27 seats less than in the previous election in 2011. The party's performance in the north was less impressive. It retained only 25 seats in 2019 in comparison to 49 seats in 2011 (*Thairath*, 7 May 2019). The Prayut government's populist policies and its mass control programme possibly caused this decline.

The programmes appear to be least effective among youth. Although the conservative elites are targeting youths nationwide, there are several signs that their royalist indoctrination and surveillance programmes had little impact among this group. First, the Future Forward Party, which campaigned on an anti-military policy and appealed to young voters, captured 6.2 million votes at the 2019 elections, despite the concerted attempts of military leaders and the rightist media to label the party as anti-monarchy and un-Thai (*Bangkok Post*, 12 October 2019). Second, after the Future Forward was dissolved by the order of the Constitutional Court there were student protests on many campuses nationwide in February and March 2020 (*Bangkok Post*, 24 February 2020). The ruling elites, including the military and the judiciary, were the targets of the protest. Third, messages on social media show the decline in the moral authority of the monarchy among youths. Since 2019, Twitter has become a platform where young users frequently show their discontent with the monarchy (*Straits Times*, 9 January 2020). One challenging hashtag reached a million overnight.[22]

State agencies are expected to routinely show their loyalty to the monarchy. Civil servants, soldiers, and members of mass organizations have to undertake volunteering activities as part of their duties. The ruling elites understand that ideological indoctrination and propaganda alone will not be effective enough after the end of King Bhumibol's reign. They need to offer economic incentives to retain their supporters working. They need to attract a variety of civil groups, ranging from remnants of the Cold War militias to former communists.

Although the conservative elites no longer command the loyalty of the majority of the population, they still have a capability to mobilize members of their mass organizations when necessary. The cases of the Thepha coal-fired power plant and the royalist communists confirm this point. The mobilization of the royalist mass will recur because the royalist elites are facing growing popular discontent.

Conclusion

The conservative elites have revived and expanded the military's counter-insurgency legacy since the 2006 coup in response to the unprecedented popularity of Thaksin Shinawatra and his parties. Electoral democracy has increasingly posed a challenge to the establishment's power and domination. The elites were unable to banish participatory politics entirely. The 2016 coup junta had to promise to return Thailand to electoral politics albeit under the unfree and unfair rules of the Constitution of 2017. At the same time, the royalist elites cannot deny that the royal hegemony has been in decline since the emergence of the colour-coded political conflict.

The royalist elites responded to the challenge by reviving the Cold War era methods of building a royalist popular base, expanded to cover all social classes and group both in the provinces and the urban areas throughout the country. They promoted Thai style democracy, officially known as "the Democratic Regime with the King as the Head of the State", in opposition to Western liberal democracy. Despite the passing of King Bhumibol, the elites remain dependent on his royal hegemony to mobilize the royalist mass and to undermine the legitimacy of politicians and electoral politics. They promote the discourse of rule by good people as the basis of royal democracy through various programmes of the army and ISOC.

Social media have been utilized heavily to connect state agencies with their members and to entrench the royal nationalist narrative. Neighbourhood watch and cyber surveillance are used to monitor the opposition. Royalist citizens have become a political weapon to counter the power and legitimacy of electoral politics, politicians and people whose aspiration is electoral democracy.

Yet the royalist elites knew that ideological indoctrination and propaganda alone will not be effective enough. They need to offer economic incentives in order to keep their supporters. In the post-2006 coup period, maintaining loyalty and mass surveillance has become very expensive.

Notes

1. www.massisoc.com/2_mass_main.php
2. General Naphon Bunthap was dismissed from the position by King Vajiralongkorn in December 2016. See *BangkokBiz News*, 12 December 2016.
3. Forest Protection Volunteers is a joint programme of the Army, Department of Royal Forestry and Department of National Parks, Wildlife, and Plant Conservation. It was created in response to His Majesty Queen Sirikit's idea. (http://www.pttreforestation.com/ForestProjectview.cshtml?Id=3 (accessed 5 November 2018).
4. https://www.facebook.com/ศูนย์ข้อมูลกลางลูกเสือชาวบ้านในพระบรมราชานุเคราะห์-304590370059353/
5. See their Facebook accounts at https://www.facebook.com/Bigbike.center and https://www.facebook.com/เครือข่ายออฟโรดไทย-ใจรักษ์แผ่นดิน-1519013815020683/
6. Interview conducted in Kanchanaburi, 2 November 2018.

7. The training is conducted at military camps once a week with each session lasting three hours. In the past, only male students participated in the programme, but now female students can voluntarily apply for the programme. The training includes general knowledge, physical exercise and the use of rifles.
8. General Ritti Intharawut is an IT expert. His current position is the advisor to the Defence Ministry's IT, Cyber, and Aero Space. His blog: http://rittee1834.blogspot.com (accessed 21 February 2020).
9. Office of Intelligence, ISOC, "*Khrueakhai khao prachachon fao rawang pai*", http://centre.isocthai.go.th/images/doc_information/sor-kor-wor/1.Network Security/NetworkSecurity2.pdf (accessed 1 December 2016); The Second Army Region, 1 December 2018; Thanjai News Online, 21 July 2018; Thairath, 22 October 2018; INN News, 5 February 2018.
10. www.massisoc.isoc.go.th/2_mass_isoc/2_mix_mass_isoc/3_pochoro/1_hist_pochoro/hist_pochoro.html
11. Interview, Bun in Ubon Ratchathani on 19 August 2017.
12. Telephone interview of a district head of a province adjacent to Bangkok, 21 November 2017.
13. Interview with Somchit in Ubon Ratchathani on 21 August 2017.
14. Interview with a vocational student in Kanchanaburi, 2 November 2018.
15. https://www.facebook.com/isoc007/
16. See pictures on the website of ISOC: https://www.isoc.go.th/?p=1630; *Prachatai*, 27 November 2017.
17. Interview with MOI official in Chiangmai on 29 November 2017.
18. Interview with Comrade Tong in Bangkok on 5 January 2018; and Comrade Muk, in Mukdahan on 1 December 2017.
19. The sum of 125,000 baht was based on the calculation that 75,000 baht was in lieu of 5 *rai* of land, and another 50,000 baht for an investment fund.
20. Pai is a village head in Mukdahan province.
21. For example, ISOC webpages: http://www.isoc.go.th/?p=3188; http://www.isoc.go.th/?page_id=112 (accessed 3 November 2018); The Royal Thai Armed Forces' webpage: https://www.rtarf.mi.th/index.php/th/2016-06-23-07-14-56/2018-07-20-08-11-15/2018-07-20-04-15-10/124-24-2561 (accessed 3 November 2018).
22. https://twitter.com/hashtag/กบัตรยีมีไว้ทำไม (accessed 26 March 2020).

Conclusion

This study has shown the extent to which the Thai military has dominated the country's internal security affairs since the Cold War period. ISOC is not the only agency in charge of internal security, but the whole armed forces, and the army in particular, are devoted to the mission. ISOC has coordinating and commanding authority over the police and other civilian agencies. ISOC can utilize the robust infrastructure of the army units as well as various civilian bureaucratic agencies. The modern Thai armed forces have never engaged in large-scale warfare with an external enemy since their formation in the early twentieth century. Internal security is the *raison d'être* of the Thai armed forces and the source of its expanding scope since the counterinsurgency period, defining its role and lending it authority over national institutions and the people.

The political offensive approach against the communist threat opened up a path for the military to engage in the nation's socio-economic and political development. Under successive military governments, the army took over political affairs. On the one hand, the operations allowed the army to lead and coordinate other state agencies in the counterinsurgency. On the other hand, the integration of development projects, mass organizations, ideological indoctrination and propaganda programmes into its operations consolidated the army's role and authority in the nation's socio-economic and political affairs.

The line that distinguishes internal security from normal domestic affairs became increasingly blurred in the post-counterinsurgency period. The definition of internal security became much broader on grounds of meeting new threats in a volatile world. Many new security threats were non-combatant in nature, yet the Thai military folded them into its mission. From fighting communist insurgency, its mission extended to defending and promoting the monarchy, eradicating poverty, managing democratization, protecting natural resources, combatting human and drugs trafficking, and building political unity. A new term was created to disguise the military's political strategy: counterinsurgency operations was supplanted by civil affairs.

The internal security mechanism became a political tool of the military and its conservative allies to protect and perpetuate their political domination and suppress political dissidents. The military's activities broadened into social, political, and economic areas, and expanded beyond the remote rural and hill areas to the urban areas. Its current operations cover every province in the country, including Bangkok, and penetrate deep into the pre-existing village governance structures. Various interest groups became targets of the military's internal security operations. The military's power in the country's socio-political sphere became steadily stronger and more pervasive, overflowing all boundaries in the aftermath of the coup in 2006. Solutions to various socio-economic problems have become militarized, such as the forced eviction of people from the forest reserve areas. Some political issues are disguised as an economic agenda. The promotion of the sufficiency economy philosophy of King Bhumibol has been targeted to undermine the legitimacy of elected governments and politicians. At the same time, the sufficiency economy principle is shielded from criticism due to the political agenda. An assessment of its economic success is not feasible.

In a democratic society, elected representatives should take the lead in debating socio-economic-political issues and directing their solutions. Issues such as natural resource management, trafficking of drugs and human, and building economic competitiveness require the knowledge and expertise of civilian agencies. The military should have an assistant role when appropriate, when necessary and when invited. In Thailand, however, the roles are reversed. The civilian bureaucratic apparatus has been subordinated to serve an army-dominated political agenda. Elected bodies allow the military to dominate without question.

The expansion of the army-led internal security mission did not happen naturally, but through the intentions, plans and support of important institutions and the ruling elite. The military's role in meeting various national security threats is defined and legitimated by constitutions, administrative orders, laws, and national development plans. If the rule of law, administrative regulations or constitutional restrictions get in the way of the military's political agenda, the powers that be will simply change the law, alter the regulations and even rewrite the constitution to eliminate any obstacles in their path. The conservative elites have issued several plans, policies, and laws to maintain the military role and power in politics. They have been quick to respond to the changing situation and have provided the military with the legitimacy to expand its role in various spheres of the society. The conservative elites understood that the command of force was not the only weapon the military could wield. They built up the military's political apparatus over several decades. The internal security mechanism has become the infrastructure through which the military and its conservative allies can control society and undermine the power of civilian governments.

While defending the monarchy is the military's top priority, the role of the monarchy under the reign of King Bhumibol was of paramount importance to the military. Royal hegemony was the most important source of political legitimacy for the military's civil duties while promotion of royal-nationalism and royal democracy was part and parcel of military operations. Internal security was the area where the synergistic relationship between the two institutions evolved and where their mutual interests are based. The military-monarchy nexus has developed far beyond a mere personal or informal relationship between the palace and military leaders.

Promotion of royal nationalism through the military's ideological programme is aimed at defending the monarchy as well as building unity amongst citizens. A historical narrative detailing the great merits of past kings and the immense moral authority of King Bhumibol has been deployed to command popular loyalty to the state. A loyal citizenry is portrayed as essential for maintaining the security and stability for the state. The people serve as assistants on community development projects, agents of surveillance, and promoters of royalism and Thai-style democracy. ISOC's responsibility for coordinating and commanding various state-sponsored mass organizations facilitates the agenda of the conservative elites to mobilize and manipulate the citizenry in a unified manner. Members of mass organizations can be quickly mobilized to fulfil particular objectives. They can temporarily change their hats as happened with *Nawaphon* in the 1970s and the *Chit-a-sa* in the 2010s. They can supply force at the vital moment. The elites have built national unity since the counterinsurgency period through mechanisms to control the people's mentality and actions.

The institutionalization of the military-dominated apparatus grants this apparatus an autonomous life. The apparatus continues its operations even when Thailand is under elected governments. Bureaucracy helps maintain routine operations and maintaining the military political apparatus proved to be the right strategy for the elites when they confronted new challenges to their domination. To counter the rise of the Red Shirts movement and the undiminished strength of the Thaksin faction, the conservative elites needed to build a loyal popular base across classes and regions, turning people into political weapons in the name of defending the Democratic Regime with the Monarch as the Head of the State.

The royal hegemony of the late King Bhumibol remained the main source of ideology for mobilizing members of state-dominated mass organizations, but his reign ended amidst deepening political polarization and increased use of force and intimidation by a military junta. The increase in short-term and long-term incentives provided to members of mass organizations is testament to the difficulties that the elites face in maintaining coercive authority today.

Entrusting the military to carry out a political offensive can be counter-productive due to the military's tendency to use violent means, as I have elaborated in Chapter 4. In the 1973–76 period, in particular, when ISOC spearheaded a political offensive along with right-wing mass organizations, these forces were complicit in several grave violations of human rights. Although the degree of violence under the NCPO junta is not comparable to that of the counterinsurgency period, since the 2014 coup the number of arbitrary detentions, arrests, charges, and instances of intimidation of political dissidents and cyber surveillance is very high (TLHR 2015). The royalist mass might be mobilized to counter the anti-military movement in the near future. In this regard, the term "political offensive" as applied to the operations of the Thai military is rather misleading. The political offensive approach was supposed to win popular loyalty and cooperation. The term sounds benevolent and conciliatory. In practice, the approach combined both persuasive/reward and oppressive/punishment measures. Although the Thai military seldom uses the term now, it still practises this dualistic method.

Unfortunately, elected bodies and civil society have not paid enough attention to the collaboration among the conservative elites to build up the military's internal security apparatus. This was partly because internal security affairs have been monopolized by the military and its allies and partly because a coup remains the military's most effective weapon for warning politicians to keep their distance from security affairs. Civilian oversight, thus, does not exist. The policies which founded and expanded the military's domination of internal security were instituted outside the parliamentary process, as in the case of Prem's Prime Ministerial Order Nos. 66/2523 and 65/2525 as well as numerous NCPO orders. Civilian governments and politicians appear to lack knowledge on the country's external and internal security affairs. They did not realize the grave political implication of the military's civil affairs projects.

This ignorance often led the politicians to rely on the military and ISOC to handle domestic problems. Whenever the country faced new security threats, even those of a non-militaristic nature, civilian governments have been quick to grant ISOC and the army the authority to address them. Civilian governments did not mind relying on ISOC's expansive apparatus to quell political disturbances, as in the case of the Abhisit government's suppression of the Red Shirts, and Thaksin's actions in the three southernmost provinces. As a consequence, there was no attempt to pursue serious security reform either. The limited reforms attempted by elected government never touched the internal security apparatus. By contrast, the conservative elites were quick to modify this apparatus to entrench their power and to combat their enemies within, who aspired to build a unified society by democratic means.

Thailand will return to electoral politics. But as long as the internal security apparatuses are in the control of the army and conservative elites, electoral democracy will remain fragile. Popular elected government will be unstable and easily undermined by the military state within the state. In light of this study, I would like to make a few suggestions for a democratic government in the future.

1. Redefine the country's national security threats to distinguish between the traditional threats, such as border security and external intervention on the one hand, and the non-traditional security threats on the other. The role of the armed forces should be limited to the traditional threats, while the non-traditional threats should be the responsibility of civilian agencies. The military can be involved in mitigating or solving the non-traditional security threats only when called on by civilian agencies.
2. Remove all civil programmes and their allocated budget from the armed forces. They should not be allowed to carry on mass control, indoctrination and psychological programmes. Nor should they take part in economic development projects for which they have no expertise.
3. Dismantle the ISOC and its operations. No democratic society should allow a military-dominated organization to lead and command civilian agencies. Internal security affairs should be the responsibility of the

National Security Council, which should be dominated by elected representatives and civilian agencies.

Certainly, it is not easy to realize these suggestions in the near future. But a clear vision is necessary for democratic-minded politicians and civil society if they wish to see a consolidation of democracy in Thailand. Dismissing a military government, as has happened in the past, is not sufficient. As long as the military's political apparatus remains intact, it will be impossible for Thai society to have a stable democracy.

Bibliography

Thammasat University Archives (TUA)
TUA. So.bo.9.7.2/46. 1969. "Krasuang mahatthai rueang kandamnoenkan tamphraratchabanyat pongkankankratham anpen kommiownit (chabap thi 2) pho. so. 2512" [Ministry of Interior Regarding Implementation of the Anti-Communist Activities Act (2nd Issue) of 1969]. 15 May 1969.
———. So.bo.9.7.2/65. 1971. "Kong amnuaykan pongkan lae prappram kommiownit, rueang kanpongkan lae prappram kommiownit" [Communist Suppression Operations Command Regarding Prevention and Suppression of Communists]. 31 July 1971.
———. So.bo.9.7.2/70. 1972. "Kong amnuaykan pongkan lae prappram kommiownit, khumue kanpongkan lae prappram kommiownit [Communist Suppression Operations Command, A Guidebook for Prevention and Suppression of Communists]. 1972.
———. So.bo.9.7.2/88. 1974. "Kong amnuaykan pongkan lae prappram kommiownit, Sarupphon kanpatipat chabap thi 234" [Communist Suppression Operations Command, Summary of the Operations No. 234]. 3 January 1974.
———. So.bo.9.7.2/147. 1976. "Bunthuek khokhwam suanratchakan ko.o.ro.mo.no., phon-ek Saiyut Koedphon to nayokratthamontri" [Official Record of ISOC, from General Saiyud Koedphol to Prime Minister"]. 7 July 1976.
———. So.bo.9.7.2/148. 1976. "Bunthuek khokhwam suanratchakan ko.o.ro.mo.no. rueang naewkit thangyutthasat" [Official Record of ISOC Regarding Strategic Idea]. 5 August 1976.

Books and Articles
Anan Ganjanapan. 2000. *Local Control of Land and Forest: Cultural Dimensions of Resource Management in Northern Thailand*. Chiangmai: Regional Center for Social Science and Sustainable Development, Chiangmai University.
Anderson, Benedict R. O'G. and Ruchira C. Mendiones. 1985. *In the Mirror: Literature and Politics in Siam in the American Era*. Bangkok: Duang Kamol.
Apichat Satitniramai, Yukti Mukdawijitra, and Niti Pawakapan. 2013. *Toptuan phumithat kanmuang thai* [Re-examining the Political Landscape of Thailand]. Chiang Mai: School of Public Policy, Chiang Mai University.
Baker, Chris, and Pasuk Phongpaichit. 2005. *A History of Thailand*. New York: Cambridge University Press.
Ball, Desmond, and David Scott Mathieson. 2007. *Militia Redux: Or Sor and the Revival of Paramilitarism in Thailand*. Bangkok: White Lotus.
Bowie, Katherine A. 1997. *Rituals of National Loyalty: An Anthropology of the State*

and the Village Scout Movement in Thailand. New York and Chichester: Columbia University Press.

Bunklom Dongbangsathan et al. 1991. *Chivit lae phon-ngan chavalit yongchaiyut: khongbeng haeng kongthapbok* [Life and Works of General Chavalit Yongchaiyut: Kongming of the Thai Army]. Bangkok: Sapan Gallery.

Bureau of the Budget, Thailand. 2009. "Electronic Documents of the Annual Expenditures of the Years 2009–2018". http://www.bb.go.th/bbweb/?page_id=604 (accessed 21 February 2018).

Chai-anan Samudavanija, Kusuma Snitwongse, and Suchit Bunbongkarn. 1990. *From Armed Suppression to Political Offensive*. Bangkok: Institute of Security and International Studies, Chulalongkorn University.

Chaloemphon Som-in, ed. N.d. *Phraratchabanyat pongkan kankratham an-pencommunit pho.so.2495* [The Anti-Communist Activities Act, 1952 CE]. N.p.

Chambers, Paul. 2015. *Civil-Military Relations in Thailand since the 2014 Coup: The Tragedy of Security Sector "Deform*. PRIF Report No. 138. Frankfurt: Peace Research Frankfurt.

———, and Napisa Waitoolkiat. 2016. "The Resilience of Monarchised Military in Thailand". *Journal of Contemporary Asia* 46, no. 3 (March): 425–44.

Chanida Chitbundid. 2007. *Khrongkan an nueang ma chak phraratchadamri: Kansathapana mmnatnam nai phrabatsomdetphrachaoyuhua* [The Royal-Initiated Projects: The Consolidation of King Bhumibol's Royal Hegemony]. Bangkok: Foundation of the Social Science and Humanity Book Project.

Chulalak Thamrongwithitham. 2016. *Thangdaeng: kansomsang prawattisat lae khwamsongcham naisangkhomthai* [Red Drumg: Restoring A History and Memories in Thai Society]. Bangkok: Thammasat University Press.

Connors, Michael Kelly. 2007. *Democracy and National Identity in Thailand*. Copenhagen: NIAS Press.

Crouch, Harold. 1988. *The Army and Politics in Indonesia*. Ithaca, NY: Cornell University Press.

Department of Disaster Prevention and Mitigation (DDPM), Ministry of Interior. n.d. *Khumue asasamak pongkanphai fai phonlaruean* [Manual for the Civil Defence Volunteers]. http://122.155.1.141/upload/minisite/file_attach/185/56a1f88376ff7.pdf (accessed 30 July 2015).

Department of Health Service Support, Ministry of Public Health. 2011. *Khumue o.so. mo. yukmai* [Manual for the Village Health Volunteers in the New Era]. March 2011. http://phc.moph.go.th/www_hss/data_center/ifm_mod/nw/NewOSM-1.pdf (accessed 30 July 2015).

Department of National Parks, Wildlife and Plant Conservation, Ministry of Natural Resources and Environment. 2015. *Phaenmaebot phitak suppayakon pamai khongchat* [Master Plan for the Protection of the National Forest Resources]. https://bit.ly/1TlZ17n (accessed 30 July 2015).

Directorate of Civil Affairs, the Army. 2002. *20 pi krom kitchakan phonlaruen thahanbok* [20 Years of Directorate of Civil Affairs of the Army]. Bangkok: Directorate of Civil Affairs.

Faculty of Education, Kasetsart University and Office of Policy and Security Strategy, The Internal Security Operations Command. 2010a. *Kanhai khwamsamkan kapsathaban phramahakasat lae kanthoetthun sathaban* [Giving Importance and Respect to the Monarchy].

———. 2010b. *Kansongsoem pratchaya setthakit phophiang* [Promotion of the Subsistence Economy Philosophy].

———. 2010c. *Kanpokkhrong rabop prachatipatai* [The Democratic Government].

Farooq, Sadaf. 2012. "Pakistan's Internal Security Dynamics and the Role of Military Regimes". *International Journal on World Peace* 29, no. 3 (September): 51–83.

Fineman, Daniel. 1997. *A Special Relationship: the United States and Southeast Asia since World War II*. New York: University of Hawaii Press.

Fitch, J. Samuel. 1986. "The Military Coup d'Etat as a Political Process: A General Framework and the Ecuadorian Case". In *Armies and Politics in Latin America*, edited by Abraham F. Lowenthal and J. Samuel Fitch. New York and London: Holmes and Meier.

Ford, Eugene. 2017. *Cold War Monks: Bhuddhism and America's Secret Strategy in Southeast Asia*. New Haven and London: Yale University Press.

Forsyth, Tim, and Andrew Walker. 2012. *Forest Guardians, Forest Destroyers: The Politics of Environmental Knowledge in Northern Thailand*. Washington: University of Washington Press.

Fourth Centre for Operations Coordination, Internal Security Operations Command. 2019. *Phonkanpatibatngan tam phaenmae-bot pracham pi ngoppraman 2562* [Action Plans According to the Master Plan of the 2019 Budget Year]. Bangkok.

4th Coordinating Center, ISOC. N.d. "Thammai tong chuai phuruam phatthana chatthai" [Why Help the Ex-Communists?]. http://rungnapah.wixsite.com/isoc04/untitledcyua (accessed 6 May 2017).

Haberkorn, Tyrell. 2013. "Making Massacre Possible: Impunity and Denial in Phatthalung, 1972–1976". In *State Violence in East Asia*, edited by N. Ganesan and Sung Chull Kim. Kentucky: University of Kentucky Press.

———. 2015. "The Hidden Transcript of Amnesty: The 6 October 1976 Massacre and Coup in Thailand". *Critical Asian Studies* 47, Issue 1: 1–43.

———. 2017. *In Plain Sight: Impunity and Human Rights in Thailand*. University of Wisconsin-Madison.

Han Phongsitanon. 1975. *9 pi nai ko.o.ro.mo.no.* [Nine Years at ISOC]. Bangkok: Rongphim Phikhanet.

Human Rights Watch. 2017. *Thailand: Junta Making Mockery a Criminal Offense*. 18 April 2017. https://www.hrw.org/news/2017/04/18/thailand-junta-making-mockery-criminal-offense (accessed 17 June 2017).

Hyun, Sinae. 2014. "Indigenizing the Cold War: Nation-building by the Border Patrol Police of Thailand, 1945–1980". PhD dissertation, University of Wisconsin-Madison.

Internal Security Operations Command (ISOC). 1992. *Khlongkan kongnun pheu khwammankhong haengchat* [The Project of Reservists for National Security]. Bangkok: Thipwisut Publishing.

———. 2002. *Khrongkan chumchon mankhong doi yutthasat ko.O. ro.mo.no. chumchon* [Strong Community Project by Strategy of Community ISOC]. Bangkok: Internal Security Operations Command.

———. 2012a. *Yutthasat kong amnuaikan raksa khwammankhong phainai ratcha-anachak pho.so. 2555-2559* [Strategy of the Internal Security Operations Command A.D. 2012-2016].

———. 2012b. *Thai asa pongkan chat* [National Defence Volunteers]. Office of the Masses and General News, ISOC.

———. 2017. *Yutthasat kong amnuaikan raksa khwammankhong phainai ratcha-anachak pho.so. 2560-2564* [Strategy of the Internal Security Operations Command A.D. 2017-2021].

Internal Security Operations Command and Ministry of Natural Resources and Environment. 2014. *Phaen maebot khaekhai panha kanthamlai sapphayakon pamai kanbukruk thidin khongrat lae kanborihanchatkan sappayakon thammachat yangyangyuen* [Master Plan for Solving Problems of Forest Destruction, Encroachment of State Land, and Sustainable Management of Natural Resources]. Bangkok: the Army College.

International Commission of Jurists. 2010. *Thailand's Internal Security Act: Risking the Rule of Law?* Geneva: International Commission of Jurists.

Ivarsson, Soren, and Lottee Isager. 2010. *Saying the Unsayable: Monarchy and Democracy in Thailand*. Copenhagen: NIAS Press.

Kanda Naknoi. 2012. "Setthasat saman samnuek: 55 pi thun hongthap thai" [Common Sense Economics: 55 Years of the Thai Armed Forces' Capital]. *Prachatai*. 23 March 2012. https://prachatai.com/journal/2012/03/39802 (accessed 17 June 2017).

Kasian Tejapira. 2016. "The Irony of Democratization and the Decline of Royal Hegemony in Thailand". *Southeast Asian Studies* 5, no. 2: 219-37.

Katoch, Prakash. 2016. "Internal Security: Need for Comprehensive Matrix". *Scholar Warrior* (Spring): 18-26.

Kauffman, Karen S. and Donna Hicks Myers. 1997. "The Changing Role of Village Health Volunteers in Northeast Thailand: An Ethnographic Field Study". *International Journal of Nursing Studies* 34, no. 4 (August): 249-55.

Kobkua Suwannathat-Pian. 2003. *King, Country and Constitutions: Thailand's Political Development 1932-2000*. London: Routledge.

Krittian, Han. 2010. "Post-Coup Royalist Groups: Re-inventing Military and Ideological Power". In *Saying the Unsayable: Monarchy and Democracy in Thailand*, edited by Soren Ivarsson and Lotte Isager, pp. 203-22. Copenhagen: NIAS Press.

Kusuma Snitwongse. 1985. *Thai Government Responses to Armed Communist and Separatist Movement*. Singapore: Institute of Southeast Asian Studies.

Lowenthal, Abraham F., and John Samuel Fitch. 1986. *Armies and Politics in Latin America*. New York: Holmes & Meier.

McCargo, Duncan. 2002. "Security, Development and Political Participation in Thailand: Alternative Currencies of Legitimacy". *Contemporary Southeast Asia* 24, no. 1 (April): 50-67.

———. 2005. "Network Monarchy and Legitimacy Crises in Thailand". *Pacific Review* 18, no. 4: 499–519.
Mérieau, Eugenie. 2016. "Thailand's Deep State, Royal Power and the Constitutional Court (1997–2015)". *Journal of Contemporary Asia* 46, no. 3 (March): 445–66.
Mietzner, Marcus. 2008. *Military Politics, Islam, and the State in Indonesia: From Turbulent ransition to Democratic Consolidation*. Singapore: Institute of Southeast Asian Studies.
Ministry of Interior of Thailand. 2018. *Khumue kankkapkhluen kanphatthana prathet tam khlongkan thai-niyom yangyuen* [Manual for National Development in Line with the Sustainable Thai-ism Project]. Bangkok: Ministry of Interior of Thailand.
Montesano, Michael. 2019. "As Thai Military Holds on to Power, a 1980 Order by Former PM Prem Looms Large". *Today*. 6 June 2019. https://www.todayonline.com/commentary/thai-military-holds-power-1980-order-former-pm-prem-looms-large (accessed 6 June 2019).
Moore, Jeff M. 2013. *The Thai Way of Counterinsurgency*. Greenville, NC: A Muir Analytics Book.
Morell, David, and Chai-anan Samudavanija. 1981. *Political Conflict in Thailand: Reform, Reaction, Revolution.* Cambridge, MA: Oelgeschlager, Gunn & Hain.
National Economic and Social Development Board (NESDB). 1982. *Rai-ngan phonkanwichai kansueksa phue kamnot naewthang lae mattrakan naikanphatthana muban yakchon phue khwammankhong* [Report of a Research in Search of a Direction and Measures for Development of Poor Villages for Security]. Unpublished document.
———. 1987. *The Sixth National Economic and Development Plan, 1987–1991*. Bangkok: National Economic Development Board, Office of the Prime Minister. www.nesdb.go.th/nesdb_en/ewt_w3c/ewt_dl_link.php?nid=3781 (accessed 1 June 2017).
———. 2017. *Sarupsarasumkan phaenphatthana setthakit lae sangkhom haengchat chabapthi sipsong pho.so. 2560-2564* [Summary of the Twelfth National Economic and Social Development Plan (A.D. 2017–2021)]. Bangkok: NESDB.
National Reform Council (NRC), The. 1976. *Khothetching kieokap hetkan mue wanthi 6 Tula 2519* [Fact about 6th October 1976]. Bangkok: Rongphim kromphaethi thahan.
Nattaka Chaisinthop. 2014. "Volunteering, Dana, and the Cultivation of 'Good People' in Thailand". *Anthropological Forum* 24, no. 4: 396–411.
Natthaphon Chaiching. 2013. *Khofanfai naifan an lueachuea: khwamkhlueanwai Khong Khabuankan Patipak Patiwat Sayam (Pho.So. 2475-2500)* [To Dream the Impossible Dream: The Counter-revolutionary Movement in Siam (A.D. 1932–1957)]. Nonthaburi: Fadiewkan.
Ockey, James. 2014. "Broken Power: The Thai Military in the Aftermath of the 2006 Coup". In *"Good Coup" Gone Bad: Thailand's Political Developments since Thaksin's Downfall*, edited by Pavin Chachavalpongpun. Singapore: Institute of Southeast Asian Studies.
Panya Khwanyu. 1988. "Kongthapbok kapyutthasat phattana" [The Army and the Development Strategy]. *Senathipat* 37, no. 2 (May–August): 89–97.

Pichai Rattanadilok Na Phuket. 2012. "Muban sueadaeng roirao haengphandin" [Red Shirt Village, the Nation's Cleavage]. *Manager Online*. 18 May 2012. https://mgronline.com/daily/detail/9550000061502 (accessed 24 November 2018).

Prajak Kongkirati, and Veerayooth Kanchoochat. 2018. "The Prayuth Regime: Embedded Military and Hierarchical Capitalism in Thailand". *TRaNS: Trans-Regional and National Studies of Southeast Asia* 6, no. 2 (July): 279–305.

Prayut Chan-ocha. 2008. *Kongthapthai kap phaikhwammankhong rupbaepmai: kanprap botbah khong kongthapthai phuea rongrap phaikhukkham rupbaepmai nai yuklokaphiwat* [Thai Armed Forces and the Non-traditional Security Threats: The Adjustment of the Thai Armed Forces' Role to Cope with Non-traditional Security Threats]. Bangkok: The Association of Political Science of Kasetsart University.

"Prime Minister Order No. 66/2523 Regarding Policy to Win over Communism" [Khamsang nayokratthamontri thi 66/2523 rueang nayobai kantosu phuea awchana kommunit]. 23 April 1980. https://goo.gl/n2o7At (accessed 6 June 2017).

"Prime Minister Order No. 65/2525 Regarding Political Offensive" [Khamsang nayokratthamontri thi 65/2525 rueang phaenruk thangkanmueang]. 27 May 1982. In *Phraratchabanyat pongkan kankratham an-pencommunit pho.so.2495* [The Anti-Communist Activities Act, 1952 CE], edited by Chaloemphon Som-in, pp. 156–67. N.p.: n.d.

"Prime Ministerial Order No. 158/2545 Regarding Establishment of the Internal Security Operations Command" [Khamsang nayokratthamontri thi 158/2545 rueang kanchattang kong amnuaykan raksa khwammankhong phainai]. 29 May 2002. In *Khrongkan chumchon mankhong* [Stable Community Programme], by Internal Security Command Operations, Appendix. 2002.

Puangthong Pawakapan. 2013. *Songkhram viatnam:songkhram kap khwamching khong ratthai* [The Vietnam War: War and the Thai State's Truth Management]. 2nd ed. Bangkok: Kopfai.

———. 2015a. "Will Thailand's New Constitution Be a Return to Authoritarianism?". *ISEAS Perspective*, no. 2015/3, 25 January 2015.

———. 2015b. "Thai Junta Militarizes the Management of Natural Resources". *ISEAS Perspective*, no. 2015/47, 3 September 2015.

———. 2015c. "Patibatkansongkhram khong kanronnarong panha yaseptid naiprathetthai" [Militarization of the War on Drugs in Thailand]. In *Khwamrunraeng son/ha nai sangkhom thai* [Seek/Hide the Violence in Thai Society], edited by Chaiwat Satha-Anand. Bangkok: Matichon.

——— and Thongchai Winichakul. 2018. "*Kanthamraisop muea 6 Tula 2519: khrai yangrai thammai?*" [Corpse Desecration on October 6, 1976: Who, How, and Why?]. *Fadiewkan* 16 no. 2 (July–December): 43–64.

Puangthong Rungswasdisab. 2005 "Thailand's Response to the Cambodian Genocide". In *Genocide in Cambodia and Rwanda: New Perspectives*, edited by Sue Cook, pp. 73–118. New Brunswick, NJ: Transaction Publishers.

Pye, Oliver. 2005. *Khor Jor Kor: Forest Politics in Thailand*. Bangkok: White Lotus Press.

Rakrat (pseudonym). 2016. "Ngan kitchakan phonlaruen nai prathetthai" [Civil Affairs in Thailand]. *Lak Muang Online*. 6 March 2016. http://lakmuangonline.com/?p=2889 (accessed 30 July 2016).

Randolph, R. Sean. 1986. *The United States and Thailand: Alliance Dynamics, 1950–1985*. Berkeley: Institute of East Asian Studies, University of California.

Raymond, Gregory Vincent. 2018. *Thai Military Power: A Culture of Strategic Accommodation*. Copenhagen: NIAS Press.

Rossi, Amalia. 2012. "Turning Red Rural Landscapes Yellow? Sufficiency Economy and Royal Projects in the Hills of Nan Province, Northern Thailand". *ASEAS: Austrian Journal of Southeast Asian Studies* 5, no. 2: 275–91.

Royal Gazette. 2008. "Phraratchabanyat kanraksa khwammankhong phainai ratcha-anachak pho.so. 2551 [The Internal Security Act of B.E. 2551] 125 Issue 39 kho (27 February 2008): 33–44.

———. "Khamsang khana patirupkanpokkhrong haengchat chabap thi nueng long wanthi 6 tula 2519" [The National Reform Committee's Order No. 1 Dated 6 October 1976], 93 Section 120 Special Issue: 6.

———. 2009. "Khamsang kong-amnuaikan raksa khwammankhong painai ratcha-anachak thi 251/2552 rueang kanchattang sun-amnuaikan raksa khwamsa-ngop riaproi" [Order of the Internal Security Operations Command No. 251/2552 Concerning the Establishment of Centre for Peace and Order]. 126, Special issue 137 Ngo. (21 September 2009): 87.

———. 2009. "Khamsang kong-amnuaikan raksa khwammankhong painai ratcha-anachak thi 283/2552 rueang kanchattang sun-amnuaikan raksa khwamsa-ngop riaproi" [Order of the Internal Security Operations Command No. 283/2552 Concerning the Establishment of Centre for Peace and Order]. 126, Special issue 157 Ngo. (26 October 2009): 113.

———. 2009. "Khamsang kong-amnuaikan raksa khwammankhong painai ratcha-anachak thi 283/2552 rueang kanchattang sun-amnuaikan raksa khwamsa-ngop riaproi" [Order of the Internal Security Operations Command No. 283/2552 Concerning the Establishment of Centre for Peace and Order]. 126, Special issue 182 Ngo. (21 December 2009): 89.

———. 2011. "Khamsang kong-amnuaikan raksa khwammankhong painai ratcha-anachak thi 59/2554 rueang hai sun-amnuaikan raksa khwamsa-ngop riaproi pen sun-amnuaikan tammattra 17 haeng praratchabanyat raksakhwammankhong painai ratcha-anachak pho.so. 2551" [Order of the Internal Security Operations Command No. 59/2554 Concerning Status of the Centre for Peace and Order a Status as an Operation Centre in accordance with Article 17 of the Internal Security Act of 2008]. 128, Special issue 31 Ngo. (17 March 2011): 56.

———. 2014. "Prakat khanaraksakhwamsa-ngop haengchat chabap thi 26/2557 rueang kansotsong dulae kanchai sue sangkhom online" [Order of the National Council for Peace and Order No. 26/2557 Concerning the Monitoring the Use of Online and Social Media] Special issue 89 Ngo. (29 May 2014): 3.

———. 2014. "Khamsang khanaraksa khwamsa-ngophaengchat chapap thi 106/2557 rueng kaekhai phoemtoem kotmai waduai pamai" [The National Council for Peace and Security's Order No. 106/2557 on Revision of the Forestry Law], 131. Special Section Part 143 Ngo. (21 July 2014): 15–16.

———. 2014. "Khamsang kong-amnuaikan raksa khwammankhong painai ratcha-anachak thi 560/2557 rueang khrongsangkanchat Lae attra-kamlang khong kong-amnuaikan raksa khwammankhong painai phak 4 suanna (ko.ro.mo.no. phak 4 so.no.) prachampi 2558 [Order of the Internal Security Operations Command No. 560/2557 Concerning Structure of Personnel Management and Manpower of the Internal Security Operations Command Region 4 Forward (ISOC Region 4 FW) of the Year 2015] 131, Special issue 274 Ngo. (30 December 2014): 40.*f*

Sahai Chuang (pseudonym), and Banchon Chawansilp. 2003. *Kraduk khao bua* [Bone Ashes in the Urn]. 3rd ed. Bangkok: Saengdao.

Saiyud Kerdphol. 1986. *The Struggle for Thailand: Counter-Insurgency 1965–1985*. Bangkok: S. Research Center.

Samnakphim Thamniti. 1989. *Krongkan namphrathai chak nailuang: Khwamkhiao khong i-san khiao* [Project of the King's Kindness: The Greenness of the Green Isan Project]. Bangkok: Phapphim Printing.

Santi Khananurak. 1990. "Phawaphunam nai-muban asa-phatthana lae pongkan ton-eng (O.pho.po.) Suksachapho korani prathan khanakammakanklang muban asa-phatthana lae pongkan ton-eng nai phuenthi kong amnuaikanraksa khwammankong phainai (Ko.o.ro.mo.no) changwat ratchaburi" [Leadership in the Volunteer and Self Defence Village (VSDV): Study of the Chairpersons of VSDV's Village Central Committee of the Internal Security Operations Command in Ratchaburi Province]. Master's thesis, Faculty of Political Science, Chulalongkorn University.

Sayam Chotmaihaet 26, 17 (26 April–2 May 2002).

Sitthiphon Khetchoi. 2017. "Botbat kanpatibat-ngan khong asasamak satharanasuk pracham muban: Rongpayaban songsoem sukkhaphap tambon nonthon ampher mueang changwat khonkaen" [The Roles of Public Health Village Volunteers's Works: Nonthon Sub-District Public Health Promotion Hospital, Muang District, Khon Kaen Province]. *Phimoldhamma Research Institute Journal* 4, no. 1 (January–June): 164–73.

Somchai Rakwichit. 1971. *Kanchai kanpatibatkan thangchitwitthaya naikan sanapsanun kanpongkan lae prappram kankokhwammai-sa-ngop* [The Use of Psychological Operations in Supporting the Counterinsurgency Operations]. Lecture Notes at the Royal Thai Army Command and General Staff College, 30 November 1971.

Srisompob Jitpiromsri. 2013. "Thailand's Security Sector and the Southern Insurgency". In *Knights of the Realm: Thailand's Military and Police, Then and Now*, edited by P. Chambers. Bangkok: White Lotus.

Stepan, Alfred. 1986. "The New Professionalism of Internal Warfare and Military Role Expansion". In *Armies and Politics in Latin America*, edited by A. Lowenthal and J. Samuel Fitch, pp. 134–50. New York: Holmes and Meier.

Stithorn Thananithichot. 2012. "Political Engagement and Participation of Thai Citizen in the Rural-Urban Disparity". *Contemporary Politics* 18, no. 1: 87–108.

Streckfuss, David. 2014. "Freedom and Silencing under the Neo-Absolutist Monarchy Regime in Thailand, 2006–2011". In *"Good Coup" Gone Bad: Thailand's Political Developments since Thaksin's Downfall*, edited by Pavin Chachavalpongpun, pp. 109–40. Singapore: Institute of Southeast Asian Studies.

Suchit Bunbongkarn. 1987. *The Military in Thai Politics 1981–1986*. Singapore: Institute of Southeast Asian Studies.

———. 1996. *State of the Nation: Thailand*. Singapore: Institute of Southeast Asian Studies.

———, and Kanala Sukphanit Khanthaprap. 1987. "Ngarn kitchakan phonlaruean khongkongthapthai" [The Civil Affairs Programme of the Royal Thai Army]. In *Rabop thahan thai: Botsueksa kongthap thai boribotthang sangkhom-kanmueang* [Thai Military System: The Study of Armed Forces in Socio-Political Context]. Bangkok: Institute of Security and International Studies, Chulalongkorn University.

Suehiro, Akira. 2014. "Technocracy and Thaksinocracy in Thailand: Reform of the Public Sector and the Budget System under the Thaksin Government". *South East Asian Studies (SEAS), Kyoto University* 3, no. 2: 299–344.

Sumet Tantiwetchakun. 1988. "Kanphatthana phuea khwammankhong adit oatchuban lae anakhot" [Development for Security, the Past, Present and Future]. *Senathipat* 37, no. 3 (September–December): 113–17.

Surachart Bamrungsuk. 1998. *Thahan kap prachatippatai chak 14 tula su patchuban lae anakhot* [Military and Democracy: From 14 October to Present and the Future]. Bangkok: Kroek University.

———. 1999. *Prapkhrongsang Kalahom pradenpanha khophicharana* [Structural Reform of the Defence Ministry: Issues and Concerns]. Bangkok: Square Print 93.

———. 2000. *Thahan kapkanmueangthai nai satawatna: Phatthanakan lae khwamplianplaeng* [Military and Thai Politics in the Next Century: Development and Change]. Bangkok: Institute of Security and International Studies, Chulalongkorn University.

———. 2002. "Krabuanthat khwammankhongmai: Khwamplianplang khongthitsadi lae korani prathetthai" [The New Security Paradigm: Theoretical Shift and the Case of Thailand]. *Journal of Social Science* 33, no. 1 (Jan–March).

———. 2016. *Senathipat: Ratthprahan kapkanmueangthai* [Militocracy: Military Coups and Thai Politics]. Bangkok: Matichon.

Surasak Kasemsuwan. 1993. "Thahan kap kanphatthana kanmueang: Sueksakorani botbat dankitchakan phonlaruean khongkong amnuaikan raksa khwammankhong phainai phak 3 naiphuenthi changwat nan" [Military and Political Development: Study of Civil Affairs Projects of the Internal Security Operations Command in Nan Province under the 3rd Army Region]. Master degree thesis, Department of Government, Faculty of Political Science, Chulalongkorn University.

Suthachai Yimprasoet. 2008. *Saithanprawattisat prachatipatai thai* [The Historical Stream of Thai Democracy]. Bangkok: Foundation of Saithanprawattisat.

———. 2019. *Thong Chaemsi tai thong patiwat* [Thong Chaemsi Under the Revolutionary Flag]. Bangkok: Cremation Volume for Thong Chaemsi.

Tanham, George. 1974. *Trial in Thailand*. New York: Crane Russak and Company.
Thaemsuk Numnon. 2005. *Mueangthai samai songkhramlok khrang thi song* [Thailand during the Second World War]. Bangkok: Saithan.
Thai Lawyers for Human Rights (TLHR). 2015. "Human Rights One Year after the 2014 Coup: A Judicial Process in Camouflage under the National Council for Peace and Order". June 2015. https://tlhr2014.wordpress.com/2015/06/05/report-human-rights-one-year-after-the-2014-coup-a-judicial-process-in-camouflage-under-the-national-council-for-peace-and-order/ (accessed 8 June 2016).
Thak Chaloemtiarana. 2007. *Thailand: The Politics of Despotic Paternalism*. Ithaca: Southeast Asian Program Publications, Cornell University.
Theeraphat Serirangsan. 1991. *"Thasanakhati khong phunamchumchon phak i-san kap kanphattana khong tahan tamkhrongkan i-san khiao"* [Attitudes of the I-san Community Leaders towards the Military's Development in The Green Isan Project]. Research report submitted to the Administrative Center of Royal Development Projects for the Northeast of Thailand.
Thongchai Winichakul. 2002. "Remembering/Silencing the Traumatic Past: The Ambivalent Memories of the October 1976 Massacre in Bangkok". In *Cultural Crisis and Social Memory: Modernity and Identity in Thailand and Laos*, edited by C.F. Keyes and Shigeharu Tanabe, pp. 243–83. New York: Routledge/Curzon.
———. 2008. "Toppling Democracy". *Journal of Contemporary Asia* 38, no. 1 (February): 11–37.
———. 2014. "The Monarchy and the Anti-Monarchy: Two Elephants in the Room of Thai politics and the State of Denial". In *"Good Coup" Gone Bad: Thailand's Political Developments since Thaksin's Downfall*, edited by Pavin Chachavalpongpun, pp. 79–81. Singapore: Institute of Southeast Asian Studies.
———. 2016. "Thailand's Hyper-Royalism: Its Past Success and Present Predicament". *Trends in Southeast Asia*, no. 7/2016. Singapore: ISEAS – Yusof Ishak Institute.
———. 2019. "Thailand's Royal Democracy in Crisis". In *After the Coup: The National Council for Peace and Order Era and the Future of Thailand*, edited by M.J. Montesano, T. Chong, and Mark Shu Xun Heng, pp. 308–34. Singapore: ISEAS – Yusof Ishak Institute.
———. 2020. *Moments of Silence: the Unforgetting of the October 6, 1976 Massacre in Bangkok*. Hawai'i: Hawai'i University Press.
Usani Kasemsan. 1999. *Phrabatsomdetphrachaoyuhua kapkongthapthai naikhhrongkan an nueangmachak phraratchadamri* [His Majesty the King and the Thai Armed Forces in the Royal Development Projects]. Bangkok: O.S. Printing House.
Williams, William Appleman et al., eds. 1985. *America in Vietnam: A Documentary History*. New York: W.W. Norton.
Yoshifumi, Tamada. 2008. *Myth and Realities: The Democratization of Thai Politics*. Kyoto and Melbourne: Kyoto University Press and Trans Pacific Press.

Newspapers and Other Media
ABC News. 2018. "Thai Cave Rescue: Volunteers from Around the Country Come to Help Support the Operation". 5 July 2018. https://www.abc.net.au/news/2018-07-

06/thailand-cave-rescue-inspires-volunteers-from-around-the-country/9946260 (accessed 4 December 2018).
Armed Forced Development Command. http://afdcict.rtarf.mi.th/afdcintra/index1.html (accessed 4 March 2019).
Army Cyber Center's Facebook Page. https://www.facebook.com/ArmyCyberCenter/ (accessed 20 April 2019).
Army Region 2's Website. http://www2.army2.mi.th/th/category/isoc2 (accessed 17 November 2018).
Ban Mueang. 2014. "Kanburanakan chattang ko.no.cho. Kongnun pheu khwammankhong hanengchat" [Comprehensive Reorganization of the Reservists for National Security]. 3 June 2014. http://www.ryt9.com/s/bmnd/1910891 (accessed 6 June 2014).
Bangkok Post. 2018. "Prayuth Denies Buriram Trip 'Political'". 8 May 2018. https://www.bangkokpost.com/news/politics/1460286/prayut-denies-buri-ram-trip-political (accessed 8 May 2018).
———. 2019a. "Corruption Rises in Thailand, Global Watchdog Says". 29 January 2019. https://www.bangkokpost.com/news/general/1619930/corruption-rises-in-thailand-global-watchdog-says (accessed 16 February 2016).
———. 2019b. "Future Forward Hits Back at Army Chief". 12 October 2019. https://www.bangkokpost.com/thailand/politics/1770679/future-forward-hits-back-at-army-chief (accessed 26 March 2020).
———. 2020. "Students Protest Party Ban as Opposition Grills Prayut". 24 February 2020 https://www.bangkokpost.com/thailand/politics/1864749/students-protest-party-ban-as-opposition-grills-prayut (accessed 26 March 2020).
Bangkokbiz News. 2016. "Protklao hai 6 naiphon pon rong samut-haratcha-ongkarak" [H.M. the King Endorsed the Announcement of the P.M.'s Office for Demoting Six Generals from Deputy Chief Aide-de-Camp Generals]. 12 December 2016. www.bangkokbiznews.com/news/detail/731410 (accessed 4 November 2018).
BBC News. 2014. "Thai Army's Struggle to Unite Polarised Country". 9 June 2014. http://www.bbc.com/news/worldasia27735992 (accessed 16 February 2016).
BBC Thai. 2017. "Thiap mattrakan chuai chaona 'yinglak' vs 'prayut' konthueng wanphiphaksa chamnamkhao" [Comparing the Farming Subsidy Measures of Yingluck and Prayut, prior to the Judgement Day of the Rice Pledging Scheme Trial]. 26 September 2017. www.bbc.com/thai/thailand-41376824 (accessed 14 May 2018).
Biznews. 1997. "Kham thalaeng nayobai khong khanaratthamontri nai chuan likphai" [Policy Statement of Chuan Leekphai's Cabinet]. 21 November 1997. http://www.ryt9.com/s/refg/166032 (accessed 4 June 2017).
Channel 3 News. 2009. "Ko.o.ro.mo.no. rap ngop 1,000 lan sakat sueadaeng" [ISOC Admits to Have Received 1,000 Million Baht to Block the Red Shirts]. 25 March 2009 goo.gl/o6kVk8content_copy (accessed 8 June 2016).
———. 2016. "Nayok mop ko.o.ro.mo.no. salai sisuea karatchakan pheu buranakan kantham-ngan" [Prime Minister Assigns ISOC to Dissolve the Color Politics Among Government Officials for Working Integration]. 10 February 2016. news.ch3thailand.com/politics/4265 (accessed 4 March 2017).

Club of Village Scouts of Bangkok's Facebook Page. www.facebook.com/profile.php?id=100006388475830 (accessed 17 November 2018).

Daily News. 2018. "No.pho.kho. 36 thahan nakphatthana songmop thanon pen khongkhwan pimai prachachon" [No.pho.kho. 36 Development Military Unit give a road as a new year gift to the people]. 23 December 2018. https://www.dailynews.co.th/article/684014 (accessed 17 November 2019).

Department of Provincial Administration. *Asa phattana lae pongkan ton-eng* [Volunteers for Development and Self-Defence]. Powerpoint presentation, www.comdopa.com/dopa/tuter/doc/tuter021_3.ppt (accessed 14 November 2018).

Directorate of Civil Affairs, the Air Forces. *shorturl.at/gstBH* (accessed 30 November 2018).

Directorate of Civil Affairs, the Army. http://doca.rta.mi.th/ (accessed 30 November 2018).

———. Facebook Page. https://www.facebook.com/pg/doca.thaiarmy/posts/ (accessed 20 April 2019).

Directorate of Civil Affairs, the Navy. *shorturl.at/mqtDV* (accessed 30 November 2018).

———. Facebook page. https://www.facebook.com/navalcivil/ (accessed 20 April 2019).

Directorate of Civil Affairs of the Air Force's Facebook Page. https://www.facebook.com/กรมกิจการพลเรือน-ทหารอากาศ-1468497056773884/?ref=page_internal (accessed 20 April 2019).

Directorate of Joint Civil Affairs's Website. https://j5.rtarf.mi.th/web/index.php (accessed 20 April 2019).

Five Provinces Bordering Preservation Foundation's Facebook Page. https://www.facebook.com/pg/fiveprovincesforest/posts/ (accessed 19 May 2018 and 6 March 2019).

Head, Jonathan. 2014. "Thai Army's Struggle to Unite Polarised Country". *BBC News*, Thailand. 9 June 2014. http://www.bbc.com/news/worldasia27735992 (accessed 16 February 2016).

Information Center of the Village Scouts under the Patronage of His Majesty the King's Facebook Page [Sun khomunklang luksuea chaoban nai phraboromrachanukhro]. www.facebook.com/ศูนย์ข้อมูลกลางลูกเสือชาวบ้านในพระบรมราชานุเคราะห์-304590370059353/ (accessed 3 November 2018).

INN News. 2017. "Ko.o.ro.mo.no. MOU kapkrasuang sueksathikan-ko.so.no. phueaiphrae laksetthakit pho-phiang" [ISOC Signs MOU with Ministry of Education's Office of Non-formal and Informal Education to Promote the Sufficiency Economy Principle]. 9 October 2017 http://www.innnews.co.th/shownews/show?newscode=815072 (accessed 18 November 2017).

———. 2018. "Chat oprom khrueakhai khao prachachon faorawangphai" [Training for the People News and Surveillance Network]. 5 February 2018 https://www.innnews.co.th/politics/news_7304/ (accessed 12 October 2018).

Internal Security Operations Command. ISOC Headquarter. Facebook page. www.facebook.com/isocnews1/ (accessed 17 November 2018).

———. "Khao kitchakan muanchon ko.o.ro.mo.no" [News and Activities of the ISOC Mass]. http://www.isoc.go.th/?page_id=112 (accessed 3 November 2018).

———. 2018. "Ruamphalang chit-a-sa 2,000 khon ruamkitchakan khlongkan chit-a-sa phraratchathan tam naewphraratchadamri" [Uniting the Power of 2,000 Volunteers of the Royal Initiated Project of H.M. the King]. 27 March 2018. http://www.isoc.go.th/?p=3188 (accessed 20 November 2018).

———. ISOC Region 3 website. https://www.isoc.go.th/?tag=%E0%B8%A0%E0%B8%B2%E0%B8%84-3 (accessed 17 November 2018).

———. ISOC Region 4 Website. shorturl.at/gnsRZ (accessed 17 November 2018).

———. ISOC Region 2 Facebook Page. //th-t.facebook.com/pg/กองบนภาค-2-176558233055660/posts/?ref=page_internal (accessed 17 November 2018).

———. ISOC Region 4 website. www.isoc.go.th/?tag=%E0%B8%A0%E0%B8%B2%E0%B8%84-4-%E0%B8%AA%E0%B8%99 (accessed 17 November 2018).

———. ISOC's 007 Security News Facebook Page. shorturl.at/sEOZ4 (accessed 17 November 2018)

Isra News. 2017a. "Pha anachak 'Com-Link' chumnum bikthurakit kondang phueanrak bik pom nai munnithi anurak pa" [Cut Open the 'Com-Link' Empire, Gathering Big Businessmen and General Prawit's Beloved Friends at the Five Provinces Bordering Forest Preservation Foundation]. 24 December 2017. https://www.isranews.org/isranews-scoop/62246-scoop-62222.html (accessed 6 March 2019).

———. 2017b. "Kammakan munlanithi pa roi to 5 changwat bik pom 24 khon pen so.no.cho. 11 khon" [11 of the 24 Committee Members of General Prawit's the Five Provinces Bordering Forest Preservation Foundation are appointed on the National Legislative Assembly]. 26 December 2017. https://www.isranews.org/isranews-scoop/62285-report001-62021-62285.html (accessed 6 March 2019).

Isaan Record. 2017. "Tham kaemling rong hua chang tae nam yang thuam" [Building the Monkey Cheek Reservoir at Rong Hua Chang But Flooding Still]. 9 September 2017. https://isaanrecord.com/2017/09/11/rong_hua_chang/ (accessed 25 April 2018).

Khaosod. 2019. "'Bik daeng lan tongpen thahan a-chip, penthiphueng khongprachachon naithuk o-kat!" [Big Daeng Proclaims Thai military Must Be Professional and Dependable for the People in Every Occasion]. 13 May 2019. https://www.khaosod.co.th/politics/news_2510116 (accessed 13 May 2019).

Khaosod English. 2015. "Ultra-royalist General Wants Charter to Permit King's Intervention". 6 January 2015. www.khaosodenglish.com/politics/2015/01/06/1420549690/ (accessed 24 January 2020).

Kom Chad Luek. 2016. "Ko.o.ro.mo.no. reng doen na tang sunsetthakitphophiang" [ISOC Speeds up to Establish the Learning Center of Sufficiency Economy]. 3 November 2016. http://www.komchadluek.net/news/regional/247753 (accessed 27 April 2018).

———. 2010. "Loekchukchuen phut so.o.so. thaen so.o.cho. chapta daeng" [End Emergency Situation, Use So.o.so instead of So.o.cho., Keep Watch over the Red Shirts]. 20 December 2010. www.komchadluek.net/news/politic/83400 (accessed 8 January 2020).

———. 2012. "Phuruam phatthana chatthai chak thongdaeng! Buengluek Ammat chathai" [Former Ex-Commies Raise Red Flags, Inside of the Conservative Elite's Scheme]. 18 June 2012. http://www.komchadluek.net/news/scoop/133060 (accessed 3 October 2018).

———. 2017. "Song ekkasan ko.o.ro.mo.no. chai hua la 2 saen dueng phuruam phatthana chatthai pen thansiang" [Examining the ISOC Document, Pay Each Ex-communist Two Hundred Thousand Baht to be Its Popular Base]. 30 April 2017. http://www.komchadluek.net/news/scoop/274327 (accessed 6 May 2017).

———. 2017. "Thahan phak phonlaruen, prakotkan antarai khayai pen rat son rat" [Military's Civil Affairs, a Dangerous Phenomenon leading to a State within a State]. 15 November 2017. http://www.komchadluek.net/news/scoop/302244 (accessed 8 June 2016).

Maenwad Kunchon na Ayutthaya. 2015. "Mueangrae thongkam song thotsawat mai khoei mi prachachon nai saita" [In Two Decades of Gold Mining, Never Any Consideration for the People]. *Prachatai*, 13 February 2015. www.prachatai.com/journal/2015/02/57911 (accessed 5 August 2015).

Manager Online. 2006a. "Sang santisuk phuea chumchon khemkhaeng pharakit thahan nakpatthana" [Building Peace for Strong Communities, Mission of Development Military]. 15 April 2006. http://www.manager.co.th/South/ViewNews.aspx?NewsID=9490000050036 (accessed 16 June 2007).

———. 2006b. "Ruam thalaengkan prakat khamsang khanapatirup kanpokkhrong" [Collected Statements, Announcements, Orders of the National Reform Committee]. 20 September 2006. www.manager.co.th/Politics/ViewNews.aspx?NewsID=9490000118389 (accessed 16 June 2017).

———. 2011. "Pho.bo.tho.bo suansanam phithi phalang muanchon khon ko.o.ro.mo.no. trang" [The Army Chief Presides over the Marching of ISOC's Mass in Trang Province]. 4 February 2011. www.manager.co.th/South/ViewNews.aspx?NewsID=9540000015640 (accessed 2 June 2017).

———. 2012. "Ammat chattem phuruamphatthana chatthai chuthong nun tulakan det khua huachai khonsueadaeng" [The Aristocrats in High Gear, the Ex-Communists Flag Their Support for the Constitutional Court, to Break Down the Red Shirts]. 23 June 2012. https://mgronline.com/daily/detail/9550000076969 (accessed 3 October 2018).

———. 2014a. "Kho.so.cho. chaek baipliw 10 hetphon thamratprahan" [NCPO Distributes Leaflets, Explains 10 Reasons of the Coup]. 2 June 2014. www.manager.co.th/Politics/ViewNews.aspx?NewsID=9570000061701 (accessed 16 June 2017).

———. 2014b. "Ko.o.ro.mo.no. chapmue krasuang satharanasuk longnam MOU sang khwamsamannachan o.so.mo." [ISOC and Ministry of Public Health sign an MOU to Build Reconciliation among the VPHs]. 26 June 2014. https://m.mgronline.com/crime/app-detail/9570000072044 (accessed 18 November 2017).

———. 2015a. "Bik tu khuen kao-i, khwanchai-chusak chong ICT pit 143 wepmin" [Gen Prayut returns positions to Khwanchai and Chusak, Propose to ICT to Shut Down 143 Websites deemed Insulting the Monarchy]. 7 September 2015. https://mgronline.com/daily/detail/9580000101509 (accessed 8 April 2019).

———. 2015b. "Ko.o.ro.mo.no. prasan ICT pit wepsaimin sathaban" [ISOC Co-ordinates with ICT to Shut Down Websites Deemed Insulting the Monarchy]. 7 September 2015. www.manager.co.th/Politics/viewnews.aspx?NewsID=9580000101476 (accessed 13 June 2017).

———. 2015c. "Ko.o.ro.mo.no. henchop khrongsang chat lae attra kamlang 59 phrom 2 rang patibatkan" [ISOC Approves Manpower Structure of the Year 2016 and 2 Operation Drafts]. 27 December 2015. www.manager.co.th/Politics/ViewNews.aspx?NewsID=9580000139653 (accessed 7 June 2016).

———. 2016. "Kongthapbok chapmue kromchon khutlok kaemling 24 khlongkan kaepanha uthokkaphai-phailaeng" [The Royal Thai Army and the Royal Irrigation Department Jointly Construct 24 Monkey Cheek Reservoirs to Solve Flood and Drought Problems]. 13 January 2016. https://mgronline.com/uptodate/detail/9590000004251 (accessed 7 June 2016).

———. 2016. "Ang pa haenglaeng! chae anuphong sen yok pa chumchon hai krathingdaeng sangrong-ngan" [Claim the Forest in Poor Condition! Anuphong Signs and Gives Community Forest to the Red Bull Company to Build a Factory]. 9 September 2016. https://mgronline.com/onlinesection/detail/9600000092561 (accessed 10 March 2019).

———. 2016. "Sap best oraphim phut duthuk khon isan mong khon mai thaokan" [Decry over Best Oraphim for Insulting Isan People]. 16 November 2016 http://www.manager.co.th/HotShare/ViewNews.aspx?NewsID=9590000115412 (accessed 2 June 2017).

———. 2017. "Ko.o.ro.mo.no. Chonburi chatsammana samphan phuea truaitsop lae khayai khrueakhai muanchon" [ISOC of Chonburi Province Organizes a Seminar to Check and Expand Its Mass Network]. 26 July 2017. https://mgronline.com/local/detail/9600000075531 (accessed 18 November 2017).

———. 2018. "Khuepna prapkhrongsang ko.o.ro.mo.no." [Progress of Structural Adjustment of ISOC]. 16 June 2018. https://mgronline.com/politics/detail/9620000057246 (accessed 28 January 2020).

Manus Min Aung's Facebook. shorturl.at/byAF2 (accessed 30 July 2016).

Mass Affair Division, Ministry of Interior. https://multi.dopa.go.th/mad/main/web_index (accessed on 12 February 2020).

Matichon. 1978. "Phichian prakottua rian to amerika" [Phichian Returned, to Pursue His Study in America]. 14 October 1978. Reprinted in Documentation of 6 October. https://doct6.com/wp-content/uploads/2019/10/นศ-เข้าป่า-คืนเมือง-ข่าว-2519-2524-2.pdf (accessed 14 February 2020).

———. 1979. "Poet tua nai ngan sutham, santiban maimi khoha" [Reappear at Sutham's Wedding, Santiban Pressed No Charge]. 21 May 1979. Reprinted in Documentation of 6 October. https://doct6.com/wp-content/uploads/2019/10/นศ-เข้าป่า-คืนเมือง-ข่าว-2519-2524-2.pdf (accessed 14 February 2020).

———. 2000a. "Nailuang rapsang kongthap prap yaseptid" [The King Told the Armed Forces to Fight Illicit Drugs]. 17 October 2000.

———. 2000b. "Kongthap tang so.o.ro.108 tan yaseptid" [The Armed Forced Set Up So.o.ro.108 to Fight Illicit Drugs]. 26 October 2000.

———. 2000c. "Nakhonban wisaman mafia ming ratchada ruap 3 mong rapkhonsong yaba phan thiewbin" [Metro Police Extra-judicially Killed Mafia Ming Ratchad, Arrest 3 Mhong Ethnics Trafficking Drugs by Flights]. 27 November 2000.

———. 2016. "Kho.ro.mo. fai khieo phoem khatopthaen asa-raksadindaen pen 13,285 bialiang wanla 200" [Cabinet Approves the Increase of Payment for the Volunteer Defence Corps to 13,285 Baht and Daily Honorarium 200 Baht]. 3 May 2016.

———. 2017a. "Bik tu nanghuatoa ko.o.ro.mo.no. wang chaekkanban 7 kho nen nganmuanchon" [Gen Prayut Chairs ISOC's Meeting, Give 7 Tasks Focusing on Mass Affairs]. 6 February 2017. www.matichon.co.th/news/453710 (accessed 6 September 2017).

———. 2017b. "Bik tu sang ko.o.ro.mo.no. phicharana 37 warapatirup doen na tam yutthasat chat 20 pi" [Prayuth Orders ISOC to Study 37 Reform Agendas in Line with the 20 Years National Strategic Plan]. 6 February 2017 <www.matichon.co.th/politics/news_453532> (accessed 6 September 2017).

———. 2020. "Ko.o.ro.mo.no rup ekkasan i.o. samchangwat tai khongching" [ISOC Admits the Authenticity of the Documents Concerning Three Southern Provinces]. 27 February 2020. www.matichon.co.th/politics/news_2008868 (accessed 28 February 2020).

Military Reservists for National Security of Phuket Province's Facebook Page. www.facebook.com/groups/1581194052132176/ (accessed 17 November 2018).

MThai News. 2013. "Mop kongthap prachachon topthao hae hai kamlangchai prayut [Mob of the People Army Gives Prayut Moral Support]. 10 July 2013. https://news.mthai.com/politics-news/253820.html (accessed 24 November 2018).

———. 2014. "Ko.o.ro.mo.no phopwepmin thueng 907 wep" [ISOC Found 907 Websites Deemed Insulting the Monarchy in 2014]. 25 December 2014. https://news.mthai.com/politics-news/408375.html (accessed 8 April 2019).

Nation, The. 2006. "Bomb Plot to Kill Thaksin Foiled, Questions Linger". 25 August 2006. http://nationmultimedia.com/2006/08/25/headlines/headlines_30011945.php (accessed 25 April 2018).

———. 2015. "Govt to Rebrand Populism". 19 October 2015. www.nationmultimedia.com/politics/Govt-to-rebrand-populism-30271153.html (accessed 8 May 2018).

———. 2016. "Paiboon Backs Orapim's Renewed Bid for US Visa". 28 November 2016. http://drive.nationmultimedia.com/news/breakingnews/30301016 (accessed 2 June 2017).

Nation TV. 2017. "Phop risot ruk pasa-nguan khaokho kwa 600 rai" [Over 600 Resorts Found Encroaching on the Khao Kho Forest Reserve]. 30 April 2017. www.nationtv.tv/main/content/378545249/ (accessed 6 September 2017).

National News Bureau of Thailand. 2017a. "Nayokratthamontri khopkhun ko.o.ro.mo.no" [Prime Minister Thanks ISOC]. 6 February 2017. http://thainews.prd.go.th/website_th/news/news_detail/TNPOL6002060010011 (accessed 1 June 2017).

———. 2017b. "Ko.o.ro.mo.no chat op-rom asa-phatthana lae pongkan ton-eng" [ISOC Organizes a Training Seminar for the Volunteers for Development and Self-Defence]. 13 March 2017. thainews.prd.go.th/website_th/news/news_detail/TNSOC6003130010067 (accessed 14 November 2018).

———. 2017c. "Ratthaban san to satphraracha nomnam lakpratchaya setthakitphophiang ma prap chai nai kanwang yutthasat 20 pi" [Government Pursues the King's

Philosophy, Applying the Sufficiency Economy to the 20-Year National Strategic Plan]. 24 November 2017. http://thainews.prd.go.th/website_th/news/print_news/WNPOL6011240010036 (accessed 5 April 2018).

National Security Council. 2015. *Nayobai khwammankhong haengchat 2558-2564* [National Security Policy 2015–2021]. Bangkok: Samnakphim khanaratthamontri lae ratchakitcha.

News1. 2018. "Malaew rabiap krasuang khlang chabap 8 khayai phedan 33 khan ngoenduen o.so.mahatthai 2.5 muen khon thuaprathet" [Finally Came, the 8th Finance Regulation, Expanding the 33-Step Salary Structure for 25,000 Volunteer Defence Corps of the Interior Ministry Nationwide]. 10 July 2018. www.news1live.com/detail.aspx?NewsID=9610000068710 (accessed 4 November 2018).

Nithi Nithiwirakun. 2017. "Kitchakanphonlaruen phaitai kansaeksuem khongkongthap" [Civilian Affairs under the Military's Penetration]. *Way Magazine*. 15 November 2017. https://waymagazine.org/behind_army/ (accessed 15 November 2017).

North Public News. 2018. "Chai ngop-klang 98 lan sang kaemling kakkaepnam khlongkan mae taeng tamnaew praratchadamri" [Use 98M of the Central Budget to Build the Monkey Cheek Reservoir at Mae Taeng District in line with the Royal Initiative]. 23 February 2018. https://bit.ly/2EGnqG2 (accessed 25 April 2018).

Office of Intelligence, ISOC. N.d. "Khrueakhai khao prachachon fao rawangphai" [People News Networks, A Crime Watch]. http://center.isocthai.go.th/images/doc_information/sor-kor-wor/1.NetworkSecurity/NetworkSecurity2.pdf (accessed 1 December 2016).

Office of the Masses Affairs and General Information, ISOC. www.massisoc.com/2_mass_main.php (accessed 5 June 2017).

———. "Khrongkan prachachon mi suanruam" [People Participation Project]. http://www.massisoc.isoc.go.th/2_mass_isoc/2_mix_mass_isoc/3_pochoro/1_hist_pochoro/hist_pochoro.html (accessed 20 November 2018).

Office of the Private Education Commission. 2017. "So.cho. chapmue ko.o.ro.mo.no. khapkhluen khwammankhong sathabanlak khong thai" [OPEC Joins ISOC Strengthening the National Pillar]. 17 February 2017. https://www.opec.go.th/old/content.php?page=content&group=executive&cid=845 (accessed 8 November 2017).

Office of the Royal Development Projects Board. 2017. "Sarup phapruam khomun khlongkan annueang machak phraratchadamri" [Summary of the Royal Initiated Development Projects]. http://www.rdpb.go.th/rdpb/projectData/files/summary_roy_project60.pdf (accessed 4 April 2018).

101 World. "Samphap Puangthong: Kongthap kanmueang muanchon lae khwammankhong phainaiprathet" [Interview Puangthong: Military, Mass Politics, and Internal Security]. 14 December 2017. www.the101.world/puangthong-interview-on-military-operations/ (accessed 14 December 2017).

Post Today. 2016. "Ko.o.ro.mo.no chaeng rang ratthathammanun triamradom muanchon nun ko.ro.tho." [ISOC Explains Draft Charter, Prepares to Mobilize Mass to Support the CDC]. 7 May 2016. http://www.posttoday.com/politic/430568 (accessed 6 May 2017).

———. 2017a. "4 lan chit-a-sa thawai ongrachan chon thueng wansutthai" [4 Million Volunteers for the King til the Last Day]. 25 October 2017. https://www.posttoday.com/politic/report/521825 (accessed 3 November 2018).

———. 2017b. "Proi prachaniyom hasiang lueaktang" [Scattering Populism in Election Campaign]. 28 December 2017. https://www.posttoday.com/politic/analysis/532635 (accessed 29 December 2017).

———. 2018a. "Bik tu chaeng thai-niyom pen nuea diao kap pracharat" [Gen Prayut Clarifies Thai-ism the Integral Part of Pracharat]. 26 January 2018. https://www.posttoday.com/politic/news/537536 (accessed 4 May 2019).

———. 2018b. "Bik tu sang plian phaplak ko.o.ro.mo.no. phoem satsuan tamruat-phonlaruen makkhuen" [Gen Prayut Orders to Change Image of ISOC, Increasing Ratio of Police and Civil Servants]. 25 December 2018. https://www.posttoday.com/politic/news/574974 (accessed 4 May 2019).

Prachachat Thurakit. 2015. "Dan ekkachon phoem phuenthi pamai 40% klum foenichoe rabu phasi thuang" [Encourage Private Firms to Increase Forest Area to 40%, Furniture Business Group Says Tariff System an Obstacle]. 12 May 2015. https://www.prachachat.net/news_detail.php?newsid=1431319208 (accessed 12 May 2015).

———. 2018a. "Kho.so.cho. sang lang samong 83,000 muban puthang lueaktang phon prachathipatai chomplom" [NCPO Orders to Brainwash 83,000 Villages, Prepare for Election to Go Beyond Fake Democracy]. 15 February 2018. www.prachachat.net/politics/news-117240 (accessed 15 February 2018).

———. 2018b. "Chutplu pluk 'sak-yang-payung' topjot sangraidaiphoem phuenthi pa" [Start to Plant 'Teak-Rubber-Siamese Rosewood' to Boost Income and Increase Forest Area]. 10 March 2018. https://www.prachachat.net/local-economy/news-128276 (accessed 10 March 2018).

Prachatai. 2007. "14 Ongkon sitthimanutsayachon ruamtan 'pho.ro.bo khwammankhong' sap hai amnat ko.o.ro.mo.no. lonfa pen rat son rat" [14 Human Rights Organizations Oppose the Internal Security Act for Giving Unrestrained Power to ISOC, Being a State within a State]. 21 October 2007. http://prachatai.com/journal/2007/10/14588 (accessed 21 February 2016).

———. 2012. "Kongthap plot-aek riakrong prachachon pokpong phrabatsomdet phrachaoyuhua lae prathetchat" [Liberation Army Calls the People to Protect the King and the Nation]. 6 July 2012 <https://prachatai.com/journal/2012/07/41422> (accessed 24 November 2018).

———. 2014a. "Khamsang kho.so.cho. 64/2557 prappram-yutyang kanthamlai pamai" [NCPO Order 64/2014 on the Suppression and Cessation of Deforestation]. 15 June 2014. http://www.prachatai.com/journal/2014/06/54015 (accessed 30 July 2015).

———. 2014b. "Rai-ngan pramuan sathanakan sitthi manutsayachon chiangmai lang ratthaprahan" [Report on the Post-Coup Human Rights Situation in Chiangmai].

1 July 2014. https://prachatai.org/journal/2014/07/54344 (accessed 21 February 2016).

———. 2014c. "Khamsang kho.so.cho. 64, 66 krathopnak fong chaoban 500 khadi i-san uam – natthok daphong wanphrungni" Fong Chaoban 500 Kadee E-san Oam – Nadtog 'Daophong' Wanphroongnee" [NCPO Orders 64, 66, Heavy Effect for Villagers, 500 Cases Filed, Meeting with Daphong Tomorrow]. 17 December 2014. http://www.prachatai.com/journal/2014/12/57041 (accessed 30 July 2015).

———. 2015a. "Thailand: Protect Human Rights Defenders in Udon Thaini". 5 March 2015. https://prachatai.com/english/node/4832 (accessed 6 June 2017).

———. 2015b. "pho.bo.to.ro. thalaeng phonngan 6 duean khadi min laew set 239 khadi chak khang pikon 443 khadi" [Police Chief Announces 6-Month Performance, Complete 239 out 443 Lèse Majesté Cases from Last Year]. 25 April 2015. http://prachatai.org/journal/2015/04/58968 (accessed 30 July 2015).

———. 2015c. "Life after Eviction". 20 May 2015. https://prachatai.com/english/node/5074 (accessed 6 June 2017).

———. 2016. "Ko.o.ro.mo.no. chaengkhao klumphatthana khunnaphap chiwit chumchon chatsonthanaphati rongfaifa ma thepa phatthana yangrai" [ISOC Sends News of Seminar organized by Community Development Group on 'How the Coal Power Plant Impacts Thepha]. 8 April 2016. https://prachatai.com/journal/2016/04/65147 (accessed 8 February 2018).

———. 2017a. "Wethi prongdong tangchangwat ham nam muethue khao" [Mobile Phone Not Allowed Inside the Reconciliation Forums in the Provinces]. 7 March 2017. https://prachatai.com/journal/2017/03/70432 (accessed 23 June 2017).

———. 2017b. "Anti-potash Mining Protester Faces Charge". 28 March 2017. https://prachatai.com/english/node/7038 (accessed 6 June 2017).

———. 2017c. "Puangthong pawakapan: muanchon chattang khongthahan nai yuk totan prachatipatai mue phuakkhao yurop tua rao" [Puangthong Pawakapan: The Military-Organized Mass in the Anti-Military Period, When They Are Around US]. 17 November 2017. https://prachatai.com/journal/2017/11/74171 (accessed 18 November 2017).

———. 2017d. "Pata-chap 16 khan rongfaifa thanhin- fainun khao khai-ingkhayut kho rengsang" [Clash-Arrest 16 Opponents of Coal Power Plant – the Proponents Enter the Ingkhayut Military Base, Urge to Speed up Construction]. 27 November 2017. https://prachatai.com/journal/2017/11/74317 (accessed 7 February 2018).

———. 2018. "Puangthong pawakapan: 10 pi kotmai khwammankhong phainai prachatipatai khue phaikhwammankhong" [Puangthong Pawakapan: 10 Years of the Internal Security Act, Democracy is Threat to National Security]. 27 February 2018. https://prachatai.com/journal/2018/02/75615 (accessed 27 February 2018).

———. 2019a. "Thuangkhuen phuenpa? 'Land Watch Thai' poet 5 pi kho.so.cho. anumat khrongkan rukpa 6 phan rai" [Reclaiming the Forest? Land Watch Thai Discloses NCPO's Approval of Projects Encroaching on 6,000 Rai of Forest Lands in 5 Years]. 8 March 2019. https://prachatai.com/journal/2019/03/81398 (accessed 8 March 2019).

———. 2019b. "Mo suphat at rat on-ngen 1.8 phanlan hai o.so.mo kon 22 mina so chetthana chai phasi suesiang yam sangkhom plian pai laew" [Dr Suphat Criticizes the State for Transferring 1.8 Billion to PHV before 22 March, Indicate intention to Buy Votes, Reiterate the Society Has Changes]. 19 March 2019. https://prachatai.com/journal/2019/03/81582 (accessed 19 March 2019).

———. 2019c. "Mi a-rai nai chit-a-sa 904: chak suphai kommunit su khwammankhong rupbaepmai" [What is the Chit-a-sa 904: From Fighting against Communists to New Security Threats]. 3 December 2019. https://prachatai.com/journal/2019/12/85400 (accessed 20 February 2020).

Reuters. 2014. "Thai Junta to Set up Reconciliation Centres across Country". 30 May 2014. http://www.reuters.com/article/thailand-politics-reconciliation-idUSL3N0OG1AG20140530 (accessed 23 June 2017).

———. 2018. "Thai King's Yellow and Blue Volunteers Boost His Support, Visibility". 3 September 2018. shorturl.at/nGHJN (accessed 3 November 2018).

———. 2019. "Thailand Passes Internet Security Law Decried as 'Cyber Martial Law'". 28 February 2019. https://www.reuters.com/article/thailand-cyber-idUSL3N20G3R5 (accessed 8 April 2019).

Royal Thai Armed Forces. www.rtarf.mi.th/index.php/th/ (accessed 30 November 2018).

——— website. "Phubanchakanthahan sungsut pen prathan nai phithi mopsingkhong phraratchathan tamkhrongkan chit-asa thamkhwamdi duai huachai" [Military Supreme Commander Chairs a Ceremony Giving Apparels to the Volunteer Spirits, Doing Dood Deeds with Heart]. 24 July 2018. www.rtarf.mi.th/index.php/th/2016-06-23-07-14-56/2018-07-20-08-11-15/2018-07-20-04-15-10/124-24-2561 (accessed 3 November 2018).

Sanook. 2013. "Khrueaikhai yangphara khuen wethi ko.po.tho. lai ratthaban" [Network of Rubber Farmers Joins the ko.po.tho. to Drive Out the Government]. 12 November 2013. www.sanook.com/news/1308306/ (accessed 20 February 2020).

Second Army Region. 2018. "Ko.o. ro.mo.no. changwat udonthani poet kanfuek oprom khlongkan phattanasamphan khayai khrueakhai muanchon runthi 5 prachampi 2561" [ISOC of Udonthani Province Opens Training Programme on Expansion of Mass Network, 5th Class, of the Year 2018.]. 1 December 2018. www2.army2.mi.th/th/isoc2/isoc2_20/2018/05/09/11851/ (accessed 30 November 2018).

Siamrath [daily]. 2001. "Kongthapthai ruamphalangthai tanphai yaseptid" [Thai Armed Forces Unite Thai People to Counter Narcotics]. 30 March 2001.

Straits Times. 2020. "Thai Turn to Twitter to Criticise Royalty". 9 January 2020. www.straitstimes.com/asia/se-asia/thais-turn-to-twitter-to-criticise-royalty (accessed 26 March 2020).

Thanjai News Online. 2018. "Oprom laksut khayai khrueakhai muanchon ko.o.ro.mo.no. klum suemuanchon phuekhwammankhong" [Training Programme for Expansion of ISOC's Mass Network, Media for National Security Group]. 21 July

2018. http://thanjainews2017.blogspot.com/p/blog-page_277.html (accessed 20 November 2018).

Thai Big Bikes Love the Nation Club, ISOC's Facebook Page. [Chomrom bik bai thai chai rak phaendin ko.o.ro.mo.no.]. https://www.facebook.com/Bigbike.center/ (accessed 30 January 2018).

Thai Civil Rights and Investigative Journalism (TCIJ). 2015. "Kho.so.cho. chai mo.44 phuekthon pa-sa-nguan cho.tak 2,100 rai triamhai ekkachon chao sin pi" [NCPO Uses Article 44 to Invoke Status of 2,100-rai Community Forest in Tak Province, to Lease to Private Firm at the End of the Year]. 19 September 2015. https://www.tcijthai.com/news/2015/19/current/5795 (accessed 10 March 2019).

Thai National Defence Volunteers' Facebook Page. www.facebook.com/thai.asa.pongkanchat/ (accessed 17 November 2018).

Thai Offroaders Love the Nation Network's Facebook Page. https://www.facebook.com/เครือข่ายออฟโรดไทย-ใจรักษ์แผ่นดิน-1519013815020683/ (accessed 30 January 2018).

ThaiPBS News. 2017. "Wikhao hhamsang 66/23 model MOU prongdong" [Analysing the Order 66/2523, a Reconciliation Model]. 24 January 2017. http://news.thaipbs.or.th/content/259766 (accessed 31 May 2017)

———. 2019a. "Prapprung laksut ro.do.-ro.ro. nairoi laothap" [Revise programmes for *Ro.Do.* and military academies). 16 June 2019. https://news.thaipbs.or.th/content/281014 (accessed 21 February 2020).

———. 2019b. "Poet kanfuek phukamkap naksueksa wichathahan" [Open a Training Programme for the *Ro.Do.* Trainers]. 16 October 2019. https://news.thaipbs.or.th/content/285231 (accessed 21 February 2020).

Thairath. 2011a. "Suthep pat ko.o.ro.mo.no klaeng buk chap witthayu chumchon sueadaeng" [Suthep Dismisses ISOC Abusively Raided the Red Shirt's Community Radio Station]. 27 April 2011. http://www.thairath.co.th/content/167268 (accessed 3 April 2017).

———. 2011b. "Ko.o.ro.mo.no. yanpit witthayu sueadaeng mai kiaokap patiwat" [Yan Pit Witthayu Suea Daeng Mai Kiaokap Patiwat" [ISOC Insists Shutting Down the Red Shirts' Radio Station Not Due to a Coup]. 28 April 2011. www.thairath.co.th/content/167527 (accessed 8 June 2016).

———. 2012. "9 phet tan maew chi pu salai muban sueadaeng chi pen phai kwa commiwnit" [9 Anti-Thaksin Webpages Urge Yingluck to Dissolve Red Shirt Villages, Say More Dangerous than Communists]. 20 May 2012. https://www.thairath.co.th/content/261913 (accessed 24 November 2018).

———. 2014. "Phakhi chaosuanyang-pam ronchotmai thuai ngoen chuailuea chak ratthaban" [Network of the Rubber and Oil Palm Farmers Issues a Letter to the Government Demanding Financial Assistance]. 2 March 2014. ww.thairath.co.th/content/407177 (accessed 20 February 2020).

———. 2015. "Ko.o.ro.mo.no. khayai kankao oprom pak prachachon pheu mi suanruam khwammunkong" [ISOC Expands Training Programme of People News Networks for Security]. 27 August 2015. https://www.thairath.co.th/content/521098 (accessed 8 June 2017).

———. 2016. "Ko.o.ro.mo.no. chuen sue kharatchakan nakthurakit khao oprom khwammankhong ko.tho.mo." [ISOC Invites Journalists, Bureaucrats and Business People in Bangkok to Join a Training Programme for Security]. 21 March 2016 <https://www.thairath.co.th/content/593822> (accessed 29 June 2017).

———. 2017. "O.pho.po.ro. mi he mo.tho. ok rabiapmai boek khachaichay thamngan asasamak laew" [Civil Defence Volunteer Cheers, MoI Issues New Regulation of Payment for Volunteers]. 17 December 2017. www.thairath.co.th/news/politic/1155150 (accessed 17 February 2018).

———. 2018a. "Phrom lui! ko.o.ro.mo.no. sang thuknuai khapkhluen nayobai rat thai niyom yangyuen" [Ready to Strike! ISOC Orders Every Unit to Propel the State's the Sustainable Thai-ism Policy]. 14 February 2018. www.thairath.co.th/content/1204415 (accessed 30 November 2018).

———. 2018b. "Tho.so.po.cho. yuk suek klai naewrop tasapparot" [TVDC in Time of Domestic Warfare, the Pineapple Eyes Battle Line]. 22 October 2018. www.thairath.co.th/content/68392 (accessed 22 October 2018).

———. 2019a. "Phon kanlueaktang so.so. baep baengkhet ruam 349 khon yaekpenphak" [Election Result of All 349 MPs for All Political Parties]. 7 May 2019. www.thairath.co.th/news/politic/1562331 (accessed 20 February 2020).

———. 2019b. "Ko.o.ro.mo.no. rapmaito lang kho.so.cho. mot amnat ngat pho.ro.bo. khwammankhong dulaepanha" [ISOC Take Over after the End of NCPO, Utilizing the Internal Security Act]. 19 June 2019. www.thairath.co.th/news/politic/1595235 (accessed 23 March 2020).

———. 2020. "Wirot Lakkhana-adison chae patibatkan i.o. yong bik tu charaeng sangtaekyaek" [Wirot Lakkhana-adison discloses IO, link to Big Tu, a divisive action]. 26 February 2020. shorturl.at/oHX35 (accessed 27 February 2020).

Thawisak Koedphoka. 2015. "Siang chak namun: thangphan khong kankhutcho pitoliam rue chiwit lae sitthi chumchon" [Voice from Namun: A Path for Petroluem Drilling or Life and Community Right?]. *Prachatai*. 5 March 2015. https://prachatai.com/journal/2015/03/58227 (accessed 8 March 2019).

Twitter. https://twitter.com/hashtag/กษัตริย์มีไว้ทำไม (accessed 26 March 2020).

YouTube Channels

Billy Airforcerider. 2011. "Banthuek kanprachum khrongkan fuek-oprom khong ko.o.ro.mo.no. runphiset samrap chao-baiker" [Record of a Meeting of ISOC's Special Training Programme for Bikers]. 11 January 2011. www.youtube.com/watch?v=eV78STJq-0o&t=275s (accessed 20 September 2018).

Hansuek Chimphali. 2016. "Ko.o.ro.mo.no. trat chat khrongkan fuek-oprom asa pongkanphai faiphonlaruen o.po.pho.ro." [ISOC of Trad Province Organized Training for Civil Defence Volunteers – CDV]. 23 February 2016. www.youtube.com/watch?v=-0vrfhiY9v8 (accessed 15 November 2018).

Military Reservists of National Security and the Military Veterans. www.youtube.com/watch?v=mlXc7ZjFl7Y (accessed 17 November 2018).

Phonchai Sae Tang. 2016. "Kanfuek oprom phunamchumchon ko.o.ro.mo.no phak 2 khrangthi 1" [The 1st Training Programme for Community Leaders by ISOC Region Two]. 15 November 2016. https://www.youtube.com/watch?v=wM8OqCeHvKc (accessed 20 September 2018).

Phonthep Sae Tang. 2016. "Kanphuek oprom phunamchumchon ko.ro.mo.no. phak 2 runthi 1" [The 1st Training of Community Leaders by ISOC Region 2]. 16 November 2016. www.youtube.com/watch?v=wM8OqCeHvKc (accessed 20 February 2020).

Thai National Defence Volunteers. https://www.youtube.com/watch?v=wGXU9iIhl5s (accessed 17 November 2018).

Woodbury Media Group. 2017. "ko.o.ro.mo.no. pheuprachachon ton thi 4 khrongkan petnaitom" [ISOC for the People, Part 4, Diamond in the Mud Programme]. 2 March 2017. www.youtube.com/watch?v=5viz5C_W640 (accessed 8 June 2017).

Interviews

Interview Mr Wan (pseudonym), 1 December 2016, Mukdahan.
Interview Mr Wat (pseudonym), 30 March 2017, Bangkok.
Interview Mr Bun (pseudonym), 19 August 2017, Ubon Ratchathani.
Interview Mrs Somchit (pseudonym), 21 August 2017, Ubon Ratchathani.
Telephone interview of a District Head of a province adjacent to Bangkok, 21 November 2017.
Interview Puen (pseudonym), 2 December 2017, Sakonnakhon.
Interview Mr Pai (pseudonym), 2 December 2017, Mukdahan.
Meeting with the group of Mr Rong (pseudonym), 3 December 2017, Nakhon Phanom.
Interview Phanlop Pinmanee, 5 December 2017, Bangkok.
Interview a vocational student, 2 November 2018, Kanchanaburi.

Index

Note: Page numbers followed by "n" refer to notes.

A
Abhisit Vejjajiva, 3
   financial aid to ex-communists, 135
   Internal Security Act, 49, 51
   Red Shirts repression, 60, 149
   state of emergency, 52
absolute monarchy, 7, 19
Accelerated Rural Development, 35, 67
American era, 22
Anupong Paochinda, General, 76, 80, 86–87
Apiko Company, 79
Apirat Kongsomphong, General, 46
Armed Forces Development Command unit or *Nuai banchakan thahan phatthana*, 30, 65, 67, 82
Arthit Kamlang-ek, General, 33, 99

B
Ban Na Sai massacre, 107
Bhumibol Adulyadej, King, 12
   anti-communist operations, 37
   benevolence, 4
   development monarch, 15, 63–67
   illicit drugs suppression, 82–84
   Isan Khiao project, 70–74
   legacy, 89
   Monkey Cheeks project, 81–82
   moral authority, 139
   poverty alleviation, 72
   royal democracy, 13
   royal development projects, 22, 36, 38, 62
   royal hegemony, 12, 36–38, 53, 88, 120, 147–48
   sufficiency economy, 3, 84–88, 126, 146
   villagers, concern towards, 109
Border Patrol Police (BPP), 22, 23, 64
   anti-drug operations, 83
   human rights violation, 107
   indoctrination programmes, 92
   ultra-rightist politics, 41
   Village Scouts, 101, 109
Bunchusi Plan, 83

C
Central Security Command (CSC), 22, 24
Centre for Digital for Security, 69
Charoen Sirivadhanabhakdi, 76
Charoenrit Chamrasromrun, 109
Chatichai Choonhavan, General, 52, 73, 74, 81
Chaturon Chaisaeng, 136
Chavalit Yongchaiyudh, General, 42, 70–73, 109
China Ming Ta Potash Corporation, 79
Chit-a-sa, *see* Volunteer Spirit
Chuan Leekpai, 30, 45, 55, 81
Chulalongkorn, King, 8, 9, 14
Civil Defence Volunteers (*A-sa samak pongkan phai fai phonlaruen*), 100
Communist Party of Thailand (CPT)
   armed struggle against state, 24–27, 111
   demise, 8, 29, 72, 117
   Khao Kho district, 65
   objective, 20
   Phayom Chulanont, 135

problems within, 112
propaganda among peasants, 22
waning threat, 60
weakening support, 43
Communist Suppression Operations Command, x, 2, 10, 24–25, 44, 106, 108
Community Development Department, 28, 35, 67
constitutional monarchy, 23
counterinsurgency operations
civilian agencies, 35
first phase, 10
government agencies, 97
Local Administration Department, 66
mass organizations, 91, 94–101
military role, 12, 23, 41, 72
monarchy and military cooperation, 37
monarchy's involvement, 22, 38
people participation, 116
political offensive approach, 24–27, 104-8, 117
reform period, 11
royalism propagation, 109
state agencies, 35
Surayud Chulanont, 135
university archives, 16
US support, 20
Cyber Center, 30
cyber surveillance, 3
cyber warriors, 127
Cybersecurity Act, 132

D
Democratic Soldiers, 42, 70
development for security (*yutthaphatthana*)
beginning of, 65–66
communist threat, 41
concept of, 27–29, 59
definition, 70

Fifth Plan (1982–86), 45
military involvement, x, xix, 2, 19, 63
objective, 88
post-counterinsurgency period, 67–69, 73
development military, 15, , 62, 67, 81
development monarch, 15, 37, 62–65, 87
Diamonds in the Mud programme, 125
Directorate of Civil Affairs (*kong kitchakan phonlaruean*), 18n11, 29, 67, 69, 90n3
Ditthapon Sasasamit, Lieutenant General, 51

E
Eastern Economic Corridor, 30
Eastern Tiger faction, 75, 76
Eisenhower, Dwight D., 26

F
Five Provinces Bordering Forest Preservation Foundation (*Mulnithi anurak pa roi to 5 changwat*), 70, 75–77
Forest Master Plan, 77–80
Future Forward Party, xiii, xiv, 130, 142

G
Green Northeast project, *see Isan Khiao* project

H
Han Phongsitanon, Colonel, 94, 108

I
Internal Security Act, 20, 49, 54–59
Internal Security Operations Command (ISOC)
army's political arm, 30–35
budget, 56
civilian agencies, control of, 10
command structure, 34, 47, 48, 50

cyber surveillance, 3
dismantling, 149
drug problem, 49
human rights violations, 106
Isan Khiao project, 71, 73
legal status, 55–59
main duty, 2
mass operations, 102–4
mass organizations, 4, 26
members, 128
natural resources, protection of, 75, 77
Nawaphon, 103–4
objectives, 1, 40
political offensive, 24, 105, 148
poverty eradication, 73–74
preventive regulations, issue of, 51
provincial ISOC director, 33, 58, 98
psychological operations, 5, 93
regional ISOC director, 58
Saiyud Kerdphol, 25, 97
semi-democracy period, 43–44
staff, 36
Isan Khiao project, 65, 70–73
Issaraphong Nunphakdi, General, 74

J
Jatuphon Phromphan, 3
Johnson, Lyndon, 22

K
Kaemling project, *see* Monkey Cheeks project
Kat Katsongkhram, Colonel, 20
Kennedy, John F., 22, 28
Khanit Saphithak, General, 76
Kho.cho.ko. project, 70, 73–74, 78
Kittiphong Ketkowit, General, 76
Kong kitchakan phonlaruean, *see* Directorate of Civil Affairs
krathing daeng (Red Guars), 41, 93, 102
Kriangsak Chamanan, General, 10, 42, 43, 91, 98, 112, 113, 114, 117

L
lése majesté, 40, 53
Local Administration Department, 35, 66, 100
Loetrit Wetsawan, General, 76

M
mass organizations
 Civil Defence Volunteers (*A-sa samak pongkan phai fai phonlaruen*), 100
 Diamonds in the Mud programme, 125
 effectiveness, 140–42
 incentives, 37, 119, 132–34
 new groups, 124–27
 objectives, 94–101, 120
 old groups, 122–24
 People's Liberation Army of Thailand, 134
 professional and community groups, 124
 Reservists for National Security, 18n9, 99, 116, 123
 Thai Big Bikes Love the Nation ISOC Club, 18n9, 125, 133, 134
 Thai National Defence Volunteers (*Thai a-sa pongkan chat* or *Tho.so.po.cho.*), 4, 18n9, 98, 114, 120, 121, 123
 Thai Offroaders Love the Nation, 125
 Volunteer Defence Corps (*A-sa raksa dindaen* or *O.So.*), 43, 94–96, 122–23, 128, 132–33, 141
 Volunteers for Development and Self-Defence (*A-sa phatthana lae pongkan ton-eng* or *O.pho.po.*), 94, 96
 Village for Development and Self-Defence Volunteers programme (*Muban a-sa phatthana lae pongkan ton-eng*), 67, 92, 96, 123

Village Health Volunteers (*Asasamak satharanasuk pracham muban* or *O.so.mo*), 100, 121, 124
Village Security Unit (*Chutraksa khwamplodphai muban* or *Cho. ro.bo*), 67, 96, 122
Village Scouts, 41, 83, 93, 101, 102, 109, 113–14, 122, 124
mass surveillance
　Cyber Center, 30
　Cybersecurity Act, 132
　expansion of ISOC's mass network, 2, 103, 126, 127
　Network of People's News and Surveillance, 127
　People's Participation Programme, 125, 127
　Pineapple Eyes project, 127
　Territorial Defence Student Cybers (*Ro.Do* Cyber), 126
military's civil works, 88
Ministry of Defence, 31–32, 127
Ministry of Information and Communication Technology (ICT), 3
Ministry of Natural Resources and Environment (MONRE), 1, 77
Ministry of Education, 36, 126
Ministry of Interior, 33, 66, 86, 122
Mobile Development Units, 28
monarchy
　lése majesté cases, 40, 53
　political power, 13, 37, 84
　protection of, 40, 53, 89, 120, 137, 145
　relationship with military, ix, 9, 10, 12–13, 23–24, 37, 46, 60, 62, 65, 68, 81, 88, 147
　relationship with the United States, 20, 22, 38,
　resacralization, xii
　role of, 15
　sufficiency economy, 84
　symbol of Thainess, 13, 22, 38

Mongkhon Amphonphisit, General, 82
Monkey Cheeks Project, 81–82
Mulnithi anurak pa roi to 5 changwat (Five Provinces Bordering Forest Preservation Foundation), 70, 75–77

N
Naphon Bunthap, General, 120, 143n2
Noppadon Inthapanya, General, 76
Nat Intharacharoen, General, 76
National Anti-Corruption Commission, 54, 76,
National Council for Peace and Order (NCPO)
　absolute power, 3
　eviction of farmers, 93, 131
　financial rewards to ex-communists, 137
　forest land, conservation of, 77–80
　military regime, 17, 53–54
　ties with big corporations, 75, 89
　2014 coup, xviii, 1, 136
National Liberation Front (Viet Cong), 22
National Peace Keeping Council (NPKC), 74, 75, 81
National Reform Committee, 40, 41, 42
Nawaphon, 93, 102–4
network monarchy, 6, 12, 13
Noppadon Inthapanya, General, 76
North Vietnam, 22

O
Office of Intelligence, 69
Office of Mass Affair and General Information, 120, 133
Office of Policy and Security Strategy, 69, 121
Office of the Royal Initiatives Projects and Security Co-ordination, 68
Oraphim Raksaphon (Best), 4–5, 126

INDEX

P

parallel state, 6
paramilitary forces, 4, 16, 23, 26–27, 41, 77, 93–94, 105–7, 141
Pathet Lao, 22
Patthawat Suksiwong, 76
People Development and Peace Keeping Unit, 98
People's Liberation Army of Thailand, 134
People's Participation Programme, 125
Prachatipatai thai niyom project, 70, 87, 122
Phalang Prachachon Party, 54
Phalang Pracharat Party, 89, 132
Phanlop Pinmanee, General, 49
Phao Siyanon, Police General, 20, 21, 23
Phatthana Phutthananon, General, 76
Phayom Chulanon, Lieutenant Colonel, 135, 136
Phibunsongkhram (or Phibun), Field Marshal, 6, 20, 21, 38, 94
Phin Choonhavan, General, 20
Phuea Thai Party, 2, 3, 54, 132, 136, 141
Pineapple Eyes project, 127
political offensive approach (*kanmueang nam kanthahan*), 148
  assessment, 59, 104–9
  civilian-police-military joint operations (CPM), 22, 24–27, 63, 92, 145
  during counterinsurgency period, 10–11, 117
  post-counterinsurgency period, 29–30
  semi-democratic period, 42–43
  66/2523, 24, 42–43, 55, 92, 111–13, 114
  65/2525, 24, 42–43, 55, 111–13, 114
Pracharat project, 54, 70, 85–86, 122, 132
Prakan Pathawanit, General, 127

Praphas Charusathian, 23, 25–26, 32–33, 44, 55, 108
Prasert Sapsunthorn, 42
Prawit Wongsuwan, General, 75–76, 127
Prayut Chan-ocha, General
  "cyber martial law", 132
  cyber surveillance, 130
  forest resources, destruction of, 1, 77–80
  ISOC's role, 59
  military regime, legitimization, 85–86
  new security threats, 46
  personnel mobilization, 36
  populist economic policy, 89, 138, 141–42
  prime minister, 57
  security policies, 120–21
  websites, shut down, 3
Prem Tinsulanonda, General
  anti-drug campaign, 84
  Isan Khiao project, 71
  ISOC Command Structure, 34
  mass organizations, 113, 115–17
  political offensive approach, 24, 29, 42
  premiership, end of, 52
  Reservists for National Security, 99
  resettlement scheme, 135
Pridiyatorn Devakul na Ayutthaya, 76
Prime Ministerial Order No. 47/2529, 43
Prime Ministerial Order No. 65/2525, 43, 111–15
Prime Ministerial Order No. 66/2523, 24, 43, 58, 92, 111–15
Prime Ministerial Order No. 83/2526, 43
Prime Ministerial Order No. 158/2545, 46, 48–50, 55, 57, 58
Prime Ministerial Order No. 187/2542, 55

Prime Ministerial Order No. 288/2534, 99
psychological operations, 16, 22, 27, 37, 38, 93
Public Welfare Department, 35, 67
Pye, Oliver, 2, 72, 74

R

Red Bull Public Company, 80
Red Drums massacre, 106
Red Guars (*krathing daeng*), 41, 93, 102
Red Shirts, 3–4, 11, 51–54, 85, 120, 124, 129, 137, 140–41, 149
Reservists for National Security, 18n9, 99, 116, 123
royal democracy, 6, 13, 143, 147
royal development projects, 22, 36, 38, 62
royal hegemony, 12, 36–38, 53, 88, 120, 147–48
Royal Forestry Department, 72, 75, 143n3
Royal Thai Air Force, 36,
Royal Thai Armed Forces, 35, 67
Royal Thai Navy, 36

S

Saiyud Kerdphol, General, 25, 26, 34, 44, 55, 67, 94, 97, 102, 103, 105, 106
Samphao Chusi, General, 82–83
Samran Phaetthayakun, General, 103
Sangad Chaloryu, Admiral, 41, 42
Sarit Thanarat, Field Marshal, xiv, 13, 21–23, 27, 28, 135
semi-democracy, 15, 43, 44, 119
Seni Pramoj, 41, 55, 97, 102, 103, 106
Siam Cement Group, 80
Sino-Vietnam conflict, 111–12, 117
Sirikit, Queen, 23, 75, 76, 113, 120, 129, 143n3
6 October 1976 massacre, *see* Thammasat massacre
Somchai Rakwichit, 108

Somkhuan Harikul, 109
Sonthi Boonyaratglin, 54
South Vietnam, 21–22, 39
Suan Kitti Co. Ltd, 73, 90n4
Suchinda Krapayoon, General, 6, 74, 81
sufficiency economy, 3, 5, 38, 56, 68, 84–89, 121, 126, 146,
Sumet Tantiwetchakun, 45, 66, 97
Sunthorn Kongsompong, General, 74
Supreme Command, 10, 16, 19, 22, 29, 67, 82
Surayud Chulanont, 54, 85, 132, 135–36
Suthep Thaugsuban, 135

T

Thahan prachathipatai, or Democratic soldiers, 42, 70
Thai armed forces
  civil affairs activities, 30, 44, 89
  civilian control, 8–9, 46
  crackdowns on protesters, 40
  creation of, 8
  duties, 39
  ideological training programme, 140
  illicit drugs, suppression of, 82–84
  internal security operations, 19–23, 60, 69, 145
  major task, 11–12
  "monarchized military", 13
  royal legitimacy, 65, 88
  US aid, 28
Thai Big Bikes Love the Nation ISOC Club, 18n9, 125, 133, 134
Thai National Defence Volunteers (TNDV), 4, 18n9, 98, 114, 120, 121, 123
Thai niyom, 70, 86–88, 122
Thai Offroaders Love the Nation, 125
Thaksin Shinawatra
  aid to the poor, 135
  limited reform of the military, 46–52, 60
  military coup, 4, 52

Phalang Prachachon, 54
Phuea Thai, 54, 141
Prime Ministerial Order No.
    158/2545, 55, 57
popularity, 11, 38, 53, 85, 89, 119, 137
Red Shirts movement, 3
southern Muslim-dominated
    provinces, 149
universal health coverage, 101
war on drugs, 83–84
Thammasat massacre (6 October 1976
    massacre), 15, 41–43, 91, 101, 103,
    104, 107, 110–12, 114, 117, 138
Thanathip Sawangsaeng, Colonel, 3
Thanin Kraivichien, 41–42, 103, 105,
    113
Thanom Kittikhachon, Field Marshal,
    23, 25, 26, 39, 44, 108, 118n5
Thirachai Nakwanit, General, 76
Thongchai Winichakul, 6, 13, 14, 103–4

U
United Front for Democracy against
    Dictatorship (UDD), 3, 17n2, 51
United States of America, 20, 23, 27, 28,
    39, 59, 95
United States Operations Mission
    (USOM), 95

V
Vajiralongkorn, King, ix, 30, 110, 129,
    139, 143n2
Viet Cong (National Liberation Front),
    22
Vietnam War, 20, 21, 23, 27, 59, 95, 102
Village for Development and Self-
    Defence Volunteers programme
    (VDSV), 67, 92, 96–97, 103,
    115–16, 123

Village Head Assistant for Peace
    Keeping Programme, 97
Village Health Volunteers (*Asasamak
    satharanasuk pracham muban* or
    O.so.mo), 100, 121, 124
Village Protection Unit (VPU), 95, 105
Village Scouts, 41, 83, 93, 101, 102,
    109–10, 113–14, 122, 124, 128
Village Security Team (VST), 26
Village Security Unit (VSU), 96, 128
Volunteer Defence Corps (VDC) or
    Kong asa raksa dindaen, 43, 94–96,
    122–23, 128, 132–33, 141
Volunteer Spirit (*Chit-a-sa*), 30, 104,
    138–40

U
Udomdet Sitabutr, General, 76

W
war on drugs, 60, 83
Walit Rotchanaphakdi, General, 76
Watthana Khieowimon, 103–4
Wirot Lakkhana-adison, 130,
Wit Thephasadin na Ayutthaya,
    General, 76

Y
Yellow Shirts, 11, 85, 129, 138, 140
Yingluck Shinawatra, 52, 55, 76, 129,
    131, 136, 141
Yutthaphatthana, 19, 27
    see also development for security

Z
007 sai khao khwammankhong (007
    Intelligence), 16

About the Author

Puangthong Pawakapan is Associate Professor in the International Relations Department, Faculty of Political Science, Chulalongkorn University. Her original academic expertise is in the field of Southeast Asian Studies with special interest in the political relationship between Thailand and Cambodia. Her current interest is on Thailand's contemporary politics. Some of her works are "Thailand's Response to the Cambodian Genocide", in *Genocide in Cambodia and Rwanda: New* Perspectives (2006); *State and Uncivil Society in Thailand at the Temple of Preah Vihear* (2013); "Warfare and Depopulation of the Trans-Mekong Basin and the Revival of Siam's Economy", in *Warring Societies of Pre-Colonial Southeast Asia: Local Cultures of Conflict within a Regional Context* (2017); *The Central Role of Thailand's Internal Security Operations Command in the Post-Counter-Insurgency Period* (2017); and "The Foreign Press and Its Changing Perceptions of the Thai Monarchy", in *After the Coup: The National Council for Peace and Order Era and the Future of Thailand* (2019). She has a PhD in History from the University of Wollongong in Australia in 1995.

www.ingramcontent.com/pod-product-compliance
Lightning Source LLC
Chambersburg PA
CBHW051524230426
43668CB00012B/1727